HOW THEY RIG OUR ELECTIONS

HOW THEY RIG OUR ELECTIONS

The Coming Dictatorship
of Big Labor
and the Radicals

DOUGLAS CADDY

ARLINGTON HOUSE·PUBLISHERS
NEW ROCHELLE, NEW YORK

Manufactured in the United States of America

Library of Congress Cataloging in Publication Data

Caddy, Douglas, 1938-
　How they rig our elections.

　Includes bibliographical references.
　1.　Elections--United States--Campaign funds.
2.　Trade-unions--United States--Political activity.
I.　Title.
JK1991.C33　　329'.025'0973　　75-25829
ISBN 0-87000-319-4

TO

that lonely handful of courageous congressmen—led by Senators
James Allen and James Buckley in the Senate and by Congressmen
William Frenzel, John Rousselot, and William Steiger in the House—
who fought so hard, though unsuccessfully, in 1974 for true campaign
reform against overwhelming odds—including a hypercritical majority
in both chambers intent on passing an "Incumbents' Protection Act,"
and radical public-interest groups and labor unions seeking to rig our
elections

What the supporters . . . really hope to achieve is not entirely clear, but what the provisions imply is the beginning of a federal structure to manage political campaigns and perhaps even the political process itself. It does not take much imagination to conceive of future legislation being proposed to further restrict political operations. In essence, this is a dangerous bill contrary to our tradition of political freedoms. Those who have condemned Watergate because it represented an effort to control political power have only to read the bill to see the potential for achieving the same end, only then it would have the cover of law as giving support to restricting political freedom.

SENATOR PAUL FANNIN (R.–Ariz.) during the Senate debate in April 1974 on the Federal Elections Campaign Act Amendments

Contents

Introduction

I defer to no one in acknowledging the need for election campaign reform in many areas. As a Member who has served on the Select Committee on Presidential Campaign Activities, the so-called Watergate Committee, I can vouch for that first hand. . . .

However, I draw the line on public financing of federal election campaigns. This is not campaign reform. It is another blatant attempt to poke the long arm of the Federal Government into an area where it has no business.

It is an effort to destroy the freedoms of the American people to choose in the election process.

It is an effort to deny the American people freedom of expression in support or nonsupport of candidates for public office.

SENATOR HERMAN TALMADGE
(D.–Ga.), in Senate debate, March 27, 1974

This book's thesis is a simple if somewhat alarming one: the federal election reform law, Public Law 93-443, which became effective on January 1, 1975, is just what Senator Talmadge (and many others) described it, "an effort to destroy the freedoms of the American people to choose in the election process." The new law is a cunning device to perpetuate radical and labor politicians in power and to foreclose from the outset conservative and moderate spokesmen from occupying federal elective offices. It is, in short, a calculated effort to rig our elections.

11

These charges are not loosely made. They were raised in various contexts in the debate in Congress during 1974, when the legislation was enacted. They are being raised again in the landmark lawsuit that is slowly wending its way up through the judiciary to the Supreme Court, and that I predict will result in the new law being struck down as unconstitutional.

The new law is extremely complex. Apart from the multitude of requirements and penalties it mandates, the new law has three essential provisions; it:

(1) establishes public financing from the U. S. Treasury of Presidential campaigns, beginning with the 1976 election;

(2) sets limitations on cash contributions by citizens and organizations to Presidential and congressional candidates;

(3) sets limitations on campaign expenditures by Presidential and congressional candidates.

When the new law was enacted, it was heralded by its congressional and media supporters as the dawning of a new age in cleansing the financing of political campaigns. Senator Edward Kennedy (D.–Mass.) said its passage meant that "at a single stroke we can drive the money lenders out of the temple of politics."

But these pronouncements of a new era have a false ring to them. Rather than a giant leap forward toward improving the democratic processes by which we elect our federal officials, the new act is emerging slowly into the public consciousness as a powerful tool that can be used by radicals to impose a totalitarian ideology and government upon the American people. (See Appendix I for "The Case Against Public Financing of Federal Elections.")

One of the new law's greatest defects is that it purposely makes no attempt to impose legitimate restrictions on the most powerful political force in the country today—organized labor. Instead, the legislation appears to be designed to strengthen the stranglehold the union bosses already have on our elected officials. As early as 1971, George Meany, president of the AFL-CIO, could boast, "We've got the finest political organization in the nation right now in the AFL-CIO." Today this political power has increased even further, to the point where the labor mogul claims he controls Congress, having supported and elected in 1974 two-thirds of the members of both the Senate and the House of Representatives.

12

IN-KIND CONTRIBUTIONS

In the 1974 national election, organized labor was the largest contributor of cash to congressional candidates. Despite the fact that its cash contributions amounted to many millions of dollars, the real political muscle of the labor bosses was found, and continues so today, in its "in-kind" contributions of goods and services.

The influential role of in-kind contributions in campaigns was noted in the message of the President to Congress on campaign reform on March 8, 1974, the eve of the Senate debate on the legislation. The message declared:

> In recent years there has been a proliferation of "in-kind" contributions in the form of campaign workers, printing supplies, the use of private aircraft, and other such nonmonetary campaign assistance. Because there is as much room for abuse with "in-kind" contributions as with financial ones, I believe we should prohibit all "in-kind" donations by any organization other than a major political party.
>
> Any "in-kind" contribution by an individual would, of course, continue to be permissible, but would have to be disclosed as to both donor and recipient, with an open report of its reasonable value. These personal "in-kind" donations would come within the same ceiling limitations as monetary contributions and would apply towards the ceiling amounts for Senate, House, and Presidential elections.

Victor Riesel, the syndicated columnist on labor affairs, estimates that organized labor spent $60 million in the 1968 national election, $50 million in 1972, and such a vast treasury in 1974 that he "stopped counting it when it passed $25 million." Riesel, in calculating his estimates of labor political spending, includes in-kind as well as cash contributions.

Most analyses of contributions to candidates, in contrast to Riesel's efforts, ignore the paramount role of in-kind donations. For example, Common Cause tabulated the cash contributions to each congressional candidate in 1974. Its report is significant not only in revealing that "Democrats outspent Republicans, $38.4 million to $32.5 million, in House and Senate races" but also in failing to reveal or tabulate in-kind donations. Organized labor is the largest provider of in-kind campaign donations and invariably these contributions assist liberal and

13

radical candidates, primarily Democrats. (See Appendix II for the Common Cause report on contributions in the 1974 national election.)

In my book *The Hundred Million Dollar Payoff* (Arlington House, 1974), which in many ways is the predecessor to the thesis of this work, thousands of internal documents, letters, and memoranda from the files of unions and Democratic Party leaders were drawn on to illustrate the vast, pervasive political operations of organized labor that are financed primarily by in-kind contributions. The book, using this incontrovertible evidence, showed that the union bosses methodically draw upon the unions' tax-exempt treasuries, whose revenues are derived from the compulsory dues of the rank and file, to finance these contributions of goods and services. Many of the internal union documents in the book were from the International Association of Machinists and Aerospace Workers (IAM), the nation's fifth largest union. The political arm of the IAM is the Machinists Non-Partisan Political League (MNPL), which coordinates cash and in-kind contributions to the hundreds of federal officeholders whom the union's leaders support. The IAM and MNPL were only temporarily embarrassed by having their clandestine political machinations exposed to the light of day. Already the union is at work to elect in 1976 a prounion President and to increase the number of labor-controlled congressmen above the present two-thirds in both houses. (See Appendix III for the 1975 Machinist report titled "MNPL Organizing Early for 1976 U.S. Elections.")

FORBIDDEN SUBJECT

Only rarely does an enterprising reporter or fair-minded commentator attempt to open the lid on the forbidden subject of the illegal political operations of organized labor. One such attempt, and a very good one indeed, was the special "CBS Reports" program "The Best Congress Money Can Buy," televised nationally on January 31, 1975 (the final day for filing campaign contribution reports by congressional candidates in the 1974 election). The program, narrated by Dan Rather, gave special attention to the Marine Engineers Benevolent Association (MEBA) and the Seafarers' Union. Although the combined membership of the two unions is under 100,000, between them they spent over a half-million dollars in the 1974 campaign. This amount, of course, represents only the cash contributions, not goods and services, which

14

were in addition. The CBS program was also unusual in that it interviewed an ex-Seafarers' Union member who told the viewing audience how the union's leadership routinely uses force to make its members contribute to the union's political slush fund.*

Organized labor was among the earliest and most fervent supporters of public financing of federal campaigns. It reached this policy position by reasoning that if limitations were set on the amounts of cash raised and spent by federal candidates, and if primary reliance were on using public funds, then it could increase its monopoly on the country's political system since most of the time the difference between victory and defeat for a candidate is the noncash contributions (that is, in-kind contributions of goods and services), which only labor is equipped to provide systematically and nationally.

Thus, the October 1, 1973, *Memo from COPE,* published by the AFL-CIO Committee on Political Education, trumpeted:

> The AFL-CIO wholeheartedly supports complete federal campaign financing for all offices and a complete bar on any private contributions to such candidates. We know there are many grave problems that may take time to solve, but there are some actions which can be taken without delay. They are:
>
> Provide for sole financing of the 1976 presidential campaign with a clear mandate for strict enforcement of the law to prevent any contribution from any other sources. In view of the politicizing of the Justice Department by the present Administration, enforcement of the law should be taken out of the hands of the Justice Department by creating a special commission with enforcement powers answerable only to the people's elected representatives, the Congress . . . .
>
> Establish and strictly enforce ceilings on the total, aggregate contributions to Congressional candidates or their political committees. Every contribution must be reported in full and reports supplied to the public before Election Day.
>
> We repeat, the goal is federal financing of elections.

---

*In 1970, eight Seafarers' Union officials, including President Paul Hall, were indicted for violations of the Corrupt Practices Act and charged with, among other crimes, forcing rank-and-file members to contribute to the union's political fund. The Justice Department refused to move promptly on the case. In May 1972 the charges were dismissed by the court because of the Justice Department's inaction. Six months later, just prior to the November election, the Seafarers' political arm made a $100,000 contribution to the Committee for the Re-Election of the President.

Prior to the enactment of the new public financing law, the campaign contributions of both cash and in-kind goods and services by organized labor to liberal/radical candidates were offset to a large degree by the large cash contributions by private donors to conservative/moderate candidates. The role of union in-kind contributions has thus increased dramatically since the new law became effective.

GOAL TO CAPTURE GOP

Radical spokesmen have already indicated that they plan to use the new law to capture the Republican Party. Russell Hemenway, executive director of the National Committee for an Effective Congress (NCEC), candidly told ace reporter David Broder, as reported in the *Washington Post* of January 26, 1975: "Our major effort in 1976 will be in the Republican primaries, to find and support progressive Republicans who will take on the mossbacks in that party."

Another NCEC official, David Brunnel, was quoted in the same article by Broder: "We want to provide some services for the marginal incumbents and target the people in Congress who ought to be challenged.

"Last time, we did very little in the primaries, but next year the Republican primaries offer our best opportunity to get new blood in. There aren't that many seats left that the Democrats can pick up, so it makes sense to make an effort to support the independent Republicans."

The NCEC is closely aligned with organized labor and many of its in-kind contributions go to labor-backed Democratic candidates. Executive Director Hemenway, quoted by Robert Walters in "Campaign Help for Liberal Republicans," in the *National Journal* of April 19, 1975, said that in the 1974 campaign, "We didn't want to duplicate or compete with existing services. For example, the Democratic National Committee provided excellent training programs for its candidates and their campaign managers as well as a highly effective get-out-the-vote program. We tried to complement their effort."

So, on the congressional level, the radical leaders plan to use their new campaign "reform" law to increase their strength even more. The new law provides them with an opportunity without parallel in American history to rig the elections in order to impose an ideological dictatorship.

16

On the Presidential level, liberal and radical leaders see a golden opportunity to promote their candidates at the taxpayers' expense. One potential candidate is Fred Harris, former Democratic Party chairman. He admitted to Christopher Lydon, in the *New York Times* of April 20, 1975: "People would ask me [in 1972]: If I did win the nomination, how would I raise the money for the campaign? I never could answer that. But now, under the new law, the public money is going to be there." Reporter Lydon concluded: "In short, the new money rules can shape the cast, the strategy, the timing, the rhetorical tone and likely the outcome of the Presidential campaign" in 1976.

One of the most troubling aspects of the new law and one likely to be examined carefully by the Supreme Court is the restriction on new or third parties. The issue is quite germane to practical politics. A Gallup poll in April 1975 showed that twenty-five percent of all voters would support a new third party more conservative than the Republican Party. The new law is rigged against new parties by allowing public financing through reimbursement *after* the election should the party's Presidential candidate receive five percent of the total vote.

"GARDNER'S FOLLY"

If the new campaign law could be traced to the efforts of any single individual, that person would be John Gardner, head of Common Cause. It was Common Cause, allied with organized labor, that mobilized the massive, well-oiled, well-financed lobby that pushed the legislation through Congress. When the new campaign bill was finally signed into law, it was John Gardner who celebrated by basking in its reflected glory. Yet the new law may well prove to be the undoing of both Gardner and Common Cause. How will Gardner be able to explain away his role as midwife to public financing if the Supreme Court should declare the law unconstitutional? For Common Cause, which has touted its activities as being incorruptible and above suspicion, the humiliation of having its most successful effort ruled illegal by the courts could fatally taint all of its future activities. In the end, history may call the present entire unconstitutional experiment with public financing "Gardner's Folly."

Even while the suit challenging the public financing law is being argued in the courts, Common Cause and its radical allies are busy proposing additional legislation, the effect of which will be to concen-

17

trate political power in the hands of a few individuals, all of whom are liberal or radical. Among the "reforms" being pushed during the 1975–76 term by Congress are:

• S.564, a bill to provide public financing of primary and general elections for the Senate and the House of Representatives. The present law provides public financing only for Presidential elections. This bill would extend it. Senator Edward Kennedy is the bill's sponsor and twenty-eight additional senators are co-sponsors. Were it not for the suit pending against the 1974 public financing law, S.564 would sail through Congress. Many congressmen, however, prefer to wait to see how the Supreme Court acts.

• S.815, sponsored by Senators Robert Stafford (R.–Vt.) and Edward Kennedy, would strictly regulate lobbying by all persons in contact with congressmen, their staffs, and employees of the executive branch. The bill defines a lobbyist (who must register) as a person who during any quarter of the year "communicates orally on eight or more separate occasions with one or more Federal officers or employees." Clearly, the intent of the legislation, which was conceived and drafted by John Gardner and his associates at Common Cause, is to intimidate the average American citizen so that he is so fearful of being prosecuted for failing to register as a lobbyist that he will cease to express his opinions and views to his elected representatives and to employees of the federal government. Such a bill is probably as unconstitutional as an abridgment of the freedom of speech as is the first "Gardner Folly."

In essence, S.564 and S.815 reflect a totalitarian mentality; they are efforts by powerful men to silence all those who would disagree with them. The leadership of this totalitarian mentality is found in politicians like Senator Kennedy, professional reformers like John Gardner, and union bosses like George Meany.

• A national voter-registration-by-mail law is part of the overall strategy to rig our elections. The AFL-CIO has promoted this legislation in past years and renewed its support at the meeting of its Executive Committee in Bal Harbour, Florida, in February 1975. Former Senator Sam Ervin predicted that if voter-registration-by-mail is passed, it will mean "there is going to be a general resurrection of the dead on every election day." The labor bosses want the new law because it would be used to register large blocs of minorities (such as Chicanos and Indians), who would vote as they were told and whose votes would offset those cast by the vast rank-and-file union members,

18

who are out of step with their radical labor leadership. *Electoral Reform and Voter Participation (Federal Registration: A False Remedy for Voter Apathy)* by Kevin P. Phillips and Paul Blackman (published in 1975 by the Hoover Institution on War, Revolution and Peace) offers a concise and informative analysis of this issue.

• H.R. 3000, introduced by radical Congressman William Clay (D.-Mo.), is titled the "Federal Employees Political Activities Act of 1975." Its intent is to enlist all federal employees in political activity by removing the Hatch Act. The 1974 public financing reform law has already removed Hatch Act restrictions on three million state and local government employees. Congressman Ed Koch (D.-N.Y.), one of the bill's admirers, declares, "Clay's bill H.R. 3000 and my bill H.R. 1326 would amend Title 5 of the United States Code so as to permit federal employees to take part in political management and in political campaigns." The federal government has over 2.8 million civil and postal service employees at the present time.

The new public financing law, the proposal to extend public financing to congressional races, the efforts to restrict the citizen's right to lobby, the movements to allow voter-registration-by-mail and to make our federal civil employees "club house" politicians—all these are part of a strategy to change the political complexion of America and, by so doing, to change America itself. As the United States approaches its 200th birthday, each American should take an inventory of the individual liberties he enjoys, or once enjoyed, as a citizen of the Republic. In doing so, he should also examine what effect on our representative government and on our freedom these new political proposals by radicals will have if they become the law of the land. When looking into the philosophy behind these radical proposals, keep in mind what George Orwell wrote in 1939: "It may be just as possible to produce a breed of men who do not wish liberty as to produce a breed of hornless cow."

1

A Question

of

Constitutionality

On October 15, 1974, President Gerald Ford, making no attempt to mask his reluctance, signed into law the Federal Election Campaign Act Amendments, which had been passed by Congress only a few days before. To the Senate and House leaders who had assembled to witness the historic signing, the President made one final attempt to express his opposition: "Although I do have reservations about the First Amendment implications inherent in the limits on individual contributions and candidate expenditures, I am sure that such issues can be resolved in the courts."

Thus, from the moment of its birth, the new law, popularly known as public financing campaign reform, has been plagued by doubts as to its legality, whether it was conceived in illegitimacy on the floor of Congress. Today its mere existence raises a question of constitutionality.

President Ford was not alone in his criticism of the new legislation. Senator James Allen (D.–Ala.), one of the conferees on the Senate-House conference committee that ironed out the final reconciliation between competing versions passed by each chamber, announced that he would neither sign the conference committee report nor vote for the compromise bill. His decision not to do so, Allen said, was "due to a strong conviction on my part that taxpayer financing of elections is not in the public interest." Allen, conceded to be the Senate's most skillful parliamentarian, charged that "to use the terms 'public financing' and 'campaign reform' interchangeably or as synonymous is erroneous."

Senator James Buckley (Cons.-R.–N.Y.) joined Allen in denouncing the legislation, declaring, "To offer this bill in the name of reform is an act of unprecedented cynicism."

Senate Minority Leader Hugh Scott (R.–Pa.), on the other hand, fairly gushed over the new campaign bill: "The regret I have principally is that we did not extend public financing on a matching basis to Congressional elections. . . . However, we will give the Presidential financing . . . a good try in 1976."

Senator Scott and many of his fellow sponsors of the bill may well be mistaken about using the new law in the 1976 election. Each passing day since its enactment finds new questions being raised about the constitutionality of many of the act's provisions, with the probability emerging that key portions of the new law will be struck down by the Supreme Court before next year's national elections are held.

The gravest threat to the viability of the new law began to take shape only one day after its last remaining provisions became effective on New Year's Day 1975. On January 2, a group of nine distinguished plaintiffs of diverse political backgrounds filed suit in federal court challenging the law's constitutionality.*

The suit, destined to be one of the great constitutional cases in our history and one which ultimately will be decided by the Supreme Court, is worthy of the close attention of every American.

The election law being challenged in the suit comprises the Federal Election Campaign Act of 1971 (FECA), the Federal Election Campaign Act Amendments of 1974, and Subtitle H of the Internal Revenue Code of 1954.

Senator Buckley heads the list of the nine plaintiffs. The others are Eugene McCarthy, former Democratic senator from Minnesota; Congressman William Steiger (R.–Wis.); liberal political philanthropist Steward Rawlings Mott; Committee for a Constitutional Presidency, a political party which intends to sponsor a candidate for President in

---

* *Buckley, et al.* v. *Valeo, et al.*, filed in the U.S. District Court for the District of Columbia. Certified to the U.S. Court of Appeals for the District of Columbia on January 24, 1975 (Court of Appeals Civil Action, No. 75–1061).

1976 (likely to be Eugene McCarthy); the Conservative Party of New York State; the New York Civil Liberties Union, which has a membership of 40,000; the American Conservative Union; and *Human Events,* a weekly Washington newspaper.

Named in the suit as defendants are the secretary of the Senate, clerk of the House, comptroller general of the United States, attorney general of the United States, and the Federal Election Commission.

Three additional defendants were added, after the suit was filed, at their own request: Common Cause, the League of Women Voters, and the Center for Public Financing of Elections. All three organizations had lobbied strenuously for the law's passage and are its most vocal supporters next to those in Congress and in the media.

A few weeks before the filing of the suit, on December 11, Senator Buckley, Eugene McCarthy, and Ira Glasser, executive director of the New York Civil Liberties Union, held a press conference to announce their decision to challenge the act. In their joint statement, the three declared:

We have come together to announce our intention to challenge the constitutionality of the Federal Election Campaign Act Amendments of 1974 and of certain related statutes enacted earlier. The 1974 Act—the so-called campaign reform bill—was passed recently by Congress and signed by President Ford.

While not all of the potential plaintiffs will jointly contest all of the law's provisions, the following are some of the major items we will challenge:

(1) Limits on the amount which any individual may contribute to any federal candidate.

(2) Limits on the total aggregate amount which any individual may contribute to all federal candidates.

(3) Limits on what an independent political organization not connected to any candidate may contribute.

(4) Limits on political expenditures by persons independent of any candidate.

(5) Limits on incidental expenses incurred by volunteers.

(6) Limits on the amounts that federal candidates may spend on their campaigns.

(7) Overbroad disclosure of political association.

(8) Establishment of an election committee with unprecedented power to investigate and regulate political activity.

(9) The public financing provisions for presidential primaries, conventions, and general elections, some of which were enacted earlier.

This is not a complete and exhaustive list of the provisions that may come under judicial review.

In concluding their joint remarks, Senator Buckley and his two prominent co-plaintiffs declared:

> We believe that many of the provisions of the new law violate the First Amendment of the Constitution. They restrict the political freedom of individual citizens by limiting political activity, circumscribing speech, institutionalizing advantages for incumbents, authorizing unprecedented government surveillance over political association and establishing broad investigative powers of doubtful constitutionality. The end result, we fear, will not be fairer elections but rather a restriction of dissenting points of view that will make it harder for independent candidates and small political parties to make themselves heard in the marketplace of ideas.
>
> We announce our intention to bring litigation with the knowledge that its eventual outcome may have a profound effect on American politics and on independent constitutional rights. The end we seek is the restoration of the freedom of expression guaranteed by the Constitution. We are confident that a careful examination by the courts of the unintended effects of this legislation will reveal the constitutional defects that unhappily escaped the scrutiny of Congress.

In their complaint filed with the court seeking declaratory and injunctive relief from the election law, the plaintiffs have listed over thirty causes of action or reasons why the campaign reform law violates the rights of one or more of the plaintiffs. These are enumerated here to illustrate the vast, almost dictatorial, scheme by which the law attempts to control the nation's electoral processes. The suit charges that the Federal Election Campaign Act of 1971 and the Federal Election Campaign Act Amendments of 1974:

• Violate the constitutional rights of one or more of the plaintiffs in that they restrict and inhibit political activity by limiting the solicitation, receipt, or making of contributions in behalf of political candidates, in violation of the rights of freedom of speech and association guaranteed by the First Amendment to the Constitution.

• Violate the rights of one or more of the plaintiffs in that they restrict and inhibit political activity by preventing candidates or their

24

immediate family from expending personal funds where available and necessary, in violation of their rights of freedom of speech and association guaranteed by the First Amendment to the Constitution.

• Violate the constitutional rights of one or more of the plaintiffs in that they restrict and inhibit political activity by limiting the incidental expenses that volunteers working in behalf of political candidates may incur, in violation of their rights of freedom of speech and association guaranteed by the First Amendment to the Constitution.

• Violate the constitutional rights of one or more of the plaintiffs in that they limit expenditures by a candidate for federal office, and thereby restrict and inhibit the candidate's ability to communicate his ideas and positions, in violation of the rights of freedom of speech and association guaranteed by the First Amendment to the Constitution.

• Violate the constitutional rights of one or more of the plaintiffs in that they are designed to have, and have, the effect of favoring most incumbent officeholders and thereby disadvantaging most challengers, in violation of their rights of freedom of speech and association guaranteed by the First Amendment to the Constitution and the Due Process Clause of the Fifth Amendment to the Constitution. Incumbents have, at the government's expense, permanent offices, the frank, expense allowances, an established staff, access to congressional television recording services, and a variety of office supplies and expenses, none of which constitutes an expenditure within the FECA and the FECA Amendments when used by them for all but flagrantly political purposes. Challengers can employ such valuable resources only by making expenditures that the act limits to an amount far below the value of what is available to incumbents by virtue of their office alone. This disparity is in addition to the political advantages that naturally inhere in incumbency, such as ability to make news and wider name recognition.

• Violate the constitutional rights of one or more of the plaintiffs in that they discriminate against third parties and minor parties, which rely heavily on large contributions, in violation of their rights of freedom of speech and association guaranteed by the First Amendment to the Constitution and the Due Process Clause of the Fifth Amendment to the Constitution.

• Violate the constitutional rights of one or more of the plaintiffs in that they discriminate against third parties or minor parties that have not previously demonstrated their ability to capture a large percentage

25

of the popular vote or that run candidates on a "balance-of-power" or "spoiler" strategy hoping to influence the policies of the major parties, in violation of their rights of freedom of speech and association guaranteed by the First Amendment to the Constitution and the Due Process Clause of the Fifth Amendment to the Constitution.

• Violate the constitutional rights of one or more of the plaintiffs in that they limit the expenditures of national committees of a political party in the cause of campaigns for federal office, in violation of the rights of freedom of speech and association guaranteed by the First Amendment to the Constitution and the Due Process Clause of the Fifth Amendment to the Constitution.

• Violate the constitutional rights of one or more of the plaintiffs in that they discriminate against political parties lacking a national committee, in violation of the rights of freedom of speech and association guaranteed by the First Amendment to the Constitution and the Due Process Clause of the Fifth Amendment to the Constitution.

• Violate the constitutional rights of one or more of the plaintiffs in that they discriminate against political parties sponsoring a candidate for President in only one state, in violation of their rights of freedom of speech and association guaranteed by the First Amendment to the Constitution and the Due Process Clause of the Fifth Amendment to the Constitution.

• Violate the constitutional rights of one or more of the plaintiffs in that they provide, through auditing procedures, for the Federal Election Commission to inspect lists and records required to be kept by political committees of individuals who contribute more than $10, in violation of their rights of freedom of speech and association and privacy guaranteed by the First, Fourth, and Ninth Amendments to the Constitution and of their right to due process of the Fifth Amendment to the Constitution.

• Violate the rights of one or more of the plaintiffs in that they require political committees to register and disclose the names of those of their contributors who contribute in excess of $100, in violation of their rights of freedom of speech, association, and privacy guaranteed by the First, Fourth, and Ninth Amendments to the Constitution and of their right to due process of the Fifth Amendment to the Constitution.

• Violate the constitutional rights of one or more of the plaintiffs in that they discriminate invidiously against them by not requiring the

26

same disclosure from incumbent officeholders of all resources available to such incumbents, such as the value of services furnished by the Senate or House recording studios or the services of certain individuals on their staffs, in violation of the right to due process of the Fifth Amendment to the Constitution.

• Violate the constitutional rights of one or more of the plaintiffs in that they provide that every person contributing or expending more than $100 otherwise than by contribution to a political committee or candidate (including volunteers with incidental expenses in excess of $600) must make disclosure to the Federal Election Commission, in violation of the rights of freedom of speech, association, and privacy of the First, Fourth, and Ninth Amendments to the Constitution and of their right to due process of the Fifth Amendment to the Constitution.

• Violate the constitutional rights of one or more of the plaintiffs in that they require any person who expends funds or commits any act for the purpose of influencing the outcome of an election or who publishes or broadcasts to the public any material advocating the election or defeat of a candidate, setting forth a candidate's position on any public issue, his voting record, or any official acts, to file reports with the Federal Election Commission as if such person were a political committee, in violation of the rights of freedom of speech, association, and privacy of the First, Fourth, and Ninth Amendments to the Constitution.

• Violate the constitutional rights of one or more of the plaintiffs in that they provide criminal penalties for violation of the disclosure provisions of the statutes, in violation of the rights of freedom of speech, association, and privacy of the First, Fourth, and Ninth Amendments to the Constitution.

• Violate the constitutional rights of one or more of the plaintiffs in that they restrain and inhibit individual political activity by limiting to $1,000 the independent (not on behalf of a candidate) expenditures of any person relative to an identified candidate, in violation of the rights of freedom of speech and association of the First Amendment to the Constitution.

• Violate the constitutional rights of one or more of the plaintiffs in that they exclude from the definition of "political committee" committees registered for less than the period of time prescribed in the statute, thus invidiously discriminating against such committees by prohibiting them from participating in the political process for a six-month

27

period, in violation of the rights of freedom of speech and association guaranteed by the First Amendment to the Constitution.

• Provide that the government may bring criminal prosecutions against anyone who violates or is about to violate Section 608 of the FECA and Section 9008 of the Internal Revenue Code of 1954. The risk of criminal prosecution deters and restrains one or more of the plaintiffs and in certain instances constitutes a prior restraint of the exercise of their rights of freedom of speech and of association in violation of the First Amendment to the Constitution, and deprives one or more of the plaintiffs of due process of law in violation of the Due Process Clause of the Fifth Amendment to the Constitution.

• Violate the constitutional rights of one or more of the plaintiffs in that they empower the Federal Election Commission and the attorney general to bring civil actions, including proceedings for injunctions against any person who has engaged or who may engage in acts or practices that violate the campaign act. The risk of being subject to civil injunction proceedings deters and restrains one or more of the plaintiffs and in certain instances constitutes a prior restraint of the exercise of their rights of freedom of speech and association in violation of the First and Fifth Amendments to the Constitution.

• Violate the constitutional rights of one or more of the plaintiffs in that they limit the freedom of the press by exempting news stories, commentaries, and editorials from the statutory definitions of "expenditure" but not from the statutory definitions of "contribution," thus subjecting those press functions to regulation, in violation of the rights of a free press guaranteed by the First Amendment to the Constitution.

• Deprives one or more plaintiffs of their constitutional rights in that it allows incumbent officeholders and successful candidates to employ surplus campaign funds to defray the expenses of their offices, thus discriminating invidiously against candidates for federal office, in violation of the rights of freedom of speech and association guaranteed by the First Amendment to the Constitution and the Due Process Clause of the Fifth Amendment to the Constitution.

• Deprives one or more of the plaintiffs of their rights in that the method of appointment of the Federal Election Commission violates the constitutional separation of powers and discriminates invidiously against them in violation of the Due Process Clause of the Fifth Amendment to the Constitution.

- Deprives one or more of the plaintiffs of their right to a hearing before an impartial tribunal by entrusting administration and enforcement of the FECA, as amended, to the Federal Election Commission, in violation of the constitutional separation of powers, Article III, and the Due Process Clause of the Fifth Amendment to the Constitution.
- Deprives one or more of the plaintiffs of their rights in that the Federal Election Commission is empowered to make rules under the FECA in violation of the constitutional separation of powers and the Due Process Clause of the Fifth Amendment to the Constitution.
- Deprives one or more of the plaintiffs of their rights in that the Federal Election Commission has power to disqualify a person from becoming a candidate for election to federal office, in violation of the First, Fifth, and Sixth Amendments to the Constitution.

Further, the suit alleges that the Federal Election Campaign Act of 1971, the 1974 amendments, and Subtitle H of the Internal Revenue Code of 1954:

- Deprive one or more of the plaintiffs of their constitutional rights in that federal tax money is thereby used to support only certain political parties, in violation of the restrictions imposed on the federal taxing and spending power by the First Amendment to the Constitution.
- Deprive one or more of the plaintiffs of their constitutional rights in that federal tax money is thereby used to support political movements and organizations, in violation of the restrictions imposed on the federal taxing and spending power by the First Amendment to the Constitution.
- Deprive one or more of the plaintiffs of their constitutional rights in that federal taxpayers are permitted to designate their preference neither for parties nor for candidates, in violation of the rights of freedom of speech and association guaranteed by the First Amendment to the Constitution.
- Violate the constitutional rights of one or more of the plaintiffs in that they establish officially supported political parties and discriminate against minor parties and independent candidates, against parties sponsoring a candidate for President in fewer than ten states, against candidates with substantial support in fewer than twenty states, against parties who have neither nominating conventions nor primaries, and against independent candidates not nominated by conventions or primaries. These provisions violate the rights of freedom of speech and association of the First Amendment to the Constitution and

the right to due process of law of the Fifth Amendment to the Constitution.

Finally, the suit charges that Titles I, II, III, and IV of the 1974 Amendments:

• Deprive one or more of the plaintiffs of the rights of freedom of speech and association and of due process of law under the First and Fifth Amendments to the Constitution because they are excessively vague and overbroad.

• Deprive one or more of the plaintiffs of their retained rights under the Ninth Amendment to the Constitution.

Senator Buckley, Eugene McCarthy, and their co-plaintiffs in their suit request that the following relief be granted by the Court:

1. Order, adjudge, decree and declare that the FECA, the FECA Amendments, and Subtitle H are repugnant to the Constitution of the United States, and that said statutes violate plaintiffs' rights under the Constitution of the United States; and further

2. Permanently enjoin and restrain defendants, their agents and assistants from the use, operation, enforcement, execution and application of the FECA, the FECA Amendments, and Subtitle H in any and all respects in which the same may be found to be repugnant to the Constitution of the United States; and further

3. Grant such order and further relief as to the Court may seem just and proper, together with the costs and disbursements of this action.

The plaintiffs in their court suit are not the only vocal critics of the campaign reform legislation. A few voices in the media managed to break through the boycott imposed on airing opposing views. Jerry Landauer, famed reporter for the *Wall Street Journal,* wrote: "Under the guise of campaign reform, hypocritical Congressmen have come up with a cunningly crafted device to help keep themselves in power."[1]

Columnist James J. Kilpatrick, who previously had endorsed public financing, expressed misgivings about the final bill: "To express these misgivings is not to condone the corrupt campaign practices of the Watergate scandal. That sordid record was a record of serious sickness in our body politic. But the more one examines the law, the more one is persuaded that in some of its provisions, the cure may be worse than the disease."[2]

Another columnist, self-styled conservative George Will, who is

30

marketed by the *Washington Post,* surprised many of his readers by predicting, "Long after the Supreme Court has dismantled the 1974 Campaign Reform Act, historians will be marveling about this fact: responding to the anti-constitutionalism of Watergate, Congress concocted a law that violated the First Amendment more systematically and comprehensively than the Alien and Sedition Acts did."[3]

Howard Phillips, onetime director of the Office of Economic Opportunity (OEO) and now head of the Conservative Caucus, examined the new law in fine detail and termed it "the most insidious threat ever posed to America's tradition of political liberty."[4]

Columnist Joseph Alsop, writing on "The Effects of Campaign Finance Reform," declared: "Finally, one must note that the new law further quite vastly increases the already vast influence on the Democratic Party of the labor groups . . . yet who pointed all this out in advance?"[5]

Additional criticism in the press began to appear at random once the full implications of the law became clearer. Outrage was expressed in some quarters after the discovery that the new law shortened the statute of limitations, on which prosecution of violations is based, from five to three years. One effect of this provision was to cut off possible prosecution of campaign violations if they occurred three years before the law became effective—that is, before 1972.* Apparently, the Ford administration acquiesced in imposing this radical reform; a subsequent news article reported that a "spokesman for the Justice Department said that the Department knew about the change before the bill was passed but that it took no stand."[6]

Public criticism has also surfaced about the quality and character of some of the eight persons nominated to the Federal Election Commission, which administers and enforces the new law. Fred Wertheimer of Common Cause, whose lobbying helped to bring the law into being, has declared, "The Commission is the heart of the law."

However, an examination of the background of most of the commis-

---

*It is widely believed that the provision was quietly inserted at the last minute by liberals on the House Administration Committee acting at the behest of organized labor. Many of the internal AFL-CIO and other union documents printed verbatim in *The Hundred Million Dollar Payoff* provided explicit evidence of campaign violations occurring before 1972. Shortening the statute of limitations served to protect the unions, union leaders and a number of Democratic politicians from prosecution.

sion members reveals them to be ethically deficient, to put the case mildly. The members are: Thomas Harris, Neil Staebler, Joan D. Aikens, Thomas Curtis, Vernon Thomson, and Robert Tiernan. Frank Valeo, secretary of the Senate, and Pat Jennings, clerk of the House, also serve by reason of the office they hold.

Thomas Harris, nominated to the commission by Senate Majority Leader Mike Mansfield, boasts the most blatant conflict-of-interest background. From 1948 to 1955 he served as associate general counsel of the CIO, and from 1955 to his appointment to the commission he was associate general counsel of the AFL-CIO. As the *Congressional Quarterly* noted in its issue of December 28, 1974, in commenting on Harris' possible nomination:

> Organized labor has a strong interest in the decisions of the new election commission. Labor is a major contributor of money and manpower to congressional and presidential campaigns. The way in which the new commission implements and interprets the campaign spending law will determine the level and kind of support that labor can give to the candidates it favors.

According to columnist John Herling, who slavishly espouses organized labor's views, in an article entitled "George Meany's Man Goes Public":

> Harris orchestrated labor's battle against the confirmation of Clement Haynsworth and G. Harrold Carswell to the Superior Court. With Meany by his side, Harris testified against Haynsworth for three hours before the Senate Judiciary Committee. He marshaled his arguments with a lean and powerful vocabulary and every word became a rock on which the Haynsworth nomination ultimately foundered.[7]

Harris, in a public document lodged in federal court, recently admitted how the AFL-CIO uses the tax-exempt dues money of its members to elect liberal candidates (see Appendix IV).

Neil Staebler, another Federal Election Commission member, was Democratic national committeeman from Michigan at the time of his appointment. On March 14, 1975, the Associated Press reported that he wanted to continue "to attend party meetings as an observer because that would be a good way to pick up information about how the law is working." Staebler has long been allied with organized labor. The

32

Detroit Free Press, in a series analyzing labor's influence in the Wolverine State, concluded:

> Organized labor's large membership funds and plentiful campaign manpower make it the most powerful single force in Michigan politics.
>
> Unions pour huge sums of money into the campaign committees of candidates they favor. The candidates are usually Democrats. Labor, in fact, contributes a major share of the funds used to finance the day-to-day operations of the Michigan Democratic Party.[8]

Robert Tiernan, a former Democratic congressman from Rhode Island, was defeated in his party's primary in 1974. His voting record in Congress was consistently prolabor, having voted fifty-three "right" and three "wrong" on the AFL-CIO COPE ratings. His prolabor bias became a matter of public concern when on February 14, 1975, AP reporter Brooks Jackson reported that

> the campaign committee of former Rep. Robert Tiernan, who has been nominated to be a Federal Election Commissioner, accepted $1,000 in gifts from a group reportedly under investigation for campaign law violations.
>
> Tiernan's campaign finance reports show his main campaign committee got $500 gifts from the Seafarers International Union on December 20 and December 28 at a time when the defeated congressman was being considered for the commission.
>
> Tiernan's committee accepted the gifts after the public reports disclosed that the union was under renewed investigation by the Justice Department. Union members complained that they were being coerced to make supposedly voluntary donations to the union's political fund.[9]

Joan Aikens, a political protégée of Senator Hugh Scott (R.–Pa.), is the former president of the Pennsylvania Council of Republican Women. Scott, an ardent advocate of public financing for both Presidential and congressional campaigns, was forced to defend Aikens' qualifications on the floor of the Senate.

Thomas Curtis and Vernon Thomson, two additional commissioners, are former Republican congressmen. Curtis is from Missouri and Thomson from Wisconsin.

Secretary of the Senate Frank Valeo and Clerk of the House Pat Jennings, who serve on the commission by reason of their offices, are both Democrats and have long been allied with organized labor.

33

If the suit filed to challenge the constitutionality of the campaign reform act does not succeed in killing it, the federal election commissioners may very well end up doing the job. For how can the American public have any faith in the impartiality of justice that will be dispensed by a commission composed of a majority who are tainted with political conflict-of-interest?

2

An Overview of
the
"Incumbents' Protection Act"

All provisions of the 1974 amendments to the Federal Election Campaign Act became effective no later than January 1, 1975.[1] The effect of the act is drastically to alter the way in which campaigns for federal offices may be financed and conducted. Failure to comply with almost any provision of the act may result in a criminal penalty. In addition, failure to comply with the provisions of the act dealing with reporting, disclosing, and handling of funds may result in the disqualification of an individual from eligibility to run for federal office.

The campaign act imposes many new restrictions on the amount of contributions that individuals and groups may make to candidates for federal office, and on the amount that candidates for federal office may expend and that may be spent in their behalf; establishes a required procedure for disclosing, reporting, and handling campaign funds; establishes a Federal Election Commission; prohibits certain campaign practices; changes the law dealing with public financing of Presidential general elections; provides for public financing of national nominating conventions of political parties; and provides for partial public financing of Presidential primary elections.

CONTRIBUTION LIMITATIONS

Definition of Contribution. Contribution is defined very broadly and includes almost anything of any value (including in-kind contributions) made available to a candidate's campaign that is not specifically excepted from the definition. The items that are specifically excepted and that may be given to a candidate's campaign without counting toward the donor's contribution limitation are:

(1) the value of the services of a person who on his own initiative volunteers his services without remuneration;

(2) the use of real or personal property and the cost of invitations, food, and beverages voluntarily provided by an individual for a candidate in rendering voluntary personal services on the individual's residential premises for candidate-related activities, up to $500;

(3) the value of the discount given on the sale of food or beverages for use in a campaign at a charge less than the vendor's normal comparable charge, but at least equal to his cost, up to $500;

(4) unreimbursed travel expenses up to $500; and

(5) slate cards, sample ballots, and other printed listings of three or more candidates for public office in a particular state prepared by the state or local committee of a political party (but not the cost of display through broadcasting stations, newspapers, magazines, and other similar types of general political advertising).

Excessive Contributions Illegal. The Federal Election Campaign Act imposes specific dollar limitations on the amount of contributions that individuals and organizations may give to a candidate's campaign. It is illegal for any individual or organization to make a contribution in excess of the legal limit, and it is illegal for any candidate or political committee knowingly to accept such an illegal excessive contribution.

General Rule. As a general rule, no person, including an individual, a political committee, or other organization (except multicandidate political committees), may contribute more than $1,000 to each stage of a candidate's campaign for nomination for election, or election to federal office. For example, an individual could contribute $1,000 to a congressional candidate's campaign for nomination for election in a primary election, $1,000 to a congressional candidate's campaign for nomination in a runoff primary election and $1,000 to a congressional candidate's campaign for election in a general election (that is, each of these stages of the electoral process is deemed a separate election in congressional campaigns). In the case of a Presidential election, however, the act provides for only two election stages: (1) the general election, and (2) all other phases of the electoral process (that is, all of the primaries and the nominating convention are regarded as one stage of the electoral process).

Aggregate Limitation on Contributions by Individuals to Candidates and Political Committees. No individual may make contributions aggregating more than $25,000 in any calendar year to candidates and political committees. An individual who makes no other contributions in a calendar year may contribute up to $25,000 to a political committee, including, for example, the national committee of a political party, *if* the contribution to the political committee is in no way earmarked for the use of a particular candidate and *if* the contribution is in no way earmarked for use in a calendar year other than the year in which it is made. (Contributions to a single-candidate political committee are necessarily earmarked for the use of that candidate.) For example, in 1975 Mr. X could contribute $25,000 to the national committee of a political party *if* he made no contributions to federal candidates or to other political committees supporting federal candidates, *if* his $25,000 contribution was in no way earmarked for the use of a particular candidate, and *if* his contribution was in no way earmarked for use in a calendar year other than the year in which it was made. Although the act is not entirely clear, it is probable that such a 1975 contribution by Mr. X would not prevent him from making an identical contribution in 1976 or, alternatively, from making twenty-five $1,000 contributions in 1976 to candidates for federal office. Clarification of the question of the permissibility of such a 1976 contribution will be sought from the Federal Election Commission.

If a contribution is made by an individual in 1975 to a candidate for use in a candidate's campaign in 1976, the contribution must count toward the donor's 1976 $25,000 aggregate limitation. For example, if Mr. A contributes $1,000 to each of fifteen congressmen in 1975 for a total of $15,000 with the intention that they use this money in their campaigns for reelection in 1976, then Mr. A may give no more than $1,000 to each of ten congressional candidates in 1976. Because his 1975 contributions were made with respect to the 1976 election, his contributions are deemed to have been made in 1976 and, when combined with his contributions in 1976, equal the maximum $25,000 allowed for any calendar year. The same rules would apply to contributions made after the calendar year of the election.

Limitations on Multicandidate Political Committees. An important exception to the general rule is that a multicandidate political committee (a committee that has been registered for six months, has received contributions from more than fifty persons, and has made contributions to five or more candidates for federal office) may contribute up to $5,000 to each congressional or Presidential candidate at each stage of the election campaign (as described above) except that state political party organizations may make the $5,000 contributions without regard to the number of candidates to whom they have contributed. Different subdivisions of the same multicandidate political committee may each contribute $5,000 to each stage of a candidate's election campaign only if the subdivision's decision to make the contribution is not under the control or direction of, and is made independently of, the parent committee and any other subdivision of the parent committee.

Earmarked Contributions. Contributions that are made at the request of a candidate or to a committee authorized by the candidate, or that are earmarked for a candidate or otherwise made through an intermediary, are counted as contributions to the candidate by the original donor. Thus the contribution limitations cannot be evaded by secret earmarking and laundering of funds.

Prohibition of Certain Contributions. Contributions by national banks, labor organizations, and corporations are prohibited.

Contributions by foreign nationals are prohibited.

Contributions in the name of another are prohibited.

Cash contributions in excess of $100 are prohibited.

In addition, many types of contributions (for example, those from government contractors) that were prohibited under prior law are still prohibited.

EXPENDITURE LIMITATIONS

Definition of Expenditure. Expenditure comprehends almost any campaign-related transaction or activity performed in support of a candidate's campaign that is not specifically excepted. The following exceptions to the definition of *expenditure* do not count toward the applicable expenditure limitation:

(1) any news story, commentary, or editorial distributed through any broadcasting station, newspaper, magazine, or other periodical publication not owned or controlled by a political party, political committee, or candidate;

(2) nonpartisan get-out-the-vote activity;

(3) any communication to its members or stockholders by any membership organization or corporation not organized primarily for the purpose of influencing a candidate's nomination or election;

(4) the use of real or personal property and the cost of invitations, food, and beverages voluntarily provided by an individual for a candidate in rendering voluntary personal services on the individual's residential premises for candidate-related activities, up to $500;

(5) unreimbursed payment for travel expenses by an individual volunteer up to $500;

(6) any communication not made for the purpose of influencing the nomination or election of a candidate;

(7) slate cards, sample ballots, and other listings of three or more candidates in a state by the state or local committee of a political party (but not including display of such a listing through broadcasting stations, newspapers, magazines, or other similar types of general public political advertising);

(8) up to twenty percent of the amount of the candidate's applicable expenditure limitation spent by a candidate (or by an individual or single-candidate committee authorized by the candidate) in connection with the solicitation of contributions; and

(9) any amount spent by a political committee (other than a single-candidate political committee) in connection with the solicitation of contributions (but not including the cost of soliciting contributions through broadcasting stations, newspapers, magazines, outdoor advertising facilities, and other similar types of general public political advertising).

Limitations on Candidates for President. A candidate for the office of President may spend no more than $10,000,000 in his primary campaigns and no more than $20,000,000 in his general election campaign. He may choose to finance these campaigns by means of public financing.

Limitations on Candidates for Senator, Representative, Delegate, and Commissioner. A candidate for *nomination* for election to the office of senator or to the office of representative from a state entitled to only one representative may spend no more than the greater of eight cents multiplied by the voting-age population of the state (as certified by the secretary of commerce) or $100,000 in each stage of his nomination campaign. In each *general election* campaign such a candidate may spend no more than the greater of twelve cents multiplied by the voting-age population of the state or $150,000.

A candidate for *nomination or election* to the office of representative from a state entitled to more than one representative, to the office of delegate from the District of Columbia, or to the office of resident commissioner may spend no more than $70,000 in each stage of his campaign for nomination or election.

Limitation on Expenditures from Personal Funds of a Candidate or His Immediate Family.   Expenditures by a candidate either from his personal funds or from the personal funds of his immediate family in all of his campaigns in any one calendar year are limited to:

(1) $50,000 in the case of a candidate for the office of President or Vice President;

(2) $35,000 in the case of a candidate for election to the office of senator or the office of representative from a state entitled to only one representative; or

(3) $25,000 in the case of a candidate for the office of representative from a state entitled to more than one representative, the office of delegate, or the office of resident commissioner.

If such an expenditure is made in 1975 for use in a campaign in 1976, the expenditure must count toward the candidate's 1976 expenditure limitation.

A candidate's immediate family means his spouse, child, parent, grandparent, brother, or sister and the spouses of such persons. No candidate or his immediate family may make loans or advances from their personal funds to a candidate's campaign, unless the loan or advance is evidenced by a written instrument fully disclosing the terms of the loan or advance. The outstanding unpaid balance of any such loan or advance must be included in computing the total amount of personal and family expenditures.

Additional Allowable Expenditures by Party Committees.   In addition to amounts allowed to be spent pursuant to the above limitations,

(1) the national committee of a political party may spend in a *general election* for the office of President two cents multiplied by the voting-age population of the United States (state and county party committees

may not make such expenditures in behalf of a Presidential campaign); and

(2) the national committee of a political party *and* the state committee of a political party (including any expenditures by subordinate committees of a state committee) may *each* spend:

(a) in a *general election* for the office of senator or representative from a state entitled to only one representative, the greater of two cents multiplied by the voting-age population of the state or $20,000; or

(b) in a *general election* for the office of representative from a state entitled to more than one representative, the office of delegate, or the office of resident commissioner, $10,000.

Application and Adjustment of Limitations.   Unless otherwise indicated, all the above expenditure limitations apply separately to each stage of the election process. Beginning in January 1976 the amount of the limitations will be adjusted annually to reflect any increase in the Consumer Price Index.

Attribution of Expenditures.   Expenditures that are made at the request of a candidate or by a committee authorized by the candidate are counted as expenditures made by the candidate.

Independent Expenditures.   Regardless of all the above expenditure limitations, any person (which includes an individual, any type of political committee, or any other group of individuals) may make on his own initiative an independent expenditure (that is, an expenditure that is not made by a committee authorized by the candidate or his agents, and that has not been authorized or requested by the candidate, an authorized committee, or his agents) in any *calendar year* in an aggregate amount not greater than $1,000 advocating the election or defeat of a particular candidate. The expenditure must be truly independent, spontaneous, and in no way approved by the candidate or his representatives. When such expenditures in a calendar year exceed $100 in the aggregate, the person making the expenditure must file a prescribed report with the Federal Election Commission. There is no limit on the number of candidates with respect to which such $1,000 independent expenditures may be made. For example, an individual could make fifty $1,000 expenditures advocating the election of each of fifty congressional candidates (for a total of $50,000), if each of these $1,000 expenditures qualified as an independent expenditure. Since such expenditures are not contributions, the $25,000 aggregate limit on

41

contributions does not limit the amount of independent expenditures. The individual would have to report such expenditures to the commission.

STATEMENTS AND REPORTS

Statement of Organization of Committee. Every political committee must file a statement of organization with the Federal Election Commission if the committee anticipates receiving contributions or making expenditures in excess of $1,000 in any calendar year. This statement must be filed within ten days of the date of the committee's anticipation that it will receive or make $1,000 worth of contributions or expenditures. In other words, the statement must be filed ten days from the date of anticipation, not ten days from the date of the actual receipt or expenditure of the $1,000.

Reports of Candidate, Principal Campaign Committee, and Other Committees. Each candidate for federal office *must* designate a principal campaign committee, even if the candidate does not anticipate receiving contributions from political committees. A multicandidate political committee may not be a principal campaign committee, with *one* exception—the national committee (a multicandidate committee) of a political party may be the principal campaign committee for its Presidential candidate in the Presidential general election. The principal campaign committee has the responsibility of receiving and compiling the reports of all other political committees that support the candidate concerning contributions made by such committees to the candidate or expenditures made by them on behalf of the candidate. These reports were formerly filed by each committee with the appropriate supervisory officer. The principal campaign committee must file a complete compilation of such reports, along with its own statement and reports, with the Federal Election Commission.

Reports must be filed with the commission by both the treasurer of each principal campaign committee and by the candidate. The treasurer of each political committee must file reports with the appropriate principal campaign committee. The reports generally must contain all contributions received and expenditures made by the reporting committee or candidate, as well as the identification of the person receiving or making a contribution. Also, the identification of any person to whom expenditures were made must be reported. Furthermore, all

42

guarantors of loans must be disclosed in the reports, as well as the circumstances under which a loan was extinguished.

Reports by Persons Other Than Candidates or Committees. A person who makes contributions or expenditures over $100, otherwise than by contribution to a candidate or a political committee, must file a report with the Federal Election Commission. Furthermore, any organization that expends money, or commits any act directed to the public, for the purpose of influencing an election must also file a report with the commission disclosing the source of the funds supporting such activity. This stipulation may require organizations like Common Cause and the American Civil Liberties Union to disclose the sources of their funds.

Exemption for Members of Congress from Reporting Value of Certain Services in Nonelection Years. In a nonelection year, members of Congress do not have to report the value of photographic, matting, and recording services furnished to them in the nonelection year by the Senate Recording Studio, the House Recording Studio, an employee of the Senate or the House, or if such services are paid for by the Republican or the Democratic Senatorial Campaign Committee, the Democratic National Congressional Committee or the National Republican Campaign Committee. However, in an election year, they do have to report the value of such recording services furnished to them in that election year.

TIME FOR FILING REPORTS

In an Election Year. Reports must be filed not later than ten days before the election and must be complete as of fifteen days before the election. (This report replaces the five-day and fifteen-day reports required by the 1971 act.) Any reports filed by registered or certified mail must be postmarked not later than twelve days before the election. A report must be filed not later than thirty days after the election and must be complete as of twenty days after the election. Any contribution of $1,000 or more that is received after the fifteenth day before an election must be reported to the commission within forty-eight hours.

For a Nonelection Year. For a nonelection year in which an individual is a candidate for federal office a report must be filed by January 31 of the following year and must be complete as of December 31 of the nonelection year.

Quarterly Reports. Quarterly reports must be filed by any candidate or political committee that receives contributions or makes expenditures in excess of $1,000 or more in any calendar quarter. These quarterly reports must be complete as of the end of the quarter and filed within ten days after the end of the quarter.

Report on January 31, 1975. Notwithstanding the 1974 amendments to the 1971 act, the report that was required under the 1971 act to be filed by January 31, 1975, must still be filed.

Filing of Reports with States. A copy of the reports filed with the Federal Election Commission by House, Senate, and Presidential candidates and their committees must be filed with the secretary of state of the state in which the election takes place. In the case of the Presidential candidate and his committees, copies of these reports must be filed in every state where an expenditure is made in the candidate's behalf. State laws are superseded and preempted. Therefore, candidates for federal office and political committees that support federal candidates are not required to file any state reports except for the above-mentioned filing with the applicable secretary of state.

Penalty for Failure to File Report. In addition to a fine or imprisonment, any person who fails to file a required report with the commission, or who files a report late, may be disqualified from becoming a candidate for federal office in a future election.

HANDLING OF FUNDS

General. Each political committee must have a chairman and a treasurer. The treasurer is responsible for keeping an account of all contributions and expenditures of the political committee as well as preparing and signing the reports filed with the Federal Election Commission. The treasurer may be criminally liable if any of the requirements relating to reporting, disclosing, or handling funds are violated. No contribution or expenditure may be accepted or made by a political committee when there is a vacancy in the position of chairman or treasurer of the committee. Every person who receives a contribution in excess of $10 on behalf of a political committee must report the contribution to the treasurer within five days after receipt or upon demand by the treasurer.

Campaign Depositories. Every authorized political committee must maintain a checking account at a campaign depository (a national or state bank) designated by the candidate. Every unauthorized political committee must maintain a checking account at a campaign depository (a national or state bank) designated by the treasurer of such unauthorized political committee. Every expenditure, except an expenditure to one person for $100 or less that may be made from a petty-cash fund, must be made by a check drawn on the checking account at the campaign depository. All contributions received by a candidate or a political committee are required to be deposited in the checking account at the candidate or committee's campaign depository.

Use of Excess Funds. If a candidate receives more contributions than he uses in his campaigns for nomination or election, he may use these excess funds to defray any ordinary and necessary expenses he incurs in connection with his duties as a holder of federal office, or he may contribute the funds to a charitable organization described in Section 170(c) of the Internal Revenue Code, or he may use the funds for any other lawful purpose. The same rule governs the disposition of funds received by an individual to support his activities as a holder of federal office.

FEDERAL ELECTION COMMISSION

General. The 1974 amendments to the Federal Election Campaign Act establish an independent Federal Election Commission responsible for administering the act.

Powers. Among other powers, the commission has the power to conduct investigations; to hold hearings; to issue subpoenas; to initiate, defend, and appeal *civil* actions; and to refer violations of the act (including violations of *criminal* laws) to the attorney general.

Advisory Opinions. The commission must issue advisory opinions on the legality of a specific transaction or activity upon the request of any individual holding federal office, any candidate for federal office, or any political committee. Such requests must be made public by the commission. If a person for whom an advisory opinion has been rendered acts in good faith in accordance with the opinion, he will be presumed to be in compliance with the act. If a question arises concerning any of the provisions of the act, an advisory opinion should be sought from the commission. The person requesting such an opinion should not do anything until the commission gives its approval through an advisory opinion.

Judicial Review. The commission's acts are subject to judicial review on the initiative of a person aggrieved by a particular act of the commission. An action testing the constitutionality of the act may be initiated by the commission, the national committee of a political party, or any individual eligible to vote in a Presidential election. Judicial actions reviewing acts of the commission or testing the constitutionality of the act must be expedited by the appropriate courts.

Regulations. The commission is required to issue regulations, but any regulations proposed by it must be submitted to Congress prior to promulgation and may be vetoed by Congress within thirty legislative days after receipt.

Enforcement. The commission has the authority to conduct investigations, which must be performed expeditiously, and to use its civil enforcement powers, as well as informal methods of persuasion such as conferences, in attempting to correct a violation. It may also report any violations of criminal laws to the attorney general for criminal prosecution.

MISCELLANEOUS PROVISIONS

Statute of Limitations. The statute of limitations for initiating prosecutions for violation of the act is three years from the date of the violation.

Use of Frank. It is illegal to use mailings under the frank to solicit campaign contributions.

Honorariums. Federal officers and employees (among others, senators, representatives, delegates, and resident commissioners) may not accept an honorarium in excess of $1,000, plus travel and subsistence expenses, or more than $15,000 total honorariums in any calendar year.

Fraudulent Misrepresentation. Fraudulently misrepresenting one's campaign authority is illegal.

Repeal of Limitation. The Campaign Communications Reform Act, which imposed limitations on media expenditures by candidates, has been repealed.

No Tax Deduction for Ads in Convention Programs. The tax deduction for advertising in a national political party convention program has been repealed.

Political Activities of State and Local Employees. State and local officers and employees, whose principal employment involves activity that is financed in whole or in part by loans or grants made by the federal government, are no longer prohibited from general participation in political campaigns *unless there is a state law prohibiting such activity.* Except for elected officials and certain other specifically excepted individuals, however, state and local officers and employees are still prohibited from actually running for election to federal office, unless all candidates in the election are nonpartisan.

Separate Segregated Funds. Corporations and labor organizations, including government contractors, may establish, administer, and solicit *voluntary* contributions to separate segregated funds to be utilized for political purposes.

Effect on State Law. The limitations on contributions and expenditures and the provisions dealing with reporting, disclosing, and handling campaign funds supersede and preempt any provision of state law with respect to election to federal office. State laws that purport to regulate contributions and expenditures in campaigns for federal office are no longer valid. Furthermore, the only reports that a candidate for federal office must file with a state are the reports required by the act to be filed with the secretary of state in each state in which a federal election takes place.

PUBLIC FINANCING

General. The public financing aspects of the 1974 amendments to the Federal Election Campaign Act are not applicable to congressional elections, but do provide for the total public financing of Presidential general election campaigns and Presidential nominating conventions and the partial public financing of Presidential primary campaigns. The money for this program will come entirely from the Presidential Election Campaign Fund. This fund receives its money solely from taxpayers who designate one dollar of their tax payment (two dollars on a joint return) to go into the fund. This system, which was in existence prior to the enactment of the 1974 amendments, is popularly known as the checkoff system. The money in the fund will be used for public financing of Presidential primary and general elections and national nominating conventions.

Presidential Nominating Conventions. The national committee of a *major party* is entitled to $2,000,000 from the Presidential Election Campaign Fund in order to defray the expenses of its Presidential nominating convention. The national committee is not required to accept this money but may choose to raise its own funds privately. However, if it chooses to use private financing, it is still limited to spending $2,000,000. The $2,000,000 limit will be increased on a yearly basis to reflect increases in the Consumer Price Index.

The commission is authorized by the act to promulgate rules and regulations defining expenses that may be incurred by a national committee in conducting its convention.

The national committee of a *minor party* may also elect to use public financing for its convention, but it is entitled to only a percentage of the major party entitlement. The minor party may raise the remainder up to the major party entitlement through private contributions. The percentage is based on the percentage of the popular vote received by the minor party candidate in the previous Presidential election.

Financing of national nominating conventions has priority over financing of the Presidential general election and Presidential primaries in the event the fund does not have sufficient money to finance fully all of its obligations.

Presidential General Election Campaigns. Candidates for President may choose to finance publicly their Presidential general election campaigns. These moneys are paid out of the Presidential Election Campaign Fund to the candidates. *Major party candidates* are entitled to $20,000,000, the applicable expenditure limitation (subject to yearly increases based on the Consumer Price Index). If a candidate elects to fund his campaign privately, he is, nevertheless, subject to the applicable contribution and expenditure limitations. Also, a candidate must either totally accept public financing or totally reject it. He cannot use partial public financing, unless the fund does not have sufficient money available to give him his full entitlement. In that case, the candidate is permitted to raise the remainder from private sources and is allotted a twenty-percent exemption for fund-raising costs.

A *minor party Presidential candidate* is also entitled to public funds to defray his qualified campaign expenses incurred in the general election campaign. Such a candidate will receive not the full amount paid to the major party candidate but a percentage thereof based on the popular vote received by the minor party's candidate in the preceding Presidential general election. A candidate of a new or minor party may receive a partial reimbursement after the election if he receives over five percent of the popular vote in the general election.

48

If the fund does not have sufficient money to provide public financing to all of the candidates who choose public financing, the secretary of the treasury, who disburses the money after certification by the Federal Election Commission, will distribute the money on a pro-rata basis. The Presidential general election is next in line for public funding after the nominating convention. The general election must be completely funded before moneys are disbursed for Presidential primary campaigns.

Presidential Primary Campaigns.　The public funding of Presidential primary campaign expenses is basically a matching program. Before a candidate qualifies for any money from the Presidential Election Campaign Fund, he must declare his candidacy and then raise $100,000 by means of private contributions (sometimes called the "threshold requirement"). This $100,000 must be raised by contributions of $5,000 or more from at least twenty states and only contributions of $250 or less will be counted in totaling the qualifying figure.

After the candidate has qualified, the threshold requirement and each succeeding contribution of $250 or less to the candidate will be matched by a similar contribution from the fund. During this period, a candidate may accept contributions of up to $1,000 from individuals and up to $5,000 from multicandidate political committees, but only the first $250 will be matched with public funds. Only money raised after January 1, 1975, will count in determining the qualifying figure or will be matched by dollars from the fund.

The maximum that a Presidential candidate may spend in defraying expenses incurred for his primary campaign is $10,000,000 (subject to annual adjustments based on increases in the Consumer Price Index). Furthermore, he may not spend in any one state more than twice the expenditure limitation imposed on a candidate for senator from that state. Half of the $10,000,000 limit ($5,000,000) may be received from the fund. Also, a candidate is accorded a twenty-percent fund-raising allowance for the money that he must raise privately. Therefore, he may spend an additional $1,000,000 (twenty percent of $5,000,000) to defray his fund-raising costs.

The Presidential primaries have the lowest priority if the fund does not have sufficient money to finance totally the nominating conventions, the general election, and the primaries. Once allowance has been made for the nominating convention and the general election expenses, then money in the fund will be supplied to the qualified primary candidates. A candidate may elect not to seek any public funds for his primary campaigns. In such a case he may raise his money through private contributions, but he will be limited to spending $10,000,000 and his fund-raising exemption will be $2,000,000.

Commission Supervision. The commission is the watchdog over the use of public money for all of the above public financing functions. It will perform examinations and audits to make certain that the political parties and candidates have used the public funds to defray expenses that were properly incurred. It will also promulgate regulations to define what are qualified campaign expenses and qualified convention expenses.

Political parties and candidates have further reporting requirements under the public financing provisions, and criminal penalties may be imposed on persons who use public money for unauthorized purposes.

Disbursement of Funds. Public funds for financing national nominating conventions of political parties will not be disbursed before July 1, 1975. Money for financing Presidential primaries and Presidential general elections will not be disbursed before January 1, 1976.

EXPLANATION OF FEDERAL TAX CONSIDERATIONS

Under the new tax regulations, all political organizations with taxable income of over $100 must file an 1120 corporation tax return and pay any taxes due. IRS rulings specifically mention three kinds of income that are taxable to political organizations: (1) interest, (2) dividends, (3) net gains from the sale of appreciated property sold after August 1, 1973. The only other kind of income that is taxable to a political organization is business income that is obviously unrelated to politics (for example, rental income). The law specifically allows each political organization a $100 exemption from these forms of income. Thus, those political organizations that have income from the sources mentioned above totaling $100 or less do not have to file tax returns or pay taxes. The other important provisions in the new tax laws affecting political organizations follow:

1. Effective May 7, 1974, the $3,000-gift tax limit no longer applies to political contributions.

2. Beginning with the 1975 calendar year, the amount of political

50

contributions (including contributions to a newsletter fund established by an individual who holds, has been elected to, or is a candidate for public office) that can be deducted on federal income tax returns has been increased to: $50 credit or $200 deduction on joint returns, and $25 credit or $100 deduction on individual returns.

3. Section 276C of the IRS Code has been repealed. Corporations are no longer allowed a tax deduction for advertising in convention programs of national political conventions.

3

Hypocrisy Triumphs

in the

Senate

For several weeks in the spring of 1974, the Senate debated the proposed federal election reform. A small, lonely but courageous band of senators waged a tactically brilliant, uphill struggle to amend the more onerous provisions. The leaders of this group of statesmen were Senators James Allen (D.–Ala.) and James Buckley (Cons.–R.–N.Y.), aided frequently by Senators John Tower (R.–Texas), Howard Baker (R.–Tenn.), Jesse Helms (R.–N.C.), and William Brock (R.–Tenn.).

In the end these valiant senators were unsuccessful, the legislation being passed by a vote of 53 to 32. This was virtually the margin of defeat for every effort to amend the legislation so as to make it more equitable. The hypocrisy that ultimately prevailed in the Senate is revealed clearly in the lengthy debate.

(Excerpts from the *Congressional Record*)
March 11

MR. FANNIN. Mr. President, the committee bill S. 3044 is described by its sponsors as a comprehensive Federal Election Campaign Act. Yet, the bill at no place seeks to provide any limitation upon the campaign contributions in either cash or services by organized labor un-

53

ions. In subsequent speeches I shall document the charge that unions have become the largest and most influential force in politics today. Mr. George Meany has demanded that his political organization produce a "veto proof" Congress this November.

Mr. President, the essence of my amendment, which the Senator from Texas (Mr. Tower) has joined me as a cosponsor, is "voluntarism." Labor unions and nonprofit corporations do not lose their tax-exempt status unless they use money, which they receive from compulsory dues, in political campaigns.

The amendment then proceeds to enumerate five things they cannot do without losing their tax-exempt status. Paragraphs numbered 1 and 2 are directed primarily at the so-called hard-money contributions. Paragraphs numbered 3, 4, and 5 are directed primarily at the so-called soft-money services contributed.

Mr. President, our amendment would not destroy COPE or any similar activity or organization that presently exists or may be created by the Chamber of Commerce or the National Association of Manufacturers, or similar organizations. It is only where the activity is financed by compulsory-produced money that their tax-exempt status would be endangered.

Mr. President, when I have sponsored similar bills or amendments in the past, I have called it the "untouchable tax loophole." If we are to have a comprehensive Election Campaign Act, the largest tax loophole cannot be left untouched.

MR. TOWER. Mr. President, I commend Senator Fannin for again bringing to the attention of the Senate one of the major abuses in our political system. Unless the power of organized labor to influence our political system is curbed, true campaign reform will never be achieved. Yet, the bill fails to directly deal with this major problem and the committee report which outlines the need for basic campaign reform is silent on the subject. I am pleased, therefore, to be, in addition to Senator Fannin, the major sponsor of this amendment.

The amendment would treat all section 501 tax-exempt organizations and trusts equally. Any one of these organizations would be denied tax-exempt status if they actively engaged in the listed activities, such as publicly supporting or opposing candidates or parties for election to office and carrying on voter registration drives, by using fees or dues that are received by the organization as a condition of employment.

Mr. President, I will find it difficult to support S. 3044 whether or not

54

the public financing title is retained, deleted or modified, if the kind of reform envisioned by the Fannin-Tower Amendment is not made part of the Senate bill. How can we truly say we have passed campaign reform legislation if we do not call a halt to organized labor's use of "soft money" which, in effect, in many campaigns is more influential than direct cash contributions?

It is, therefore, very important that the Senate consider this amendment. It serves to bring to the attention of the American people whether the Senate will allow to be considered all of the campaign abuses recently witnessed, or just some of them.

March 26

MR. WEICKER. So the gut question about the Government financing of elections is not, "Is it plague or panacea?" For we know it is neither, but rather, "Do the advantages outweigh the disadvantages?" And more important, "Are the alternatives insufficient to do the same job?"

My answer to both questions must be "No."

Federal financing only acknowledges the size of the problem; it does not reform it. There are several ways to effectively reform campaign spending without resorting to Government financing. One is to reduce the length of campaigns. Another is to require full disclosure before the election, rather than after. Another is to limit campaign financing to one committee per candidate, to end the juggled books and "laundered" contributions. And yet another is to eliminate the use of cash in campaigns.

MR. BUCKLEY. Mr. President, the distinguished Senator from Connecticut (Mr. Weicker) has just spoken of the indisputable advantages of incumbency. I would like at this time to focus on just one aspect of the truly mischievous campaign financing proposal now under debate. I believe that S. 3044 might well be termed the Incumbent Protection Act of 1974. While I do not believe that those who drafted the bill intended to do so, they have nevertheless come up with a scheme whose practical effect will be to help us insulate ourselves from effective challenge.

I do not make this statement lightly, but only after a serious examination of the potential impact of the provisions of S. 3044. The evidence available suggests rather strongly that the spending limits included in this bill would help incumbents who might otherwise be targets of serious challengers.

55

This is most readily observed in relation to House races where figures can be fairly easily quantified because of the similarity of the districts in terms of population.

In this regard I would direct your attention to a Common Cause study of the 1972 elections entitled "The 1972 Congressional Campaign Finance—A Study by Common Cause."

The authors of the study are numbered among the principal supporters of public financing and use its results to bolster their case. But I am convinced that they misread their own data; that in fact it argues against public financing generally and the provisions of S. 3044 specifically.

In 1972 more than three-quarters of all House races were decided by pluralities of 60 percent or more. In these races the average winning candidate spent $55,000 or less and the average loser spent even less.

These races all took place in what political analysts like to call "safe" districts. The districts involved were either so totally dominated by one party that a serious fight for the seat impressed almost everyone as futile, or the seat was occupied by a personally popular incumbent who just was not about to be beaten.

The authors of the study apparently believe that real races might be run in these districts if enough dollars are poured into the campaigns of those challenging now firmly entrenched incumbents. I am not persuaded that this would happen.

For reasons outlined above the incumbents holding these seats are probably impervious to real challenge. Those running against them have not failed, because they have lacked funds; they have lacked funds because their campaigns were doomed to failure. Common Cause has simply confused cause with effect in a way that has led Mr. Gardner and his friends to precisely the wrong conclusions.

The average spent by candidates who unseated incumbents in 1972 was $125,000 as opposed to the average of $86,000 those incumbents spent. Thus, it can be argued on the basis of these figures that a challenger must be able to outspend an incumbent opponent by a significant margin if he expects to beat him and that he will have to spend in excess of $100,000 to stand a realistic chance.

But what effect will the $90,000 limit imposed by S. 3044 have in these races? It is not at all unrealistic to assume that it will prevent challengers in marginal districts from overcoming the advantages inherent in incumbency. It is not at all unreasonable, in other words, to

56

assume that those limits, had they been in effect in 1972, might have saved most, if not all of those 10 incumbents.

Mr. BAKER. Let me begin by stating my adamant opposition to the public financing of campaigns for Federal office. I think there is something politically incestuous about the Government financing and, I believe, inevitably then regulating the day-to-day procedures by which the Government is selected. Obviously, it is neither reasonable nor desirable to expect a laissez-faire approach to the conduct of political campaigns. The Government has been involved in one way or another in the electoral process since we undertook our present form of government; and I have no doubt that the Government will increase its involvement in the future. However, if we continue to delegate responsibility for regulating campaigns to the bureaucracy, as we would do by enacting public finance, then I fear that a situation could arise in which the executive branch had the power to manipulate political campaigns in a manner which would make Watergate pale in comparison.

I think it is extraordinarily important that the Government not control the machinery by which the public expresses the range of its desires, demands, and dissent. And finally, I genuinely believe that a statutory prohibition against political contributions, whether it applies to primaries, general election campaigns, or both, may abridge the individual's First Amendment right of freedom of political expression.

Mr. ALLEN. There are many atrocities committed in the name of campaign reform, and I submit that public financing is one such atrocity. Every change does not necessarily mean it is a reform, and paying the bill out of the public Treasury is not reform—it is just shifting the burden to the taxpayer.

Mr. KENNEDY. A detailed summary of the public financing provisions of S. 3044 is attached as an appendix to my remarks. In essence, these provisions do two things:

First, the bill takes Senator Russell Long's dollar checkoff, the imaginative device enacted by Congress in 1971 for public financing of Presidential general elections, and extends it to Senate and House general elections. Under the checkoff, full public funding will be available for the general election campaigns of candidates of the major political parties, and proportional public funds will be available for candidates of minor parties.

Second, in a genuine breakthrough, the Rules Committee bill does not stop with public financing of general elections. It also offers public financing for all primaries for Federal office—President, Senate and House—through a system of matching public grants for small private contributions.

Thus, S. 3044 proposes a system of comprehensive public financing for all Federal elections.

Taken together, these provisions of the bill can spark a renaissance in American political life, because public financing of elections is the answer to many of the deepest problems facing the Nation, especially the lack of responsiveness of government to the people. Only when all the people pay for elections will all the people be truly represented in their government.

At a single stroke, we can drive the money lenders out of the temple of politics. We can end the corrosive and corrupting influence of private money in public life. Once and for all, we can take elections off the auction block, and make elected officials what they ought to be—servants of all the people instead of slaves to a special few.

March 27

MR. GRIFFIN. One of the important things, as we try to consider whether or not this is reform, is the level of expenditures that is going to be involved under this legislation. I put some figures in the *Record* yesterday. They were somewhat preliminary. I asked my staff to do some more work and they have come up with better figures and they are even more startling than the ones I had yesterday. These figures have come from three sources: The Clerk of the House, who has accumulated information about House races based on the 1972 reports; the Library of Congress, and their figures have come from Common Cause, as I understand it; and also from the GAO. It certainly should be in the *Record* and it should be of some interest, I would think, that in 1972 there were 1,010 candidates in the United States who ran in primary and general elections to seek election for the House of Representatives. The total amount spent by all of those candidates in all of those races was $39,959,276. That is what was spent in 1972 without public financing.

Now, what does the GAO estimate will be the cost for House races, out of the public treasury for the most part, if this bill is passed? Well, that information is on page 27 of the committee report. The GAO estimates that the total cost for races in the House of Representatives, if

58

this bill is passed, and goes into effect, will be $100,307,988, or almost three times as much as the 1972 cost.

MR. McGOVERN. Let me say I am not an advocate of full public financing of campaigns. At some point, if it is not done by another Senator, I shall offer a modification of this bill that would make it impossible for anyone to get full public financing. What I would strongly prefer is a system where private citizens are allowed to make modest contributions to campaigns, and that would be matched by public contributions, up to a reasonable amount.

I am not going to debate with the Senator whether $90,000 is the right amount or not. It may be too high. I am not going to advocate the proposal for full public financing. I do not believe in it. I think in 1972 we demonstrated in the Democratic Presidential campaign that it was possible to raise a great deal of money from a large number of people, and do it in a very wholesome and honest way.

MR. CANNON. The only importance I attach to public financing is that it gets rid of the undue influence of big contributors. A big contributor, under this bill, cannot have any undue influence and still come within the bill. That is where the reform issue comes up in public financing. It means that a candidate is not dependent upon big contributors.

MR. BEALL. But this is a nonincumbent's bill, I would hope. This bill is not to perpetuate incumbents in office, much as we would like it to be. I thought the purpose of this was to give anybody an opportunity to seek public office, in the U.S. Senate or the House of Representatives, regardless of whether he is in office at the present time.

MR. CANNON. The Senator is not correct. This bill is not designed to give anybody the opportunity to seek public office. This is an election reform bill, to try to reform the electoral process by providing limits to reduce the influence of large contributions, and it is not directed toward either political party. So far as we can tell, it is not weighted toward either political party.

MR. BROCK. I think the Senator is saying that whether or not it was the intent of the bill, as it is written it is an incumbent protection act, particularly in the sense of the primary. Further, if a candidate is a viable candidate and all his supporters happen to be people of low economic standing, he just does not have an opportunity to demonstrate his voter appeal, because the dollars are not there.

MR. BEALL. That is correct.

MR. BROCK. So he is penalized, even though he may have enormous appeal for the majority of his constituency. That is the thing here: The incumbency is perpetuated. The process is damaged. It is made almost impossible for challengers to bring any freshness into the system. That is the terrible thing about this kind of approach, and it seems to me that we can do a better job on it.

MR. BUCKLEY. This strikes me as one of the most objectionable features of this entire scheme. The checkoff as modified by the authors of S. 3044 is a fraud on the American taxpayer. It is an attempt to give people the feeling that they can participate in decisions that the authors of this bill have no intention of letting them participate in. This provision alone would force me to vote against S. 3044 and should be stricken along with the rest of title I.

As you may recall, the checkoff was originally established to give individual taxpayers a chance to direct $1 of their tax money to the political party of their choice for use in the next Presidential campaign.

When it was extended by the Congress last year, however, the ground rules were changed so that this year taxpayers are not able to select the party to which their dollar is to be directed. They are simply allowed to designate that the dollar should go into the Presidential election campaign fund to be divided up at a later date. Thus, while the taxpayer may still refrain from participating he may well be directing his dollar to the opposition party if he elects to participate.

MR. HUGH SCOTT. Mr. President, I rise in opposition to the Allen amendment which, if adopted, would strip public financing from the bill. As a member of the Rules Committee which held long hearings and markup sessions before favorably reporting the bill to the Senate floor, I support the entirely flexible and realistic approach it takes.

Supporters of the amendment claim that public financing, as proposed in title I, would place full Federal control over the election process. This is inaccurate. As a *New York Times* editorial said this morning:

The bill would not lock parties and candidates into a novel or rigid arrangement. Rather, it curbs the abuses of private financing and offers public financing as an alternate route to elected office.

I hope that the Allen amendment will be soundly defeated.

MR. FANNIN. What the supporters of S. 3044 really hope to achieve is not entirely clear, but what the provisions imply is the beginning of a Federal structure to manage political campaigns and perhaps even the political process itself. It does not take much imagination to conceive of future legislation being proposed to further restrict political operations. In essence, this is a dangerous bill contrary to our tradition of political freedoms. Those who have condemned Watergate because it represented an effort to control political power have only to read this bill to see the potential for achieving the same end only then it would have the cover of law as giving support to restricting political freedom.

MR. TALMADGE. Mr. President, I defer to no one in acknowledging the need for election campaign reform in many areas. As a Member who has served on the Select Committee on Presidential Campaign Activities, the so-called Watergate committee, I can vouch for that firsthand.

I have supported legislation designed to achieve campaign reform, including limiting amounts of money that may be contributed and spent in political campaigns, reporting and disclosure of campaign contributions and expenditures, and provisions for enforcement of the law to insure that the election process in our free society is not subverted.

In fact, even before Watergate and campaign reform became highly charged household words, I sponsored legislation to allow tax credits or tax deductions for modest contributions to political campaigns in an effort to broaden the base of public political support.

However, I draw the line on public financing of Federal election campaigns. This is not campaign reform. It is another blatant attempt to poke the long arm of the Federal Government into an area where it has no business.

It is an effort to destroy the freedom of the American people to choose in the election process.

It is an effort to deny the American people freedom of expression in the support or nonsupport of candidates for public office.

It would constitute a raid on the Federal treasury, at a time when our country and hard-working taxpayers are caught in the grip of rampant inflation, when we are unable to even come anywhere near balancing the budget, and when we cannot make both ends meet on programs that are needed in our society.

What we have before us today is a program that is neither needed, desirable, or in the best national interest.

The right to vote is as sacred a right as the American people have in our free society. Voting is an expression of support of a particular candidate for public office and an endorsement of his views at the ballot box.

A citizen's contribution to the election of a particular candidate is likewise an expression of support. To make such a choice and to give such a contribution is in my estimation also a sacred right.

How a free citizen casts his vote and how he supports a candidate of his own choosing is a decision only that citizen can make. No one has a right to make that decision for him.

A citizen can support this candidate or that candidate. Or, he can choose to support no candidate. That is his right in our system of free elections.

I know of no American taxpayer who fully understood the situation who would agree to having his tax money spent on the political candidacy of a person whose views were totally repugnant to him. I certainly do not want my tax money spent that way.

Yet, that is precisely what would result from public financing of Federal election campaigns.

It is unthinkable that the Federal Government would presume to tell voters and taxpayers how they ought to contribute to political campaigns. Yet, that would be the effect of this legislation.

It would cut both ways. If I were an arch conservative, I would not want my tax dollars going to the candidacy of an arch liberal. If I were an arch liberal, I would not want my taxes supporting the candidacy of an arch conservative. Such an idea as this flies in the face of everything I understand about freedom to choose in the electoral process.

Under this proposal, the Federal Government first forces the American taxpayer to fork over his money. Then, the Federal Government takes that money and turns it over to the election campaign of a candidate who perhaps could not get even his wife to vote for him. The only way this could be avoided, would be for the citizen to evade the tax collector.

MR. KENNEDY. Others, like myself, feel that there are better ways to bring a person into the system than by reaching for his pocketbook, and that the best way to a voter's heart is through his opinions on the issues, not through the dollars in his wallet.

The result was announced—yeas 33, nays 61.

So MR. ALLEN's amendment (No. 1064) was rejected.

March 28

MR. HOLLINGS. I am opposed to establishing public financing for the congressional and senatorial races. This onslaught on the public treasury to pick up the tabs for campaigning and "politicking" all across America would create chaos. It would entice every Tom, Dick, and Harry to jump into the political arena and take his money, and hence take advantage of the public financing. It is nothing more than a subsidy program for all would-be politicians.

MR. ROBERT C. BYRD. Mr. President, I have said on numerous occasions that the most important task now before us is to restore the confidence of the people in their Government. Public feeling toward elected officials is at an extremely low point. In fact, this Congress—despite its fine record—could muster a favorable rating from only 21 percent of the people interviewed in a recent Lou Harris survey.

It appears to me, then, that this is the worst possible time for Congress to enact legislation that would provide for the use of tax dollars to finance congressional campaigns. I have grave doubts that public financing of House and Senate races would ever be advisable, but I have no doubts as to this being the wrong time, of all times, to provide for Federal financing of House and Senate races.

With all the problems facing the taxpayers of this country today, we should be trying to find more ways to save their tax dollars—not new ways to spend them.

Therefore, I support the amendment to delete public financing of congressional campaigns from this bill.

The result was announced—yeas 39, nays 51.

So MR. ALLEN's amendment (No. 1109) was rejected.

March 29

MR. HELMS. Mr. President, there is one further provision in amendment number 1071 to S. 3044 to which I want to address myself. Too often, political candidates receive support from groups not directly connected with their campaigns but which nonetheless provide assistance to them. I speak here not only of so-called soft money contributions from powerful labor union bosses that we hear so much about these days; but also, I speak of the aid provided by other organizations, formed for the specific purpose of rallying support around a particular candidate by rallying support for a particular issue which he espouses, thereby evading the letter and the spirit of the 1971 Act. Amendment

1071 takes care of these groups also by requiring that they report their expenditures made on behalf of a candidate; and further, by requiring that each candidate who has knowledge of any contribution made to him shall report the contribution and the person making it. This, in effect, places the burden on the candidate and his committee to report the receipt of "soft money" contributions, aid from issue groups, et cetera.

The result was announced—yeas, 20, nays 43.

So MR. HELMS' amendment (No. 1071) was rejected.

April 1

MR. WEICKER. The fact is that we have gone through two administrations, one of each party, where clearly an excess of power has been turned against the best interests of the people of this Nation, and they have every reason to have a distrust of both parties.

Why should we be subsidized, Mr. President? Why should we not be out there on our own merits, facing the American people, rather than have Federal campaign financing and have our mediocrity and our inattention to detail subsidized by the people of this country?

MR. FANNIN. Those who advocate public campaign financing through the checkoff plan cannot ignore the reality that the taxpayer is deprived of the right to designate the party he wishes to support. Instead, if he chooses to participate, his dollars will be divided not only among the major parties but, perhaps, minor parties as well. This is not fair to those who want to support one party over the others. It is not fair for the simple reason that the taxpayer, if he desires to participate, has no choice.

MR. BUCKLEY. It is difficult to place a dollar value on incumbency, especially in Senate races. Senator Brock last week referred to one estimate that placed the value of House incumbency at some $600,000. I suspect this figure is a bit high, however, because it includes money spent on things that have only marginal value at reelection time.

The true value of incumbency is difficult to determine primarily because it is only one of a number of factors that determine the outcome of any election.

For example, a number of studies have shown that party is even more important as the vast majority of congressional districts especially are dominated by a single party. Indeed, while 90 percent of those incumbents running are reelected in House races 75 percent or more of

64

the candidates representing a retiring incumbent's party are also elected. With this in mind, it is indeed difficult to separate out the dollar value of incumbency in a meaningful way so that we can structure our laws to allow all candidates to start the race at the starting line.

April 3

MR. BAKER. Mr. President, this amendment would allow only individuals to make contributions to political campaigns. It would strictly prohibit contributions by organizations, associations, co-ops, caucuses, committees, or any other group which aggregates funds from its members and gives those funds in the name of a cause, interest, or section of the country.

Having served for over a year as vice chairman of the Senate Select Committee on Presidential Campaign Activities, I can conceive of no more effective way to eliminate the distortive influence of special interests than by banning group contributions altogether. Obviously, not all contributions by groups distort or, in any way, influence the political process. However, there is no effective way to eliminate the groups that do, short of prohibiting group contributions or segregated funds completely—and that is precisely what I propose to do.

I do not think corporations or labor unions should be permitted to contribute. They cannot now, but they do through AMPAC, BIPAC, COPE, and a half dozen other devices. Moreover, I do not think purely political action groups should be permitted to contribute.

They cannot vote. The American Medical Association cannot vote. The U.S. Chamber of Commerce cannot vote. Common Cause cannot vote—except as individuals. So, why should they be allowed to contribute. Only individuals can vote, and I believe only individuals should be allowed to contribute.

I do not wish to infringe upon the freedom of association. That freedom is guaranteed by the first amendment to the Constitution; and I do not believe that my amendment would diminish that right in the least. However, it would diminish the ability of groups to assert influence beyond what they wield by virtue of their numbers and that, in my judgment, is the way it should be.

The special interest givers are alive and well in 1974, Watergate and potential indictments notwithstanding. Moreover, I could not agree more that confidence will only be restored if we correct the glaring abuses of past campaigns. Nevertheless, S. 3044, with the avid support

65

of Common Cause, allows the same old things to continue. It will allow groups or organizations, whether they are occupational or otherwise, to distort the most sensitive of all processes. It will perpetuate the worst part of our electoral process. And it will continue the serious erosion of public trust in our major governmental institutions.

I cannot accept the argument that group contributions are necessary to adequately fund an effective two-party system. But even if they were necessary in the past, they certainly should not be under a new system of public financing, or even under a refined form of private financing through realistic tax incentives such as I have proposed with Senators Ervin, Talmadge, Gurney and others.

I would be willing to bet, though, that under the provisions of S. 3044, in which the role of private contributors has been substantially reduced, the reduction will not be felt so much by the special interests as by the individual contributor. In fact, I doubt very serious whether S. 3044 will reduce at all the number of special-interest givers. It may only reduce slightly the amount of money they can give to individual candidates.

Now, is that real reform? It seems to me that the only realistic way to eliminate the distortive effects of special interests is to prohibit contributions by groups altogether. They cannot vote. Only individuals can vote; and I, therefore, propose that only individuals be allowed to contribute. In my view, it would be the single most constructive improvement we could make in the political process, in the wake of the events of the past two years.

MR. HUMPHREY. Do I correctly understand, in other words, that the COPE organization of the AFL-CIO, under the amendment, would be able to make a contribution?

MR. BAKER. No, it would not.

My reason for it, in answer to the question of the distinguished Senator from Minnesota, is that I think the aggregation of money in that way creates an enormous sum of money, in many instances, that has a distortive impact far beyond the importance of the individual committee, whether it is a labor organization, a business association, a cooperative, or COPE.

I think it is perfectly appropriate and much to be desired that the individual worker make his $2 contribution, but he should send that $2 contribution to the central campaign committee of a candidate, or a congressional or senatorial campaign committee, and not under the

66

aegis or auspices of his company, his union, or any other group that itself is not a bona fide member of society.

This strikes at the very reason and rationale for this amendment, I might say to the Senator.

It is my belief that only individuals should contribute, and that special-interest groups, whether they are business-oriented, labor-oriented, industry-oriented, geography-oriented, ethnic-oriented, or whatever kind of groups, should not be able to make these huge contributions that they do frequently make.

The result was announced—yeas 36, nays 53.

So MR. BAKER's amendment (No. 1126) was rejected.

April 4

MR. ALLEN. The issue is whether we are going to pass a measure, a so-called reform, which in actuality is for a Federal subsidy. We already have Federal subsidy to a great extent—Federal subsidy in every field one can think of, for that matter—and we are now getting around to subsidizing the politicians directly. There has been a great deal of talk about subsidizing them indirectly. This would subsidize them directly.

MR. GRIFFIN. Tragically, in my view, the American people will find it difficult to get the facts. Three of the four titles left in this bill can be described as genuine campaign finance reform. But unfortunately, title I, which would establish public financing of campaigns—financing directly out of the Public Treasury—does not contribute reform at all. It represents, instead, a raid on the Treasury and a huge escalation of the levels of campaign spending.

Returning to the merits of title I, taxpayer financing, I find it interesting—although I have not read this in the news report—that five out of the seven Senators who serve on the Watergate Investigating Committee have registered opposition to public financing. The members of that committee have uncovered and exposed the abuses we are supposed to be seeking to correct. The Watergate Committee has been charged with the responsibility not only of investigating but also of recommending needed reforms to correct the abuses.

Senate attention should be taken, by the Senate as well as the press, of that fact that a substantial majority of the committee best qualified to pass judgment does not view public financing as reform.

MR. KENNEDY. The issue is an ancient one. No man can serve two masters. No Senator or Congressman can serve both the people of America and his big campaign contributors. So long as we in the Congress continue the practice of financing our campaigns with the dollars of a wealthy few who have a stake in the laws we pass, corruption will keep increasing and democracy will keep decaying.

MR. ALLEN. Mr. President, the distinguished Senator from Massachusetts has said that the issue is who owns Congress, indicating, I assume, that some Members of Congress are subservient to special interests. He did not bother to name any and I wonder who those Senators are.

The Senator from Alabama is not one of them. I dare say that the Senator from Alabama, in the upcoming race in his home State this fall, will not spend one-twentieth of the amount of money that would be available to him under this public financing, so it would be interesting to know who some of these Senators are who are subservient to special interests.

MR. BAKER. Mr. President, the purpose of this amendment is to purify the process of public disclosure of campaign contributions by requiring the completion of that process before rather than after the election has taken place. In other words, my amendment would require political candidates to disclose the size and source of all contributions a certain time before each election. In this way the public is afforded their full and legitimate right to examine the sources of a particular candidate's financial support, and then draw their own conclusion prior to voting.

The result was announced—yeas 33, nays 57.

So MR. BAKER's amendment (No. 1075) was rejected.

MR. BAKER. But I cannot accept that alternative. I cannot accept it because there seems to me something politically incestuous about the Government financing and, I believe, inevitably then regulating the day-to-day procedures by which the Government is selected. It is extraordinarily important, in my judgment, that the Government not control the machinery by which the public expresses the range of its desires, demands, and dissent. And yet, that, in a sense, is what we are debating here. I do not question the motives of those who drafted this legislation, but rather the possible consequences of its enactment.

Indeed, I can even visualize a scenario in which bureaucrats, empowered to write checks on the Public Treasury—checks essential to the success of various political campaigns—can abuse, manipulate, or otherwise influence the outcome of those elections by generating the kind of bureaucratic red tape which is characteristic of our burgeoning Federal Government.

For these reasons, I would urge that we avoid delegating significant funding authority to the Government until it is absolutely necessary. The American people should retain exclusive responsibility for funding political campaigns, and they should be encouraged to do so, on a much broader scale.

MR. ERVIN. We have gotten into an unfortunate state in this country —when anything goes wrong, we say, "Go down to the bottom of that empty hole we call the Treasury of the United States and get some money out of that empty hole to cure the problem." In my judgment, it would multiply the problems, because here is an indirect encouragement to anybody who wants to have a lot of money at his disposal to have a good time traveling through this country by becoming a candidate for the Presidency of the United States. This bill is going to be a stimulation to get more money out of the Treasury of the United States so people can indulge their political fantasies, and I do not think that is something to be encouraged.

MR. HARRY F. BYRD, JR. Mr. President, I wish to commend the difficult and lonely fight being made by the distinguished Senator from Alabama (MR. ALLEN) against an unjustified raid on the Treasury of the United States. The Senator from Alabama has led the fight against taking tax funds to finance political campaigns.

As one Senator, I shall not vote to take money from the pockets of the hard-working wage earners of our country and turn that money over to the politicians. The polls show that politicians these days are not in very good standing. Yet many in Congress say, "Oh, the people want us to vote this money. They want us to take tax funds for our campaigns." I do not believe that. I do not believe that the wage earners of the country want to have the House and Senate dip into their pockets and take money from the hard-working people of the country and turn it over to the politicians to use as they wish.

April 8

MR. DOLE. Mr. President, if campaigns for Federal office are to become federally financed projects like housing developments, highways, and flood control levees then they deserve to be accorded the same treatment. Therefore, I am introducing an amendment to the so-

69

called public financing bill that will require tax-supported political materials to be clearly identified and called to the attention of the American people.

My amendment requires that any candidate for Congress, the Senate, President or Vice President who accepts Federal tax funds for his campaign shall print on all of his campaign literature, advertisements, bumper stickers, billboards, or matchbooks a clear notice that they are paid for with tax money.

The result was announced—yeas 30, nays 48.

So MR. DOLE's amendment, as modified, was rejected.

April 9

MR. AIKEN. Mr. President, the so-called "clean elections" bill now pending before this Senate was laid before the Senate on March 22, 18 days ago.

If this bill had any faint resemblance to a "clean elections" bill at the time it became the pending business, it is hardly deserving of the title any longer.

To be sure, we have had dishonesty, cheating, and law violations in every election campaign since my earliest recollection.

But, at no time has there been so much encouragement to continue such practices as may be found in the bill before us—as it now stands.

The bill before us, as it now stands, only makes matters worse.

I am not going to burden the Senate with a recital of all the things pertaining to this proposed legislation that simply lend more encouragement to the practices which we publicly condemn.

I am not going to waste any time in discussing the merits or demerits of financing political campaigns at taxpayers' expense, which means expense to our Government, since the money authorized by the income taxpayer for political financing simply means that that money does not get into Uncle Sam's coffers.

MR. ALLEN. The Senator from Alabama has already tried to add amendments cutting the amount of individual contributions. The first amendment was to cut the amount that could be contributed in a Presidential election to $250, and in House and Senate races to $100, the theory being that that is all the Treasury would match and that, therefore, there should not be any contributions over that. That amendment was turned down.

Then the Senator from Alabama offered another amendment which

70

would raise those figures a great deal, to provide a $2,000 contribution permitted in Presidential races, a $1,000 contribution in the House and the Senate. That amendment was voted down by the Senate.

That leads the Senator from Alabama to the inescapable conclusion that the proponents of this bill, this public financing measure, are not interested in campaign reform. What they are interested in, particularly in the primaries, is providing campaign expenses for themselves. They want the best of two worlds. They want contributions permitted up to $3,000 per person, $6,000 per couple. They want those contributions, and then they want a matching system, too. So they do not want reform. They want public subsidy added to the amount garnered from the private sector. . . .

Does the Senator feel that candidates would be subject to improper influences during their campaigns?

MR. HUMPHREY. I have never believed; but I will tell the Senator that a great many folks I know do believe that. I do not happen to believe it, but I believe the Senator from Alabama makes a valid point. But I wish I could convince everybody who writes to me.

MR. ALLEN. The Senator said that in being for this amendment he had to resist certain entreaties and demands of certain pressure groups that were demanding all or nothing, I believe the Senator said. I want to commend the distinguished Senator for not being completely in the pockets of those pressure groups.

MR. HUMPHREY. I thank the Senator.

MR. ALLEN. Some Senators are not quite as brave as the distinguished Senator from Minnesota. . . .

So apparently there are great pressure groups at work in behalf of public financing, and I think we know who those groups are. I see them in consultation with Members of the Senate from time to time. They have not consulted with the Senator from Alabama. However, there are great pressure groups involved here, as indicated by the statement of the distinguished Senator from Minnesota.

MR. NUNN. Mr. President, it is most enlightening to note that of the seven members of the Watergate Committee, five, including my distinguished colleague from the State of Georgia (Mr. Talmadge), are opposed to this bill's public financing provisions. This committee has labored long and hard over many months to investigate campaign abuses and to determine how to reform our electoral process to prevent future improprieties. The Watergate report is scheduled to be filed in

71

the near future. However, the proponents of public financing refuse to defer action until after this body has had an opportunity to study the report's recommendations. All too well do they realize that the report will not favor their view; all too glibly do they dismiss the wise counsel of the committee's majority; and all too readily do they seek to expend the taxpayer's dollars.

April 10

MR. DOLE. The pending legislation is the so-called Public Financing bill.

A better name might be the Politicians Subsidy Act. It has been the subject of long and heated debate both in and out of the Senate, on and off of the "Today" show. And the end is not yet in sight, since a motion to close debate failed on Thursday.

Public financing is unnecessary because, regardless of all the crocodile tears on Capitol Hill, there is money to support the political system—cleanly, honestly and sufficiently—without milking the Federal Treasury. The campaigns of Barry Goldwater in 1964 and George McGovern in 1972 are the best evidence available that small contributors can be tapped—even against hopeless odds—to support major campaigns.

Public financing is simply not a solution for human stupidity, individual criminality, or personal greed. Perhaps some might have felt better about the Watergate mess if the hundred-dollar bills that were floating around had come from the U.S. Treasury instead of a Mexican bank. But I do not see how it would have made much difference to the overall outcome of the affair or to the criminal charges in question.

When everybody gets the same amount of money, when everybody can only spend the same—what stresses will be put on the system as people jockey for new advantages?

Will it mean that the wealthy individual will quit his job 2 or 3 years ahead of the election, so an elaborate "non-political" publicity campaign can gain the exposure required for a successful race? If so, where does this leave an equally or better qualified man, say a young lawyer with a wife and family to support, who might also want to throw his hat in the ring? How could he hope to compete against such an opponent on an equal dollar basis after a headstart like that?

As financial equality was imposed would we see more newscasters, astronauts, football players, and TV stars suddenly cashing in on their fame to become politicians?

And what about incumbents under such a system? How are you possibly going to give some unknown first-time candidate equality with an incumbent Senator or Congressman—or an incumbent President. I suppose you could lock every Member of the Senate and House in his office from June to November every election year, but then what would prevent NBC from broadcasting the sounds they made trying to get out?

MR. FANNIN. Mr. President, the Senate apparently is on the brink of passing a campaign financing bill designed to fool the American people into thinking that it solves the major problems in our political system. Nothing could be further from the truth.

In addition to its many other shortcomings, this bill fails completely to advance any remedy for the illegal and undesirable activities of unions in the campaign process.

Unions make their greatest impact by providing services for their chosen candidates for office. These services are provided by union staff, union supplies, and union equipment paid for out of union dues.

The great concern we have heard in the debate over campaign reform involves the amount of money donated to candidates, and the money these candidates spend on their campaign.

This money simply is used to purchase campaign services on behalf of the candidate.

If we are going to prevent people or organizations from donating money to candidates, then it follows that we also must prevent the donation of services which are the equivalent of money.

Unions simply short circuit the system by providing campaign workers who are on union payrolls, union computers, union presses, union vehicles, union phones, and other such services. These services are the same as money to the candidate.

If it is illegal for someone to donate money to candidates to purchase these services, why then is it not illegal for anyone or any organization to donate equivalent services? We are talking about services that are worth tens and hundreds of thousands of dollars—even millions in some national campaigns.

Mr. President, I am deeply concerned about what is happening here. Union leaders are seeking a "veto-proof" Congress, and they are going to great lengths to accomplish this goal.

MR. BUCKLEY. It is clear that the pressure for reform is enough to force many Senators to go along with a proposal that might easily create more problems than it will ever solve. The argument has been

73

cast in a way that allows those in favor of S. 3044 to appear as heroes in the press while those of us who oppose it are made to look like the villains of the piece.

In fact, however, the legislation under discussion is far too important and far too complicated to be decided on the basis of slogan and lobbyist pressure. We have an obligation to look at the facts, to analyze the specifics of the legislation before us and at least to guess at the consequences that might follow its passage.

That, in my view, is what those who question the wisdom of the bill have been trying to do for some time now. . . .

I think that the constitutional aspects of the legislation before us have been almost totally ignored by the press, the Congress, and in most of the discussions we have seen in columns and editorials. Yet, the importance of protecting the first amendment in all its aspects, especially in its political aspects, is so essential to a free society that I urge this body not to be swept into enacting legislation that we will all live to regret; legislation that will most assuredly be found to be unconstitutional once its key provisions are tested.

April 11

MR. TOWER. This is a very simple amendment. Nevertheless, without it this bill cannot be objectively considered to be the "comprehensive" proposal that the proponents of it maintain it is.

This proposal amends title III of the bill, specifically section 615, dealing with limitations on contributions. As the bill now stands, an individual contribution is limited to $3,000 per candidate for each election and $6,000 for a political committee. The amendment specifically addresses the nature of a contribution by such a political committee by stating that "for purposes of this section with respect to a political committee which establishes, administers, and solicits contributions to a separate segregated fund supported by payments from a corporation or labor organization, as permitted under section 610, the term 'contribution' includes the fair market value of services which an individual who is an employee or member of such corporation or labor organization, respectively, provides to such a committee for, or for the benefit of, a candidate, or which such an individual provides to, or for the benefit of, a candidate at the direction of such a committee."

This amendment would, therefore, have the fair market value of services provided at the direction of a political committee established

74

by a labor organization or a corporation to a particular candidate counted toward the political committee's contribution limitation.

Mr. President, unless this amendment or an amendment similar in scope is approved, this so-called campaign reform bill will be nothing more than a sham. I, myself, have some philosophical reservations about imposing a contribution limitation on individual expenditures. Nevertheless, such a limitation seems inevitable. Therefore, if this legislation is to achieve the goal of controlling the aggregate impact which special interests have on our electoral process, then the limitation must apply to all contributions and not just direct cash contributions.

As far as the impact of special interests is concerned, what difference does it make whether that influence is obtained by direct cash contributions or services rendered. The influence obtained, and the danger to the political process that this bill is said to address, is not retarded or controlled when organizations are allowed to contribute thousands upon thousands of dollars in non-cash services to candidates.

Under the bill as currently before us, the individual American who wishes to contribute a small sum to the candidate of his or her choice is given a subservient status when placed alongside the types and levels of contributions this amendment seeks to control and limit. The integrity of the small contributor and his or her contributions remains in doubt.

This amendment treats corporations and organized labor equally. Admittedly it has been labor unions which have impacted upon our political system by making their members available to engage in political activity by working in a candidate's campaign, doing direct mail solicitations and other traditional forms of activity. Nevertheless, I wonder whether, if this bill is passed without this amendment, corporations also will shift their emphasis to providing services to a candidate rather than direct contributions. The end effect will be that the political process will be subject to the same abuses that were apparent long before this bill was drafted.

MR. MAGNUSON. Suppose a person wanted to spend 10 days working on my or the Senator's campaign who happened to be a member of a union. How would the Senator handle that?

MR. TOWER. This is a matter that I dealt with in my remarks. That would be legal, provided he was not doing so under the direction of his union or as an officer of a corporation, and it was not being done for or under the direction of the corporation or organization.

75

MR. MAGNUSON. He could not be directed by the union?

MR. TOWER. That is correct. In other words, if an official of BIPAC, let us say, which is a business and industrial political action committee, if an officer of that organization was working in a campaign at the direction of that committee, then his services would have to be counted.

MR. MAGNUSON. But it in no way acts to prohibit an individual—

MR. TOWER. No. I made that very clear, that this impacts not at all against the activities of individuals not under any control or direction.

MR. MAGNUSON. They might take time to do it on their own?

MR. TOWER. That is right. I have individual volunteers working in my campaigns.

MR. MAGNUSON. What would happen if a group of individuals got together on their own?

MR. TOWER. That would be legal if they were not working under the direction of a political action committee.

MR. THURMOND. Mr. President, will the Senator yield?

MR. TOWER. I yield to the Senator from South Carolina.

MR. THURMOND. In the event that an individual of that group was or several were inspired by a union, then what would be the effect?

MR. TOWER. I think this would have to be a matter of adjudication, probably, to determine it. If there was a complaint that someone was working at the direction of the organization, it could, of course, be a matter for adjudication.

MR. THURMOND. In other words, if the individual or the group, of their own free will and accord, without any direction, suggestion or inspiration from the union, goes out and works, that is all right?

MR. TOWER. The Senator is correct.

MR. THURMOND. But if they do so under direction, suggestion, or inspiration from them, that would violate this section, is that correct?

MR. TOWER. That is right.

MR. BIDEN. Mr. President, will the Senator yield?

MR. TOWER. I yield.

MR. BIDEN. If the union endorses a candidate, and it so happens that an employee who is a member of a union ends up working for that candidate on his own, is it assumed that he is working for that union?

MR. TOWER. No, it is not, and this would not be charged against any legal contribution that was made to the candidate by the organization endorsing him, as long as he is a self-starter, working on his own initiative and not under the direction of the contributing organization.

MR. BIDEN. How is the direction determined?

MR. TOWER. Well, if, for example, the union says, "All right, tomorrow morning you and you and you report to somebody's campaign headquarters and get to work and work 4 hours during the day," then you have to figure the fair market value of that 4 hours of labor as a part of the contribution. But if the individual union member, regardless of the fact that his union has endorsed a candidate, walks in and volunteers to work, that is his own business.

MR. BIDEN. It sounds like a fairly equitable thing, but will it not turn out to be a sham? Will it not be understood that we are pulling another fraud on the American people?

MR. TOWER. I think it depends on how the law is enforced. The whole act could be a sham, for all I know.

MR. BIDEN. How could anyone legitimately enforce it, when there is no tighter determination as to what constitutes whether or not someone is working at the behest of a union leader? Suppose the union leader just says, "I think, Tower, I like that guy Biden. Were I you, I would be out supporting the amendment and that ends it." Then you show up at my headquarters.

MR. TOWER. If I had been coerced against my will—

MR. BIDEN. You would not do that, would you?

MR. TOWER. I would file a complaint.

MR. BIDEN. I am not worried about coercion. I am worried about who determines whether you are chargeable to me.

MR. TOWER. The court would make a determination of that, in a situation like that. The election commission—the organism set up in the bill.

The point I am trying to make is if someone were directing a person to work in a campaign on the organization's time, someone who is an employee of that organization—

MR. CANNON. That would be a direct violation of section 610 right now. That would be a violation of existing law.

MR. TOWER. No, no—in a political committee.

MR. CANNON. It is a violation for a union or a corporation to direct someone—

MR. TOWER. That is not my understanding.

MR. CANNON. To work in a campaign.

MR. GRIFFIN. Mr. President, I was not intending to comment on the question of the distinguished chairman. If it is really a violation, then there would be no objection—

MR. TOWER. That is right.

MR. GRIFFIN. To accept the Senator's amendment. But I should like to ask a question on a different point, for purposes of trying to determine what the amendment does and would mean.

In 1970, in the election in Michigan for Governor, as I recall, there were allegations that the UAW gave members who were striking against General Motors at that time—in order to draw their strike benefits, they had to march in a picket line—the option, as I understand it, of going to work in the Democratic campaign. If they did work in the Democratic campaign then they were given credit as though they had walked the picket line and drew their strike benefits.

Would the Senator from Texas have some comment on what impact his amendment would have on that?

MR. TOWER. It would be prohibited under the provisions of the amendment.

MR. GRIFFIN. I thank the Senator from Texas.

MR. TOWER. Mr. President, I reserve the remainder of my time.

The PRESIDING OFFICER (MR. STAFFORD). Who yields time?

MR. CANNON. Mr. President, I yield myself two minutes.

The PRESIDING OFFICER. The Senator from Nevada is recognized for 2 minutes.

MR. CANNON. Mr. President, I simply point out that under section 610 of the Corrupt Practices Act at the present time, it is unlawful for any corporation whatever, or any labor organization, to make a contribution or expenditure in connection with any election, and so forth. Certainly, if a corporation or a labor union pays the salary of an individual and puts that person out to work for a candidate, that is unlawful. It is unlawful under existing law. I should like to know whether the Senator intends to go beyond that.

In section 610 as modified—we have amended 610 to clarify the definitions, and it says, as used in the section, the phrase "contributions or expenditures"—then it goes on to define them as follows:

But shall not include communications by a corporation to its stockholders and their families or by a labor organization to its members and their families on any subject; nonpartisan registration and get-out-the-vote campaigns by a corporation aimed at its stockholders and their families, or by a labor organization aimed at its members and their families; the establishment, administration, and solicitation of contributions to a separate segregated fund to be utilized for political purposes by a corporation or labor organization. . . .

MR. TOWER. Mr. President, most of this talk has been about labor organizations but the same kind of abuse can be practiced by a corporation as well. As I pointed out in my remarks, if this amendment is not passed, then corporations might be encouraged to contribute time and effort which is not measured in monetary terms.

The unions are solidly against this amendment which is true, so in all probability it will not pass. Nonetheless, it should be understood it cuts both ways, against labor organizations as well as business organizations.

MR. CANNON. Mr. President, I yield myself one minute.

The PRESIDING OFFICER. The Senator from Nevada is recognized for one minute.

MR. CANNON. It would appear that what the Senator is attempting to do is to prohibit any volunteers who are in a separate organization, on a voluntary basis, from working, without charging that time. I presume that would apply to the young Republicans, to the young Democrats, or to any other organization.

MR. TOWER. No. It applies only to section 610. The specific reference is made to section 610.

The result was announced—yeas 40, nays 48.

So MR. TOWER's amendment (No. 1131) was rejected.

MR. BROCK. So perhaps we had better proceed with the charade. I cannot obviously support the bill as it is written. I consider it an insult to the American people and to their intelligence. I consider it an abridgment of their freedom and rights. But that is something they will have to decide when they face the issue.

MR. ROBERT C. BYRD. Mr. President, I ask for the yeas and nays on final passage.

The yeas and nays were ordered.

The result was announced—yeas 53, nays 32, as follows:

YEAS—53

Abourezk	Hartke	Moss
Bayh	Haskell	Muskie
Beall	Hatfield	Nelson
Bentsen	Hathaway	Packwood
Bible	Huddleston	Pastore
Biden	Hughes	Pearson
Brooke	Humphrey	Pell
Burdick	Jackson	Percy
Cannon	Javits	Proxmire
Case	Kennedy	Ribicoff
Chiles	Magnuson	Schweiker
Clark	Mansfield	Scott, Hugh
Cranston	Mathias	Stafford
Domenici	McGovern	Stevens
Eagleton	McIntyre	Tunney
Gravel	Metcalf	Williams
Gurney	Mondale	Young
Hart	Montoya	

NAYS—32

Aiken	Curtis	McClellan
Allen	Dole	McClure
Baker	Dominick	Nunn
Bartlett	Eastland	Roth
Bellmon	Ervin	Stevenson
Bennett	Fannin	Taft
Brock	Griffin	Talmadge
Buckley	Hansen	Thurmond
Byrd, Robert C.	Helms	Tower
Cook	Hruska	Weicker
Cotton	Johnston	

PRESENT AND GIVING A LIVE PAIR, AS PREVIOUSLY RECORDED—1
   Stennis, against.

NOT VOTING—14

Byrd, Harry F., Jr.	Hollings	Randolph
Church	Inouye	Scott, William L.

Fong	Long	Sparkman
Fulbright	McGee	Symington
Goldwater	Metzenbaum	

So the bill (S. 3044) was passed.

MR. KENNEDY. Mr. President, the final passage, achieved today, of the legislation for campaign reform and public financing of elections is one of the finest hours of the Senate in this or any other Congress.

Most, if not all, of the things that are wrong with government today have their roots in the way we finance campaigns for public office. The corrosive influence of private money in public life is the primary cause of the lack of responsiveness of government to the people.

Now, through public financing, we can change all that. Once public financing is signed into law, it will begin to have an immensely salutary effect on every dimension of government, as it sends ripples through every issue with which Congress and the administration have to deal.

At least, the stranglehold of wealthy campaign contributors and special interest groups on the elections process will be broken, and democracy will be the winner. Only when all the people pay for elections will all the people be truly represented by their Government.

Finally, I would like to commend the public interest groups, led by Common Cause and the Center for Public Financing of Elections. I do not think the public interest has ever been better served than by the joint efforts of those in and out of Congress with whom they worked. These two groups, and others with whom they worked were extremely successful in making these issues plain and clear to the Members of this body and to the country, and I am hopeful that they will be as successful with the House of Representatives.

I think this is really one of the finest efforts for reform I have ever seen in this body. Public financing of elections will rank with the great reforms of the political process in our history, a milestone of which every Member of this body should be proud.

I think the American people can be reassured that the Senate is alive and well in Washington, and that in what we achieved today, we acted in the best interests of all the people of this Nation. Public financing can be one of democracy's finest hours, and I hope that the issue will do as well as it navigates its difficult course through the House of Representatives and to the President for his signature.

4

The House Mocks Representative Government

In contrast to the Senate, the House of Representatives took only two days to debate election reform. This short period was not due to a lack of interest by the members. Rather, the Democratic leadership in the House succeeded in rigging the discussion by limiting general debate to only two hours and by allowing only selected amendments to be offered from the floor.

At a time when the American public in the wake of Watergate were crying out for passage of true campaign reform, the liberal majority in the House was intent solely on making certain its "Incumbents' Protection Act" would sail through to passage by using a parliamentary procedure that would shame a banana republic.

The House considered the bill on August 7–8, passing it by a vote of 355 to 48 on the day that President Nixon announced his resignation. It was a day of disgrace for both branches of government—executive and legislative.

(Excerpts from the *Congressional Record*)

February 27

MR. JAMES V. STANTON of Ohio. Obviously, when we give public money to the parties, we are subsidizing the ideologies that they espouse. If we subscribe to the wisdom of Jefferson, who called for the separation between church and State, we ought to carry this policy to its logical conclusion and prohibit also any conjoining of ideology and the State. I submit that we should be especially sensitive to this danger in today's world, when ideologies are proclaimed and promoted with religious fervor. To the extent that we subsidize majoritarian ideology, I question whether this is wise or constitutional. Does not this perforce discriminate against individuals and groups that hold minority viewpoints? Does not this make it more difficult for new ideologies, better attuned to a rapidly changing world, to gain a foothold? We ought to beware, Mr. Speaker, of so entrenching the party that we belong to, as well as the opposite party to which our colleagues across the aisle adhere. We should keep in mind that it is under fascism and communism that the State and ideology are entwined.

Further, when we grant to a party a continuing subsidy, we strengthen not only the party at the time the subsidies start. We can imagine circumstances under which the leadership, having control of the money, could arrange things so that it would be difficult to oust them from power even after they had lost an important election, or in the face of a movement by younger leaders or reform elements to take over.

March 20

MR. JAMES V. STANTON of Ohio. Mr. Speaker, in a lengthy presentation to the House on February 27, as reported in the *Congressional Record* of that day, I outlined what I consider to be "The Case Against Public Financing of Political Campaigns." I am pleased to note that the *Cincinnati Enquirer,* one of this Nation's most thoughtful newspapers, shares the viewpoint held by me and a growing number of other Americans who, nonetheless, do favor reform of the political process in other ways. I would like to insert in the *Record,* Mr. Speaker, for the information of our colleagues, several editorials that have appeared in the *Enquirer* on this important topic. The editorials follow:

(From the *Cincinnati Enquirer,* Jan. 27, 1974)

PUBLIC FINANCING: A CALAMITY TO AVOID

It is ironic to find among the supporters of public funding a number of organizations and individuals who, in general, have advocated "opening up" the political process and making both government and the party structure more responsible to popular tastes and aspirations.

Public funding, it seems to us, would have precisely the opposite effect. The citizen, after all, has only two unfailing devices to influence the political process—his vote and his financial contribution. To deny him his right to contribute, to insulate the parties from the pressures of opinion, would not, in any accepted sense of the word, make American political parties more responsible. Indeed, it would invite them to become even less dependent on the people whose convictions and aspirations they were created to reflect.

March 21

MR. HAYS of Ohio. Mr. Speaker, I could take the will of the House on a question of personal privilege on a full page ad that appeared this morning in the *Washington Post,* but I do not want to waste 59 minutes; one minute will be enough.

Mr. Speaker, John Dingell, Sr., who was a longtime Member of this House, had a saying which I think is very timely. He used to say: "Love those who seek the truth; distrust those who have found it."

That certainly applies to John Gardner, the head of Common Cause. A more succinct saying we have in Ohio is "Beware of a man who keeps telling you how honest he is."

Every time Mr. Gardner comes into my office, I put my hand on my billfold.

Yes, the Democrats are having a fundraising dinner tonight, and the name of every contributor will be on a list open to the public. We cannot say as much for those who contribute to Common Cause. The people who send in contributions to Common Cause are misled into believing that they have something to say about the policies of this organization. The truth of the matter is that policies are made by two people: John Gardner and Fred Wertheimer.

Such an ad as was run in the *Washington Post* could not be run in my State of Ohio because it is a political ad, and political ads in Ohio are required to have the signature of some individual.

One of the delays in bringing a bill to the floor is in writing an amendment to force Common Cause and other lobbyists like it to make public their list of contributors. We will have a bill within a few weeks, maybe within a few days, which will have strict ceilings on contributions, reasonable limits on campaign spending, publication of all contributions. It will apply to all candidates of all parties, and we hope to be able to apply it as well to common crooks like John Gardner, the head of Common Cause.

That is all I have to say, Mr. Speaker. A strong letter to Mr. Gardner follows.

May 16

MR. ERLENBORN of Illinois. Mr. Speaker, in the name of reforming the financing of political campaigns, the Senate has approved legislation which will pass all or most of the cost of Federal election campaigns along to the Treasury of the United States. The short name is public financing; and it has the support of several groups which are usually identified with the cause of reform and good government.

Those who favor some form of public financing make lofty-sounding statements, extolling its virtuous intent, but I believe such a measure would be more fraught with danger than with benefits. It would be expensive, discourage the involvement of people, and fracture basic principles of taxation.

There is a better way to achieve the goal of election reform. The bill the gentleman from New York (Mr. Conable) and I are introducing today would get at the roots of abuse by permitting contributions to political candidates only by individuals and regularly organized political party committees. Donations by special interest groups, whether they be big labor, business associations, or lobbying organizations, would be prohibited.

June 26

MR. BADILLO of New York. Mr. Speaker, the continued procrastination of the House in reporting out and voting on an election campaign reform act is unacceptable in this year of Watergate disclosures. The events of the past two years have convinced the American people that their Government has been subtly transformed into government by, of, and for special interests. By now the impact of wealthy contributors on Government policies is too well documented to allow us any excuse for delaying further on doing what we can to clean up Federal election campaigns.

The American people want and deserve an accounting for our views on campaign practices that are now held in universal disrepute. The

86

Senate on April 11 approved a good campaign reform bill by a vote of 53 to 32. Many State legislatures have enacted election laws with teeth in them. Once again, the House of Representatives wallows along in the wake of the rest of the country.

Public financing of elections is not a giveaway. The real giveaway comes with sales of ambassadorships, preference in awarding of Federal grants and contracts, selected exemption from antitrust laws, increases in subsidy levels, and a thousand other sub rosa ways in which wealthy contributors can be rewarded.

August 6

MR. ARMSTRONG of Colorado. Mr. Speaker, for several weeks there has been a rumor the House Rules Committee would recommend a gag rule for debate of the campaign reform bill.

Frankly, I have not paid much attention to such rumors until now. Obviously, a gag rule, or a "modified" rule as it has been elegantly described, is so blatantly and highhandedly out of tune with the times that I did not believe the committee would do it. But yesterday the rumors came true.

Just imagine the gall of the committee in using such tactics to ram through a bill which supposedly will clean up politics and bring about fair play in campaigning.

On a straight party line vote, the Rules Committee approved a ruling which will make it impossible to fully debate the merits of the bill and to offer needed amendments.

Let me call attention to some of the many amendments which will not be in order—which cannot even be offered in debate tomorrow—if the Rules Committee proposal is approved by the full House.

Some provisions of the bill are probably unconstitutional. For example, portions of the bill which limit campaign spending by persons other than candidates are strikingly similar to sections of the present law which a New York court recently struck down as violating first amendment freedoms—*American Civil Liberties against Jennings.*

Although this case was decided on fairly narrow legal grounds, and is presently under appeal, the basic principle is clear to me: the idea of giving candidates a veto power over the right of other persons to express their opinion is totally inconsistent with American traditions.

I do not want to argue the legal issues involved. But from a purely common-sense standpoint the anti-free-speech, anti-free-press provisions of this bill are directly in violation of the spirit and intent of the first amendment of the U.S. Constitution, in my opinion.

The rule proposed by the committee will not even permit the House to consider the issue.

Nor will loophole-closing amendments be permitted if the proposed rule is adopted. The bill purports to limit campaign contributions, but it ignores the so-called in-kind contributions of personal services, food, automobiles, planes, storefronts, and other goods and services. In fact, the bill creates new exceptions to existing definitions of such contributions and expenditures.

Nor does the proposed rule permit amendments aimed at specific abuses uncovered in the Watergate investigations; campaign dirty tricks, espionage, and so on. These abuses are probably far more in need of reform than the self-serving campaign law changes presently in H. R. 16090. But these amendments would not be in order under the rule recommended by the Rules Committee.

Mr. Speaker, this is not a time for partisanship. I have therefore withheld, at least for the time being, comment about the partisan considerations which are apparent in the handling of this legislation in the House Administration Committee and before the Rules Committee. I have done so in the hope that Members of both parties will rise above strictly partisan considerations and vote against this gag rule. Let us have a free and open debate of the bill on its merits, permit amendments to be offered and vote them up or down so the legislation can be judged accordingly. To do otherwise—to bring so-called reform legislation—to the floor under such a rotten rule—is a travesty.

I, therefore, hope all Members will join me in voting against the previous question when the proposed rule is presented. If we can defeat the question, it will then be possible to amend the rule and give the House full opportunity for amendment and consideration of this legislation.

August 7

MR. MARTIN of Nebraska. Mr. Speaker, House Resolution 1292, as the gentleman from Texas (Mr. Young) has explained, provides for two hours of debate on this very important piece of legislation.

Unfortunately, however, this resolution provides practically for a closed rule on the bill that will be debated by this body this afternoon.

The Members can carefully go through the rule and the bill itself and they will find that really only three amendments are in order:

First, in regard to the amount of money which a candidate may expend or the amount of money which may be contributed to a candidate's campaign.

Second, an amendment may be offered in regard to changing the composition of the Board of Supervisory Officers, which amendment will be offered by the gentleman from Minnesota (Mr. Frenzel);

And then the third amendment will be in order in regard to endorsers of loans from banks to political campaigns. This is another loophole in this present bill.

Those in essence are the only three amendments to be allowed in the bill itself.

Mr. Speaker, again I point out there are far too many loopholes in this legislation, and there is no chance, and I repeat, no chance at all, to offer amendments to change these provisions. Therefore, Mr. Speaker, we propose, on our side of the aisle, to make an attempt—and I hope it will be successful—to vote down the previous question, and I urge the Members to vote "no" on the previous question. I intend then to offer a resolution which provides for an open rule, not requiring that the amendments to be offered be published in the *Congressional Record* one calendar day previously. Also, that the bill shall be read by title rather than by section. I urge the Members to vote "no" on the previous question.

Mr. Hays of Ohio. Mr. Speaker, I was a little surprised to see the gentleman from Nebraska riding in here on a white horse, because the gentleman has never been noted in my time here of being such a champion in carrying out election reforms.

Mr. Anderson of Illinois. Mr. Speaker, Members of the House, it is certainly not an overstatement to say that this is a bill for which the country has been waiting, and one in which every one of the 435 Members of this body is very, very much interested. The only question before us during this hour is the kind of rule under which we are to debate this bill.

I am asking the Members to vote down the previous question. I want a rule. I want a bill, but I suggest that it is a travesty on the legislative process and an insult to every one of the 435 Members of this House to tell us that we should be limited by the kind of rule that is proposed in this case. The Democratic caucus in February 1973, at least adopted

89

some rules that were postulated in order to meet Democratic aims to do away with what they said was the iniquitous procedure that had been followed by the Committee on Ways and Means in presenting closed rules. Yet, we have the distinguished chairman—I think he is here—of our Committee on Rules take office in this Congress, and I remember reading an interview where he said he wanted the Members—referring to the Members of this body—to vote. "That is what they are sent here for."

Yet, they are going to muzzle the Members of this House today with the kind of rule suggested for adoption. Vote down the previous question; give us a chance to legislate. We will do that responsibly and intelligently.

Mr. Speaker, the gentleman is correct. There is the utmost irony in a situation where we find that we are legislating reform under the kind of rule that is proposed here this afternoon.

Vote down the previous question; let the gentleman from Nebraska offer an open rule so that we can work our will on this vital piece of legislation and get on with the kind of reform that the country is waiting for.

MR. YOUNG of Florida. The Rules Committee has unfortunately decided that H.R. 16090 will be considered under what is essentially a "gag rule." Whole crucial sections of the bill will, under House Resolution 1292, be totally exempt from amendment. We will not be able to toughen up the provisions of H.R. 16090, nor will we be able to close some very glaring loopholes in the bill.

MR. CLEVELAND of New Hampshire. Mr. Speaker, as a member of the Committee on House Administration which produced this bill, I rise in opposition to its consideration under what amounts to a closed rule. It would be an utter disgrace for the House to act on the critical issue of political campaign reforms while denying Members meaningful opportunity to improve it by amendment.

The record will show that this legislation was finally reported, more than two years after the Watergate break-in, by a committee dominated —like the rest of the House—by the majority party. Many amendments offered in committee were rejected by party-line vote. Some amendments such as the Brademas proposal to use checkoff funds for matching of small contributions to candidates in presidential primaries were adopted with bipartisan support, including my own. Yet the bill with all its deficiencies is essentially a Democratic product.

90

It is significant to me that many of the amendments barred from consideration by this rule deal with special-interest contributions, the problem of pooling of funds so as to prevent identification of original donors, and in-kind contributions.

The affinity of organized labor for the majority party makes all too evident the basis for resistance to this type of reform, as well as other measures to tighten up this legislation. Because the majority does operate from a privileged sanctuary, the media and election reform advocates will probably remain respectfully and benignly silent.

MR. HAYS of Ohio. Let me say this to you, Mr. Anderson: I can understand the speech you made, and if I had been the author of the bill which produced Watergate, as you were, with no limitations I would be making the same kind of speech you made.

MR. FRENZEL of Minnesota. Mr. Speaker, during the past two years, the American public has been forced to witness the depressing spectacle of massive violations of our campaign laws under a coverup atmosphere. Do we now dare to subject the American people to the irony or perhaps the outrage of considering the campaign finance reform bill under a closed rule?

The confidence of the American people in their Government is too low for us to embark on such a risky undertaking. With public cynicism and alienation so rampant, a campaign reform bill that is considered under a closed rule will be short on credibility.

The rationale for the closed rule is that the House cannot be trusted to deal with one of the most important issues it will consider all year. If our own leadership does not have confidence in us, then how can we expect the American people to have any confidence in us?

I think we can be trusted to handle the people's business. I think that is what we were elected for. If the public is to regain confidence in the Congress, then we have to show confidence in ourselves. I think the best way to display that confidence is for all Members to commit themselves to the principle that open proceedings are the way to obtain the best bill possible.

The closed rule will both stifle debate and discussion and drastically limit the amendments that can be offered. Only about half a dozen amendments will be in order.

MR. ARMSTRONG of Colorado. The very idea of bringing an election reform bill to the floor of the Congress of the United States under a closed rule is absurd, and it would be laughable if it were not tragic.

MR. DENT of Pennsylvania. Mr. Speaker, I take this moment just to say that I endorse the rule and the previous question on it, because I started this little bill on its way with the hearings in our subcommittee over a long period of time. Most of the closed parts of the bill are matters that in my honest opinion have very little to do with campaign behavior. Most of them are kinds of regulations and criteria that have to be put into legislation for guidelines.

MR. RHODES of Arizona. Mr. Speaker, I rise in opposition to the rule on H.R. 16090, the Federal Election Campaign Act Amendments of 1974, and I ask that the previous question be voted down so that the rule may be amended.

In a straight party-line vote, the Committee on Rules adopted House Resolution 1292, a "modified closed" rule. Instead of full and open consideration of campaign reform, the rule permits Members to amend only a few, specific portions of the bill.

On such a vital issue, where real, workable reform is essential, it is unconscionable that the major party would impose a gag rule.

I do not believe that the gentleman from Ohio really is getting his hats mixed up, and that he is wearing his hat as the chairman of the Democratic Congressional Committee with as much more pride as he wears the hat of the chairman of the House Administration Committee. I just think it is at least suspect that this "soft money" phase of the bill is not covered adequately.

MR. PRITCHARD of Washington. Numerous crucial amendments have been drafted for this Federal election campaign reform bill. But many of these cannot even be considered because of this modified closed rule that we have been given by the Rules Committee. How are we to be able to develop the best possible legislation for Federal election campaign reform if we are unwilling to subject the entire bill to proper scrutiny? Does this Congress fear consideration of all these amendments? Is this true reform?

I suspect that my colleagues on the other side of the aisle are anticipating the predicted landslide congressional victories for their party this fall. So naturally they are anxious to pass this bill, heavily weighted in favor of the incumbent, which will become law next year with Congress heavily controlled by the Democratic majority. Such a bias to the advantage of the incumbent will insure their continued strength and domination in this body. The new election campaign laws would not apply to this fall's election campaigns.

MR. ARCHER of Texas. Unfortunately, we will not be allowed to offer those amendments on the House floor. The chairman of the House Administration Committee saw to that when he went before the Rules Committee. The result is a rule allowing only the five amendments he approved. Others will not be allowed because, by his own admission before the committee, they would not benefit Democrats.

In my opinion, this is an irresponsible answer to the Nation's plea for open election processes. The bill that should accomplish that goal has become itself a closed partisan issue. As it now stands, there can be no amendment to restrict the "in-kind" contributions Democrats enjoy from big labor. Instead, the limitation has actually been increased from $100 provided in present law to $500 per individual. Nor can any amendment even be considered to restrict contributions by organized groups, whether they be big labor or big business, which deny the individual's right to decide which candidate receives his contribution.

According to the present bill, incumbents still have too great an advantage over their challengers in congressional races. I also question whether or not the American people want to finance Presidential nominating conventions of political parties with their tax dollars.

We need responsible nonpartisan campaign reform to guarantee fair competition in our election processes, not a package that simply carries the title of "reform" but in fact is designed to assure advantages to only one political party. If we indeed want true reform and open elections in this country, we also need to open up the debate and amendment procedure by which this reform legislation is written.

MR. MICHEL of Illinois. The Senate-passed bill is for all practical purposes an incumbent protection act. All of us here today are incumbents. As a practical matter, none of us are about to give our challengers an advantage; but I think just simple equity dictates that at least we debate this overall question. . . .

MR. HAYS of Ohio. I will assure the gentleman that he will have five minutes if I have to get it and give it to him myself.

MR. CONYERS of Michigan. I am not only concerned about getting the five minutes but I am equally concerned about the provisions that limit new and small parties which ought to be thoroughly considered in passing this legislation.

THE CHAIRMAN. The time of the gentleman has expired.

MR. ROUSSELOT of California. Mr. Chairman, I appreciate the gentleman yielding. I wanted to ask my colleague, the gentleman from Michigan, did he vote for the closed rule?

MR. CONYERS. I think that is irrelevant.

MR. ROUSSELOT. I do not think so. As a matter of fact, it is a most relevant question because an open rule would have guaranteed the gentleman from Michigan more adequate time for appropriate amendments.

MR. CRANE of Illinois. Mr. Chairman, for openers, I would like to extend my congratulations to my colleagues on the Committee on House Administration for the time and energy they have put into preparing this rather prolix campaign "reform" bill. I put the word "reform" into quotation marks, Mr. Chairman, because, unfortunately, my colleagues in this body saw fit earlier this afternoon under our vote on the rule to prohibit me from introducing some amendments which I had anticipated I might have the opportunity to present for consideration, and which, in my judgment, represent the real substance of campaign reform, while much of that contained in the proposed legislation I do not view as reform at all. On the contrary, I think it is going to set our political system back rather considerably.

In this connection we had an amendment introduced before our committee by the distinguished gentleman from Wisconsin (Mr. Froehlich) which would have dealt with this question of influence-peddling by special-interest groups, and which would remove any doubt in anyone's mind as to whether any vested-interest group was exercising undue influence on the decisionmaking of a Member. This amendment that the gentleman from Wisconsin (Mr. Froehlich) had initially proposed before the committee, and was defeated in the committee, I intended to bring before the whole House. It would have prohibited contributions from political committees to candidates except for contributions from the respective congressional campaign committees of the Democratic and Republican Parties, and the Senate campaign committees.

As the gentleman from Wisconsin (Mr. Froehlich) very capably explained to the committee at the time he introduced this amendment, this would have had the effect of removing any area of doubt as to whether the realtors through REALPAC, or business and industry through BIPAC, or the American Medical Association through AMPAC, or for that matter, even the American Conservative Union through its Conservative Victory Fund (sic).

Also, the Political Education Committee of the AFL-CIO was exercising undue influence over Members through campaign contributions. That, in my estimation, was a salutary amendment. It was one

94

that I think should have been adopted by the committee and incorporated into this bill.

The second amendment I intended to offer deals with contributions in kind. This has been an area where we are all too aware of a number of abuses—and they are not confined exclusively to unions. When corporations provide, for example, unreported aircraft travel, that surely is an abuse as much as when unions engage in the providing of services of a similar nature. Such contributions should have an appropriate fair market value attached to them and classified and reported as in-kind contributions. That was the second amendment that I had hoped to bring up before this committee.

The third is one that I introduced first before the committee at the time we had our Reporting Act legislation two years ago. This would have prevented the use of involuntarily raised union moneys for political purposes, whether those were voter registration drives or get-out-the-vote drives. I do not think there is any question in anyone's mind that these have distinctly partisan overtones.

I can understand so long as silence in the law permits this injustice to continue, that those people who are so inclined will exploit this deficiency in the law. I have been waiting vainly for the American Civil Liberties Union to get involved in the fight on behalf of the civil liberties of these people whose involuntarily raised union moneys, which must be paid frequently as a condition for employment, are being used to subsidize political objectives contrary to their own.

MR. DENNIS of Indiana. I simply want to say that in my judgment the gentleman from Illinois in the well is making a very important contribution to this debate, although unfortunately there are very few people here to hear it. The essential cynicism of the process we are going through this afternoon is illustrated by the consideration of this so-called reform bill, which is being considered under a rule where the three important amendments mentioned by the gentleman, indeed, essential amendments for any real campaign reform, to anyone who knows anything about the subject realistically cannot even be considered by this body, cannot even be voted upon. The essential cynicism of this situation is a sad commentary on our whole operation here, and I am glad the gentleman at least is still allowed to point out the need, even though in this body we are not allowed to have a vote.

MR. ARMSTRONG of Colorado. The thing I do not understand, and I wish we could have some explanation, is how we can limit the right of free speech to $1,000 worth. The first amendment says we may not abridge free speech, we may not curtail; we may not diminish; we may not shorten.

MR. BROWN of Ohio. Mr. Chairman, I wish to associate myself with the gentleman's concerns. I think there is a real question as to whether or not we can put a quantified limit on the individual's constitutional rights of free speech, whether it is about political campaigns or anything else, but in particular political campaigns, which strikes at the heart of the operation of our Government.

I think the gentleman has raised a substantial point which, if this legislation is thoughtfully considered, will sustain his viewpoint.

MR. BAKER of Tennessee. Mr. Chairman, in the catalog of abuses, compulsory political donations by union members rank right up there with the worst.

Absolutely no one argues against union officials' right to assist their political friends. It is precisely the same right enjoyed by business groups. The trouble begins when unions take dues money to finance that assistance.

How do they do this? Mostly through the services they perform for prounion candidates. Union political front organizations, notably the Committee on Political Education, COPE, conduct get-out-the-vote drives in neighborhoods likely to go for right-thinking candidates; they turn over buildings, trucks, telephones, and computers to friends of the union viewpoint.

Now if the dues-paying union man happens to like the candidate his union is helping, he may not worry much about where his dues are going. But what if he hates the fellow, cannot stomach his views for a minute? It is too bad, but there is no help for him. Like it or not, he is going to subsidize a candidate for whom he refuses to vote.

The issue, then, is one of political freedom. Either the union member has the right to withhold support from a given candidate or he has not the right. There is no other way of looking at it.

In 1972 the unions spent some $50 million on their political friends, only about 10 percent of which, according to labor columnist Victor Riesel, came from voluntary giving.

Accordingly, I would have been supporting the proposed amendments to curb "in kind" as well as directed donations.

MR. MICHEL of Illinois. One final point I would like to make in transgressing upon the Member's time in general debate here is what I see is left out of the bill and which I would like to have seen offered in the form of an amendment to appropriately treat the in-kind services and goods, for the special interest groups often make substantial contributions by providing in-kind services and goods, such as telephones, cars, airplanes, computer time, staff "volunteers," and the like.

The committee bill would exempt these contributions from both the limitation and in some cases the disclosure requirements.

To prevent this type of campaign abuse, the amendment I had intended to offer before adoption of the closed rule would have prevented or prohibited such in-kind contributions in excess of $100. [For the full text of Rep. Michel's important remarks about union-in-kind contributions, see Appendix V.]

MR. BLACKBURN of Georgia. Mr. Chairman, we are now engaged in trying to pass a campaign reform bill—a bill which most Americans want to see adopted. I believe it is almost incredible, however, that this long and detailed bill makes absolutely no mention of what is probably the largest single abuse of our present campaign laws. I refer to the giant loophole which, in effect, allows union dues to be used in vast quantities, perhaps $100 million in a general election, to be funnelled by the union leaders to their favored candidates. Two international unions—caught red-handed in these practices—have recently agreed as a result of court cases to refund to their members those portions of their union dues which have been spent on political campaigning. These were the Brotherhood of Railway and Airline Clerks and the International Association of Machinists. A recent article in the *Wall Street Journal*, January 29, 1974, makes it very clear that cash-equivalent political expenditures by union officials far outweigh their direct cash aid to candidates.

MR. PHILLIP BURTON of California. Mr. Chairman, I would like to associate myself with the remarks of the gentleman from New York and add my own personal commendation to the distinguished chairman of the Committee on House Administration. The gentleman from Ohio (Mr. Hays) is really in many, many respects a very misunderstood Member. His basically kind and generous nature is not understood universally. Very importantly, his commitment to make the House a responsive instrument to resolve the public policy issues confronting this country is known by all who watch him and work with him.

MR. ARMSTRONG of Colorado. Mr. Chairman, this bill has been brought to us under the theory that "if we keep them panting long enough, for reform, they will take anything that is called reform." But this is not a reform bill.

Mr. Chairman, this bill purports to cut back on contributions, but it only limits and calls for the reporting of one kind of contribution, dollar contribution. The often more important, usually decisive, contributions in kind—the donation of storefronts, of goods and services, of personnel coming in from out of State—are not curtailed in this bill.

This legislation introduces public financing of nominating conventions, a procedure which is no reform but is nothing more nor less than a raid on the public treasury.

Finally, we all know—and I think most of us know in our hearts—this is a sweetheart incumbent bill. This is a bill which is going to make it harder than ever to defeat an incumbent of either party. It sets the kind of limits that makes it almost impossible for an unknown to become known and thereby heightens existing advantages which incumbents enjoy.

MR. HAYS of Ohio. Mr. Chairman, I move to strike the requisite number of words.

Mr. Chairman, there are two things we can do about a speech like we just heard, which is about 90 percent baloney. We can ignore it or we can set the *Record* straight. I do not want to take too much of the time of the committee but I think it might be well to set the *Record* straight, and if the gentleman wants to vote against this and go home and try to tell his constituents that he voted against it because it is not reform and he can sell that bill of goods, that is all right, but I do not think he can. From the reports I get from his district, I think he is going to be lucky if he can sell them anything. However, that is neither here nor there.

MR. ROUSSELOT of California. I wish to make this brief statement. The reason I feel this amendment is most appropriate is because national political conventions have been in the past clearly outside the realm of government and should be. To believe for one moment that by this kind of public financing out of the U.S. Treasury that we are being fair to the small political party or the so-called potential poor-boy Presidential candidate, I think, is a joke. My belief is that because this is a highly discriminatory portion of the present bill H.R. 16090 in favor of the major parties of this country, this approach is wholly unfair to small minority parties. To use public funds to give total advantage to the two major parties to have convention extravaganzas is, I think, a major disgrace, to the concept of civil rights. . . .

MR. CONYERS of Michigan. I yield to the gentleman from California.

MR. ROUSSELOT. I thank the gentleman for yielding.

Is the gentleman also saying that if we are going to, under this bill, actually open up the Federal Treasury to certain groups, we ought to make it fair for all regardless of their size? Is that true?

MR. CONYERS. Precisely.

MR. ROUSSELOT. I think that is a wholly reasonable and correct position and I appreciate the gentleman's explanation.

MR. CONYERS. I urge the support from the membership in behalf of this amendment.

I should like to point out that the handful of people who may want to form a political party is the same kind of a handful of people who might form and have formed some of the great parties in the past, and specifically the two great parties that exist in this country today. There was a handful of people that formed the Whig Party that elected two Presidents. There was a handful of people that formed the party that the gentleman and I are members of, back in 1800. At the same time I think that we should not deprecate those citizens who may reserve judgment.

MR. ROUSSELOT of California. This is going to be managed by the Treasury Department? Where did that wonderful magic term of five percent come from?

MR. FRENZEL of Minnesota. The Congress determined that when it passed the original checkoff fund.

MR. ROUSSELOT. I really do not know who can explain this arbitrary five percent formula.

MR. HAYS of Ohio. Of course it is an arbitrary decision, just like the $60,000 figure is arbitrary.

MR. ROUSSELOT. This bill has many arbitrary decisions in my opinion.

Then nobody can answer that question about the five percent and how it was arrived at? I am therefore constrained to vote for the amendment. . . .

I take this time to ask my good colleague, the gentleman from Arizona, who voted against the amendment to eliminate public financing of Presidential campaigns, why he now comes before us and eliminates financing for congressional campaigns in a primary contest. I find that highly inconsistent and discriminatory to Members of Congress and the Senate.

MR. UDALL of Arizona. If the gentleman will yield, one does the best he can.

MR. ROUSSELOT. I will be glad to yield to the gentleman from Arizona.

MR. UDALL. I have long favored the original Anderson-Udall bill, which covered both primaries and general elections.

MR. ROUSSELOT. Why did the gentleman eliminate that concept from this amendment?

MR. UDALL. Because it could not pass with primaries contained in the bill.

MR. ROUSSELOT. What we are now hearing from my good friend, the gentleman from Arizona, is that he has become very political on this issue of public funding for congressional primaries. I think that is an unfortunate discrepancy and obvious deficiency in the gentleman's amendment. The gentleman sincerely believes it should be in Presidential campaigns for both the primary and the general elections, but to garner votes here on the floor, he has come before the House and played a kind of Mickey Mouse game with his own principles.

MR. FRENZEL of Minnesota. Mr. Chairman, I oppose the Udall-Anderson amendment.

I have previously listed for the members of this committee some of the ill effects of public financing, but a rerun might be helpful now. Here is what we get with public financing:

First, we get weakened political parties; second, we get more candidates in every race and duller elections, and duller elections mean reelection of incumbents. We get additional protection of incumbents. We get discouragement of challenges. We get discouragement of personal participation in political campaigns. We get starvation of funds for State and local condidates. We get restriction of freedom of speech. We get a compelled use of your money and my money for candidates that we may personally object to. Worse, we get an increase in the bureaucracy.

Finally, we get more spending than we have now, although the people who put up this amendment are telling us they want to cut back.

100

The worst effect of all is the promise of clean elections cannot be fulfilled by using public money.

Public money is the same color as private money. It is green. Translated in another way, a lawbreaker can break the law with public money as well as with private money. There is no essential cleanliness in public money.

MR. ASHBROOK of Ohio. Mr. Chairman, the revelations of the last few months have convinced me of the need for a meaningful election reform bill. Our Nation cannot afford a continuation of the massive campaign abuses that have marred our electoral process in the past.

The so-called campaign reform bill now before the House, however, is not the type of reform that we need.

First, the bill leaves open one of the largest loopholes in our current law: in-kind contributions by labor unions. Tens of millions of dollars —taken from workers as union dues—are used in behalf of selected candidates to cover the costs of printing, materials, office space, telephones, and many other campaign items. Why should these labor union contributions be treated any differently than other contributions? Unlimited in-kind contributions by an special-interest group must be stopped if we are to have truly meaningful campaign reform.

MR. ZION of Indiana. Mr. Chairman, we desperately need a good campaign reform bill. It is long past time that special-interest groups be prevented from buying an election. Unfortunately, this act does not accomplish this purpose. This bill was authored by the chairman of the Democratic Campaign Committee, who is also chairman of the House Administration Committee having jurisdiction over the legislation. It came out of the Democratic-dominated Rules Committee in a fashion that prevented Republican Members from introducing perfecting amendments.

It does nothing, for example, to prevent big unions from spending $50 million in cash and contributions in kind. It does nothing to stop the use of involuntary dues to pay union officials for campaigning purposes, or to pay printing, postage and telephone costs for union-endorsed candidates. A recent AFL-CIO publication, mailed by a tax-supported subsidy, called for a veto-proof Congress. It does not permit a union member to determine what candidate his money is used to support, either by dues or voluntary contributions.

MR. FRENZEL of Minnesota. Mr. Chairman, there has been plenty of talk in the last two days about in-kind contributions. I want this record to show that that section 205 of the 1972 act, amending chapter 610 of title 18, clearly provides in its definition of contribution that "any services, or anything of value" is a contribution and must be reported as such.

Obviously, such contributions are subject to all the requirements that any contribution is subject to.

The problem with in-kind contributions is that they have not been properly reported by either donor or recipient. With the creation of the new Board of Supervisory Officers, I believe that supervision adequate to cause reporting, disclosure, and limitations of in-kind contributions.

MR. BAUMAN of Maryland. Finally, the most glaring weakness in this legislation involves the section regarding "in kind" contributions. We cannot ignore the fact that special-interest groups, principally labor unions, contribute the equivalent of upwards of $100,000,000 a year in "in kind" gifts to candidates: mailings, get-out-the-vote drives, printing, mailing lists, equipment, transportation, storefronts, and numerous other campaign benefits which are more valuable than cash. Not only does this bill fail to deal effectively with this type of contributions, it encourages them, and fails to either limit or require disclosure of such activity. This represents a glaring loophole big enough to drive every Teamster-operated truck in the Nation through. It makes a farce of any effort to bring about campaign "reform," and instead promises to expand campaign contributions of a very substantive nature which never need be reported or kept track of. This section makes the title "campaign reform" the biggest violation of "truth in packaging" since 19th-century hawkers roamed the prairie selling snake oil as a cure for cancer.

MR. TIERNAN° of Rhode Island. Mr. Chairman, the electoral process has been suffering a most serious illness. One need not be a medical doctor to diagnose the problem. Every citizen is sadly aware of the fact that campaigns in the United States have been riddled with unethical and illegal contributions and expenditures. The treatment for this cancerlike disease is simple, yet this honorable body of Congress has done little to cure the electoral process and revitalize the voice of our democracy.

°Appointed in 1975 as one of the eight members of the Federal Election Commission.

I ask the Members of Congress, can we remain idle while the future of our great Nation stands in jeopardy. To remove only a fraction of a malignant tumor is futile. We must thoroughly remove all traces of the cancer. We must stitch the loopholes in order to make campaign reform a meaningful and successful operation.

THE SPEAKER. The question is on the passage of the bill.

The vote was taken by electronic device, and there were—yeas 355, nays 48, not voting 31.

5

Final Passage:
"An Act of
Unprecedented Cynicism"

Election reform legislation, having been passed by the Senate on April 11, 1974, and by the House on August 8, 1974, was sent to Conference Committee for a reconciliation of differences. The most significant and controversial difference was that while both bills provided for public financing of the Presidential elections, the Senate version also called for public financing of congressional elections and the House version did not.

(Excerpts from the *Congressional Record*)

In the Senate

October 8

MR. CANNON. Mr. President, the conference report pending before the Senate on the Federal Election Campaign Act Amendments of 1974, S. 3044, represents many months of hearings, executive sessions, floor debate, and Senate and House conferences.

MR. HUGH SCOTT. I thank the chairman of the committee who has done such a magnificent job in shepherding this bill through the conference. It has been a long and hard road. I think we have achieved a reasonably good bill. We have had to make concessions that we did not want to make. I think the Members of the other body felt the same way. I am personally delighted that my own original amendment to provide for an independent Federal Election Commission has been included as part of this bill. The regret I have principally is that we did not extend Federal financing on a matching basis to congressional elections as proposed by the distinguished Senator from Massachusetts (Mr. Kennedy) and myself. However, we will give the Presidential financing through matching funds a good try in the 1976 election.

I would like to ask a question as to the amount presently available, if the distinguished Senator has it, in the checkoff fund for Presidential elections where the voter can check $1 or if it is a joint return he and his wife can check off $2 to be used for this purpose.

MR. CANNON. As of July 1 of this year, the amount was roughly $29.5 million. Of course, we would have two more taxpaying periods that would be up before the financing provision would become effective.

MR. HUGH SCOTT. What projection do we have as to what can reasonably be anticipated as available in the 1976 election?

MR. CANNON. I do not think we can really make a very accurate projection, but the best guesstimate that we have is roughly $75 million.

MR. KENNEDY. It is no secret that the Senate conferees, in a real bipartisan effort, worked hard to obtain a compromise acceptable to the House, a compromise that would establish at least a beachhead for public financing of congressional elections.

On every other provision in the bill, the conferees were able to hammer out a reasonable agreement on the various conflicting provisions of the bill. But on the overriding issue of public financing, the opposition of the House conferees was total and unyielding. Day after day, session after session, the Senate conferees sought progressively weaker compromises, until finally only token public financing for congressional elections was requested by the Senate.

But even this minimal compromise was refused.

In the end, to get a bill at all that the President would be obliged to sign or veto before election day, it was necessary for the Senate conferees to abandon public financing altogether for congressional elections. Reluctantly, we did so.

I like to think that, because we yielded on public financing, the

106

Senate conferees fared better on two other very important issues in the bill—the spending limits for Senate and House races, and the enforcement powers of the new Federal Election Commission.

And the effort in this Congress has been genuinely bipartisan. Senators Hart, Mondale, Stevenson, Cranston, Clark, Pell, and I were joined by Senators Hugh Scott, Mathias, Schweiker, and Stafford in introducing various forms of public financing legislation in this Congress and in working to keep the issue in the forefront of debate throughout both sessions.

I also give great praise to Common Cause, the people's lobby. For the first time—at least in my service in the Senate, and perhaps for the first time in the history of Congress—a powerful and truly effective representative of the public interest has emerged to speak for the ordinary citizen in the halls of Congress. Now, on campaign financing and many other issues, there is a real countervailing force against the narrow special interest groups that have held unchallenged sway for so long. Things are changing now in Congress, and Common Cause deserves the credit. I hope they keep the pressure on.

MR. CLARK. In addition, a number of organizations provided valuable support and information, including the Center for Public Financing of Elections and especially Common Cause, whose representatives played a leading role in strengthening this legislation, as Senator Kennedy has said.

MR. ALLEN. The Senator from Alabama understands that the bill would provide no subsidies to candidates except from funds going into the checkoff fund; is that correct?

MR. CANNON. The Senator is correct. The public financing provision would go only to the extent that funds were in the pot, so to speak, from the checkoff provision under the income tax laws at the present time.

MR. ALLEN. Then the first priority would be the Presidential election; is that correct?

MR. CANNON. The Senator is correct. The first priority would be the Presidential election.

MR. ALLEN. If there is not enough to go around.

MR. CANNON. That is correct.

MR. ALLEN. Then what would follow?

MR. CANNON. The allocation, then, from that point on, would go to the primary elections and to the national committees on a prorata basis,

107

because that is the lowest priority, and that is in the process of selecting the candidates for the general election.

MR. ALLEN. Due to a strong conviction on my part that taxpayer financing of elections is not in the public interest, I could not, in good conscience, sign the report even though I was a member of the conference on the part of the Senate. And yet the report, composing the differences between the Senate and House versions of the bill, contains much that is good, much that I support, and much that was shaped or influenced by positions that I have advocated—and other Senators on the floor have advocated—on and off the Senate floor and in committee.

There is no stronger advocate of campaign reform than I, for it is a fallacy to feel that anyone who opposes a raid on the Treasury to support political campaigns must be against campaign reform.

Public financing of elections re-forms the campaign laws, it does not reform them. True reform comes from strict limitations of the total amount of permissible campaign contributions and expenditures, full disclosure of all contributions and expenditures, limitation of the size of contributions, limitation on amount of cash contributions and expenditures; and an independent election commission—and which was, of course, the Senate's position—and many other similar reforms in the private sector.

First, public financing of elections is a raid on the taxpayers' pocketbooks for the benefit of politicians. Subsidizing the candidates with funds from the Treasury only adds to the escalating costs of elections when we should be limiting and reducing election costs.

Second, much of the volunteer spirit of citizen participation in elections will be lost where the public treasury is required to pay the cost; and it deprives the citizens of First Amendment rights in depriving them of freedom of expression implicit in the right to contribute to the candidate or candidates of their choice.

Third, it forces a person to contribute to a candidate whose views might be violently opposed to the views of the taxpayer. This objection cannot be met by the contention that only checkoff funds are being used, for these funds belong to all taxpayers and not just to those who participated in the checkoff.

Fourth, Presidential primaries are already spectacle enough without the Federal Treasury adding from $5 to $7½ million more to each candidate's funds.

I have been told that there are some 6, 8, or 10 candidates for the

108

Presidency right here in this Chamber, not here on this floor at this time, but they are Members of this body. I have been told there are some 6, 8, or 10 Members of the Senate who will be candidates for the Presidency.

This bill, of course, would make them a present provided they get enough popular support to get in excess of $5 million, up to as much as $6 or $7½ million, which, if true, each of the candidates from the Senate or from the House, over $5 million for their campaign chest (*sic*).

Mr. President, I was discussing the reason why I opposed the conference report. I was discussing the item of the financial subsidy not only for the Presidential general election, to the candidates for President of the respective parties, but also to finance the literally dozens of candidates who will seek the nomination of the major parties as well as the minor parties, to some extent.

Mr. President, this bill would provide a subsidy of between $5 million and $6 million—up to that amount—for each candidate for Presidential nomination. Literally dozens of them will be encouraged by the subsidies provided by this bill, as well as any hope of obtaining the nomination.

It has been pointed out that it is reputed that there are some 6, 8, 10, or 12 Members of Congress who will seek the Presidency, or will seek the Presidential nomination, and they will be able to receive $5 million or more each, provided they get the necessary contributions from the public generally. But far from cutting down on the spectacle of these Presidential preference primaries, this would escalate the cost by $5 million or $6 million for each candidate and would run up into astronomical terms.

Mr. President, those of us who have sought campaign reform and have opposed just turning the bill over to the taxpayer have had some little success in shaping the campaign reform aspects of the legislation that is now before us.

It is interesting to note that when the distinguished senior Senator from Tennessee (Mr. Baker) offered his amendment to require candidates to disclose the size and source of all contributions and to provide that no contributions could be accepted after 10 days before the election, the reform-minded opponents of public financing supported this fine amendment that would have provided for disclosure.

By and large, whenever an opponent of public financing of taxpayer-

109

subsidized financing, is found, one finds a person who advocates true campaign reform: cutting down the amount of authorized expenditures, cutting down on the amount of the permissible contribution, providing for more disclosure. This amendment of the distinguished Senator from Tennessee (Mr. Baker) provided that a candidate had to disclose the size and source of all contributions and that he could not accept any contributions after 10 days before the election. During that period, he could not accept contributions.·

It seems to me to be a fine disclosure provision, offered by an opponent of taxpayer-financed and subsidized elections, but a strong advocate of campaign reform. . . .

MR. BUCKLEY. Mr. President, I was smiling when the eloquent Senator from Delaware was talking about the advantages of incumbency and the stringent limits proposed by this bill because this is precisely one of my major complaints, but not the most major. I shall recite some of those later.

I addressed myself a week ago to the frustration of coming to this floor in order to debate legislation and then finding out that the report was not available.

When we began this debate at 3 o'clock the conference report was still not here.

Mr. President. This morning I attempted to obtain a copy of the conference committee report on the bill we are now debating. It was unavailable so I have not had a chance to study it. I question the wisdom of voting substantially in the dark on legislation that could alter the way we select our representatives without ever having a chance to see the bill.

When we debated the Senate version of this legislation early this spring, a number of us pointed out practical and constitutional deficiencies in the bill. I said at that time that the bill might accurately be described as the Incumbent Protection Act of 1974.

To offer this bill in the name of reform is an act of unprecedented cynicism.

When enacting legislation that deals with the political activities of American citizens, the Congress is well advised to remember the words of Mr. Justice Holmes, dissenting in *Abrams against United States:*

> . . . when men have realized that time has upset many fighting faiths they
> may come to believe even more than they believe the very foundations of

their own conduct that the ultimate good desired is better reached by free trade in ideas—that the best test of truth is the power of the thought to get itself accepted in the competition of the market . . .

The campaign reform bill, as reported by the conference committee, does much to weaken the ideals of Holmes that have now become law. In Yale Law School Professor Ralph Winter's felicitous phrase, these "price controls in the marketplace of ideas" are necessarily violative of the freedoms guaranteed to the citizens by the First Amendment. That amendment has long been used to defend the rights of unpopular groups to make their positions known, but it applies with no less force when the rights of the great majority of Americans are threatened and infringed.

Limiting the amounts that candidates can spend in election campaigns offends the First Amendment in several ways. As Ralph Winter put it:

> Setting a limit on candidate expenditures sets a maximum on the political activities in which American citizens can engage and is thus unconstitutional. The reasoning that speech which costs money is too persuasive cannot be contained. For one can also argue that demonstrations of more than a certain number of people, extensive voter canvassing, or too many billboards with catchy slogans also "distort" public opinion and also ought to be regulated.

It is particularly disturbing that Senators who had heretofore been considered civil libertarians have rushed to support this measure without considering alternative means, less drastic in their scope, of accomplishing their purposes. The fear of overly persuasive campaigns, particularly when expressed by incumbent Members of Congress, strikes dangerously close to prohibited suppression of speech because of its content. It must certainly give the Supreme Court pause when they see officeholders with vested interests in remaining officeholders passing legislation that restricts the ability of potential opponents and average citizens alike to alter the political makeup of the Congress.

It is hard to imagine a measure that is better designed to protect incumbents. I say this on the authority of Common Cause which presented figures showing that the only successful challenges in House races two years ago were those that spent in excess of $100,000 on the average, to overcome the notorious advantages of incumbency.

111

The result was announced—yeas 60, nays 16.
So the conference report was agreed to.

In the House

October 9

MR. STEIGER of Wisconsin. Mr. Speaker, although S. 3044 tightens the campaign disclosure requirements of the 1971 law in one or two ways, there are at least three ways in which the bill weakens the present disclosure law:

First. It reduces the number of reports that candidates must file.

Under the current Federal Election Campaign Act of 1971, candidates must file 15-day and 5-day preprimary and preelection reports.

S. 3044 strikes this requirement and says candidates must file a single report to be submitted 10 days before each primary and general election. These preelection reports unfortunately must be complete only "as of the 15th day before" the election.

In 1976, therefore, any receipts or expenditures after October 18 —except in excess of $1,000—will go completely unreported until "not later than the 30th day after" the election.

Second. It reduces the information required of candidates and political committees.

Under current law, contributors must be fully identified by mailing address, occupation, and principal place of business if any. S. 3044 will strike this requirement and substitute simply "identification."

Third. It grants a considerable reporting loophole exclusively to incumbent Members of Congress.

The wording of this provision is clear and bold:

(d) This section does not require a Member of Congress to report as contributions received or as expenditures made, the value of photographic, matting, or recording services furnished to him by the Senate Recording Studio, the House Recording Studio, or by an individual whose pay is disbursed by the Secretary of the Senate or the Clerk of the House of Representatives and who furnishes such services as his primary duty as an employee of the Senate or House of Representatives, or if such services were paid for by the Republican or Democratic Senatorial campaign committee, the Democratic National Congressional Committee, or the National Republican Congressional Committee.

Hence, instead of limiting the use of House and Senate resources for re-election purposes, the bill actually encourages the use of incumbent resources and specifically exempts at least some of them from the disclosure law.

In fact, given this exemption from reporting our costs for in-house photographic and recording services, what is there to prevent the Members of Congress from ordering all campaign photographic and recording services through the House Recording Studio? We all know the prices we pay for color video tapes. This could amount to literally thousands of dollars—all of them unreportable for the lucky incumbents.

Such a special exemption for incumbents, combined with the strict limits on spending, will help to lock incumbents to their seats in both parties and both Houses for years to come.

Perhaps the most inequitable feature of the bill is not, however, in its loopholes for incumbents of its limits on spending, but in the way it deliberately injures independent candidates who seek congressional office. While the bill sets a spending limit of $70,000 for a House seat, the conferees decided to allow major party committees other than the principal campaign committees to make expenditures on behalf of congressional candidates. An additional expenditure of two cents per voter is available to congressional candidates who are Republicans or Democrats, but no such extra spending is possible for those who run without benefit of party. Thus, for most of us the spending ceiling is actually about $88,000, but for an individual running as an independent—an opportunity we in the United States pride ourselves in granting—the spending limit is the strict and inequitable $70,000.

There are further inequities as regards the public financing for Presidential primary races.

A candidate who is given $250 by a big contributor will be rewarded with $250 from the U.S. Treasury. But a candidate who is given $1 will receive only $1 from the U.S. Treasury.

And, most seriously of all, any party that has a great many Presidential candidates will receive far greater sums from the U.S. Treasury.

But there are many features of this conference report that will haunt the American people for years to come. In addition to the loopholes and problems already mentioned, I must object to the needless and mischievous provision regarding "Reports by Certain Persons." I refer to the so-called Common Cause Amendment. There is no reason to

113

require of Common Cause, the League of Women Voters, the Americans for Constitutional Action, and other groups of voluntary citizens who do not contribute to candidates, any special reports—simply because they have exercised the basic right of telling Members of Congress what they think. This is frivolous lawmaking at best.

In the face of these serious reservations, I find no alternative to voting against S. 3044, and I strongly urge my colleagues to reject it with me.

October 10

MR. DEVINE of Ohio. Mr. Speaker, I rise not to discuss the technical aspects of this bill, but to speak particularly to my colleagues from this side of the aisle who have had a great deal of concern about the public financing aspects of this legislation.

I was one of about 45 Members who voted against this bill when it came through the House, on the basis of my concern for the public financing features of it, and knowing the strong position of the other body on Presidential, Vice Presidential, senatorial, and congressional public financing, I must compliment the chairman of the Committee on House Administration, who was also chairman of the conference, on the tremendous amount of work and patience he exhibited during the conference. The gentleman had some rather strong persons from the other body, such as Senator Kennedy, Senator Scott, Senator Griffin, Senator Cannon, and others, and they were almost adamant in their position of public financing across the board, including the House and the Senate.

Our chairman and the House conferees stood steadfast against the conferees on the other side, and it was not easy.

Our chairman, the gentleman from Ohio (Mr. Hays), was unjustly accused by the organization he identified as "C.C." I will call it Common Cause. It was no surprise. It accused him of throwing a roadblock in this legislation.

He worked hard to get a bill out that he thought meaningful and which we all felt meaningful, to the point where I, as one of the conferees who voted against this bill when it came through, intend to vote for the conference report.

MR. HAYS. Will the gentleman yield?

MR. DEVINE. Yes, I yield to the gentleman from Ohio.

MR. HAYS. Speaking of roadblocks, one thing that slowed the con-

114

ference down is the fact that the Common Cause lobby was outside the door all the time sending messages in to staff people, which went to conferees, and that took several hours. Otherwise, we would have gotten through a lot quicker.

MR. DEVINE. As far as the House is concerned, the House and Senate no longer are included in the public financing feature.

MR. ARMSTRONG of Colorado. Mr. Speaker, there is some good in this legislation. I am particularly pleased that the conference report provides a strong independent commission to enforce provisions of this act.

But I would be remiss if I did not voice my objection to Federal financing of conventions and to the failure of this bill to adequately define and outlaw certain improper in-kind contributions, and for the fact that it is in tone and in detail a proincumbent bill. It is really a "sweetheart" bill, one that will serve primarily to reelect incumbents and make it harder than ever for challengers to unseat an entrenched incumbent.

But, Mr. Speaker, the part of this bill that makes it most objectionable, the part that makes an antireform bill, is the provision that limits the right of voters to speak out on candidates who are running for public office.

It is one thing to limit candidates expenditures. But it is completely wrong to limit the rights of citizens in this regard.

MR. SANDMAN of New Jersey. Mr. Speaker, I intend to support this bill because it has some improvements over the system we have.

One thing disturbs me about this, and this is again only for my own information, but has anybody bothered to check into the constitutionality of what we are doing? Does the gentleman believe we are meeting the requirements of the 14th Amendment when we set particular standards on what a candidate has to raise before he qualifies to get so much money, because we are not giving all candidates the same amount of money?

MR. FRENZEL of Minnesota. Yes; the gentleman makes a valid point.

There are many members of the conference committee, including, I believe, the chairman, who believe that this feature may be unconstitutional.

I believe within this conference report there are at least 100 items questionable from a constitutional standpoint. Any time we pass legislation in this field we are causing constitutional doubts to be raised. I have many myself. I think the gentleman has pointed out a good one. We have done the best we could to bring out a bill which we hope may pass the constitutional test. But we do not doubt that some questions will be raised quickly.

I do call the attention of the gentleman to the fact that any individual under this bill has a direct method to raise these questions and to have those considered as quickly as possible by the Supreme Court.

MR. YOUNG of Georgia. Mr. Speaker, at this point in the *Record* I would like to insert a list of those members of the reform coalition who contributed so much to this legislation:

PUBLIC FINANCING/ELECTION REFORM COALITION

Center for Public Financing of Elections
AFL-CIO
Common Cause
League of Women Voters
United Auto Workers
Ralph Nader's Congress Watch
Amalgamated Clothing Workers
American Association of University Women
American Civil Liberties Union
American Institute of Architects
American Federation of State, County and Municipal Employees
Americans for Democratic Action
Communications Workers of America
Friends Committee on National Legislation
International Association of Machinists
International Ladies Garment Workers Union
Leadership Conference on Civil Rights
League of Conservation Voters
National Association for the Advancement of Colored People
National Council of Churches
National Committee for an Effective Congress
National Education Association
National Farmers Union
National Rural Electric Cooperative Association
National Women's Political Caucus

116

Network
Religious Committee for Integrity in Government
Service Employees International Union
Steelworkers Union
Union of American Hebrew Congregations
United Mine Workers
United Methodist Church

The vote was taken by electronic device, and there were—ayes 365, noes 24, answered "present" 1, not voting 44.

So the conference report was agreed to.

6

" What Do You Do for an Encore ?"
(Or Why Organized Labor
Likes the New Law)

"What Do You Do for an Encore?" read the headline of the post-1974 election issue of *Memo from COPE,* official publication of the AFL-CIO Committee on Political Education. The opening sentence beneath the headline appropriately stated, "It's a good question: What *do* you do for an encore after a day like November 5?"

No matter how one looks at it, organized labor has good reason to be proud of its success at the polls in the last national election. The same *Memo* tallies the unions' political success story:

> COPE rang up its best results ever November 5 in terms of victories for endorsed candidates.
>
> Over-all, 455 candidates for U.S. House and Senate and for governor were endorsed, with 321 of them winning, a 70.5 percent record.
>
> In the House, 389 endorsements were made, with 270 winning for 70 percent; in the Senate, 25* for 33, 76 percent, and in the gubernatorial races, 26 for 33, 79 percent.[1]

*This may increase to twenty-six if the Democratic candidate in New Hampshire's contested senatorial race is seated in the Senate.

Organized labor's declared goal in 1974 was to elect enough liberal, union-backed candidates to achieve a "veto-proof" Congress. Declared George Meany, "We need a Congress that has the numbers and the will to override every veto the President can throw at us." Did Meany get his veto-proof Congress? Many observers say he did or that he came very close to doing so. According to an election summary titled "Labor's Candidates Score Election Wins" in the November 1974 issue of *Allied Industrial Worker,* official publication of the international union of the same name:

> The House margin hits the magic two-third's veto-proof goal, but the Senate margin falls short. Nonetheless, the voters provided a strong mandate against the policies of the Ford-Nixon Administration by repudiating Administration-backed candidates throughout the country.
>
> Actually, the Senate margin does not include three liberal Republicans, all of whom were supported by organized labor and who are expected to vote with Democrats on labor issues. The three Republicans, all who won, were Senators Richard Schweiker of Pennsylvania, Jacob Javits of New York and Charles Mathias of Maryland.

HOW MUCH DID LABOR SPEND?

Final reports from political committees on their spending in the 1974 election reveal organized labor was the biggest cash contributor in the election. As Pulitzer Prize–winning reporter of the *Washington Star-News* James R. Polk has noted, "The big winner in the biennial sweepstakes for special-interest groups in the political act of putting money where it counts was the AFL-CIO, a granddaddy of the Washington game." At the beginning of October over forty union political committees had spent, or had on hand to spend, more than $11 million raised from the "voluntary" contributions of union staff personnel and members. "Voluntary" is put in quotation marks because evidence exists that some unions use compulsion to exact these cash contributions.

The total sums received and spent by each of the union political committees vary widely. The AFL-CIO COPE spent $1,970,570.40. The national political arm of the National Education Association

120

poured in $225,000 and its 9,000 state and local affiliates spent an additional $2.5 million. The Marine Engineers (retirees group) spent $1 million and the Autoworkers close to another million.

When one reads that the AFL-CIO COPE spent nearly $2 million in cash in 1974 it must be recognized that this represents only a small portion of labor's total political spending since there are more than forty other labor political committees. COPE is only one among many. While there are a multitude of business political committees, their political interests are diverse and many times work at cross-purposes. For example, the political interests of the American Medical Association, the National Association of Manufacturers, and the milk lobby differ widely, whereas those of the COPE, Steelworkers, and Autoworkers are identical. (See Appendix VI for a listing of union cash contributions in 1974 to members of the House Education and Labor Committee.)

Actually, the cash contributions reported by union political committees are only the tip of the iceberg. For labor's "in-kind" contributions of goods and services to its candidates, it is estimated, exceed its cash contributions by a ratio of ten to one. This means that for each one-dollar cash contribution to a candidate, organized labor also provides ten dollars' worth of goods and services. Organized labor likes the new campaign law because it believes it need not fear prosecution for its in-kind contributions and because it controls the Federal Election Commission.

1974 "TARGET LIST"

Early in the election year COPE drew up its "target list" of forty-seven incumbent Republican House members whom it wanted to defeat. All forty-seven were conservatives. During much of the year organized labor contributed cash to the campaigns of the challengers to these incumbents and mobilized in-kind contributions of goods and services, including full-time manpower.

The spreading stain of the Watergate scandal, the resignation of President Nixon, and his subsequent pardon by President Ford all served to embolden union political strategists. On October 22, a date

121

picked by the union strategists so as to avoid having to publicize additional contributions before election day, COPE increased its target list to ninety congressional districts in which it planned to concentrate its efforts to elect its candidates. Only one of the ninety that COPE supported was a Republican: Congressman Peter Peyser of New York, a member of the House Education and Labor Committee.

According to the *National Journal,* in the remaining eighty-nine districts

> COPE had a 53–36 record. The complete list is divided into primary and secondary priority races, and COPE had a 28–9 record in the former category, compared with a 25–27 record in the latter.
>
> The "target list" included 65 Republican districts, 51 in which the incumbent GOP Representative was seeking reelection and 14 which were being vacated. In a phenomenal performance, COPE came close to defeating half of the incumbents, emerging with a 23-28 record. In the open districts, COPE-endorsed candidates won eight and lost six races.
>
> Finally, COPE "targeted" 24 Democratic districts, 12 in which the incumbent was seeking reelection but was believed to be weak enough to require outside assistance and 12 seats being vacated by Democrats. Republican candidates won only one seat in each category.[2]

Organized labor also scored significant gains on the state and local levels. Labor-backed Democratic candidates won twenty-seven of thirty-five gubernatorial races for a new total of thirty-six state mansions held by labor-backed governors. Many state legislatures were also swept into the Democratic-labor tide. California, the nation's most populous state, provides a typical example. The *California AFL-CIO News* in a front-page article, "Labor and the Elections," proclaims:

> The November election results gave the state AFL-CIO an historic sweep in both State and Federal races.
>
> State AFL-CIO affiliates made it possible. State AFL-CIO affiliates deserve the praise.
>
> We have increased the liberal majority by nine votes in the State Assembly.
>
> We have added three liberals to the State Senate, defeating two deeply conservative incumbents in the process.
>
> We have increased by four the liberal majority in our congressional delegation.
>
> And we now have in the Governor's office a liberal who will return the

essential agencies of state government to public control. We have in Governor-elect Brown a man who will give California a new life and direction.

All of our other endorsed candidates for statewide offices were successful in November. A perfect score!

The affiliates of our State AFL-CIO movement have built one of the most effective political structures in American labor. November 5 was a continuance of what we have been doing through united union action. We're not going to stop![3]

Mary Zon, COPE director of research, provided the following analysis in "The 1974 Elections: Good Omens," which appeared in the December 1974 AFL-CIO *American Federationist:*

The effect of the size of the vote was, in 1974, as erratic as the coattail factor. Following the pattern of the 1974 special elections the size of the November turnout was low. Estimates now range between 38 percent and 40 percent of those eligible to vote (18 years old or older). This would make the 1974 turnout the smallest since 1946 when the figure was a 37.4 percent.

The size of the vote is clearly no longer a reliable basis for predicting results. COPE's registration and get-out-the-vote efforts can provide the winning margin in a large voter turnout and can account for more than its normal proportion of the electorate when the vote is low. This shown in those metropolitan areas with an important blue-collar and trade union presence, which accounted for more than their share of new congressmen in 1974. For some years union members have joined the flight to the suburbs where, more often than not, they were lost to the COPE program. Expansion of the use of data processing has made it possible to find these members and to involve them in all organizational and educational aspects of COPE.

The organizational efforts of allied groups working with minority members, young members and retired unionists contribute importantly to the COPE effort.

The state and local COPEs are becoming more selective in bestowing endorsements and more skilled in backing an endorsement with solid organizational support.

In 1974 state COPEs endorsed more candidates than in any earlier election and a higher percentage of COPE-endorsed candidates for Congress and for Governor were successful in 1974 than in any previous election. The 70.5 percent score in 1974 compared to 60.9 percent in 1970 and a dismal 51.8 percent in 1966, the two preceding non-presidential years.

123

Overall, the figures were good enough for liberals to look forward to the 1976 campaign—which began on the morning of Wednesday, November 6, 1974.

UNIQUE ADVANTAGES

As noted earlier, organized labor's political contributions can be broken into two categories: (1) cash contributions derived from "voluntary" contributions, and (2) "in-kind" contributions of goods and services. For every one-dollar cash contribution by labor, ten dollars are spent by it in in-kind contributions, including paid manpower assigned to campaigns, postage, telephones, automobiles, sound trucks, campaign materials, and partisan voter-registration and voter-turnout drives.

Just as it is true that labor's political contributions are of two categories, the source of labor's political funds can also be divided into two categories: (1) voluntary political contributions, and (2) involuntary or compelled payments by union members. No matter how broadly one may construe the category "voluntary" or how narrowly the category "involuntary," two facts are clear:

• Voluntary contributions by members are sizable but inadequate to the total needs of organized labor's political activities.

• In order to fill those needs, organized labor relies heavily on "taxes" or assessments imposed upon the dues paid by union members.

Since the bulk of organized labor's political spending is in goods and services, it follows that the bulk of the sources of labor's funds to pay these contributions is from "taxes" or assessments imposed on members' dues and not from voluntary cash donations by the rank and file. Just as labor's cash contributions represent only the tip of the iceberg of union political spending, the voluntary donations by the rank and file to union political committees are only the tip of the iceberg of the source of labor political funds.

Several dramatic examples of how the taxes or assessments on members' dues are used in politics can be found in a legal document filed in 1973 in the U.S. District Court for the Central District of California. The case in which the document is now part of the public record is *Seay, et al.* v. *International Association of Machinists and Aerospace Workers, et al.,* in which a group of aerospace employees who are

124

agency fee payers to the Machinist union have sought an injunction to prevent their dues money being used for partisan politics. The plaintiff-protesting Machinists are being represented in the suit by the National Right to Work Legal Defense Foundation. In the court records Thomas Harris, associate general counsel, AFL-CIO, and now a member of the Federal Election Commission, stipulated the following statements as true:

> With minor exceptions, the expenses of COPE, including the salaries of COPE staff personnel, travel expenses, office supplies, telephones and telegraph, printing and general overhead expenses are paid by the AFL-CIO out of the general fund of the AFL-CIO, a fund which is derived principally from per capita taxes received from affiliated national and international unions. . . .
>
> A portion of COPE Educational Fund monies, derived ultimately from membership dues, are frequently used for the preparation, printing and dissemination of political brochures and other materials which support particular candidates for federal office. Such funds are also used for the purpose of making direct cash contributions to candidates for nonfederal offices such as state gubernatorial races.[4]

Another example of how the AFL-CIO uses its tax-exempt resources for partisan politics is described by Rex Hardesty in an article, "The 1974 Elections: A New Opportunity," published in the October 1974 issue of *American Federationist:*

> In recent years, the AFL-CIO has been systematically computerizing lists of union members' names for registration drives, precinct walking lists and selective mailings by various local COPE bodies. From a tiny experimental project 10 years ago, the program has now expanded to 38 states and has passed the 1974 goal of 10 million names. While fancy computer printouts are only as valuable as the volunteers who handle them, one big plus already discernible is that COPE endorsements can now zero in on specific candidates, thanks to computer coding by ward and precinct.

The bottom line, then, on the source of union political funds used for contributions of goods and services in partisan campaigns is the taxes or assessments on members' dues. The union bosses, such as Thomas Harris before his appointment to the Federal Election Commission, determine to which candidates these multi-million-dollar contributions are directed, the rank and file having virtually no input

125

in the decision-making process even though they ultimately foot the bill.

PUBLIC EMPLOYEES

Two unions rapidly emerging as political powerbrokers are the American Federation of State, County and Municipal Employees (700,000 members) and the National Education Association (1.5 million members).

AFSCME is headed by left-wing activist Jerry Wurf, who makes no pretense that he uses the compulsory dues money of his rank and file to promote his liberal causes and to elect liberal candidates. He makes these admissions in an affidavit filed in court records in a suit brought by AFSCME members protesting the use of their dues for partisan political purposes. (Wurf's affidavit is found in Appendix VII.)

Wurf is especially optimistic these days about the success of his political operations because the new federal election law opens the door to state and local government workers to engage in partisan politics. In announcing the return of the spoils system to American politics, AFSCME's official publication, *Public Employee,* declared:

Congress has eliminated the provision of the federal Hatch Act that outlawed voluntary political campaign activities by state and local public employees in agencies that receive federal money.

The new Hatch Act legislation does not repeal the law, but it does remove its most objectionable provision. This means that—after January 1, 1975—state, county and municipal employees can voluntarily work on their own time for the election of candidates of their choice running in a partisan campaign for public office.

AFSCME representatives in the Union's Legislation Department who worked for enactment of the measure said it was passed with strong bi-partisan support. It was approved and recommended for passage by a unanimous vote of the House Administration Committee, which drafted the main elements of the campaign spending reform bill and its amendments.

The AFSCME represenatives expressed special appreciation for the efforts of Rep. Wayne Hays (D–Ohio), who chairs the House Administration Committee and who introduced the amendment, and Reps. John Dent (D–Pa.), John Brademas (D–Ind.) and Frank Thompson (D–N.J.), all of whom supported it.[5]

126

The National Education Association has moved into political action in a big way in recent years. With an annual budget of $32 million, NEA is able to mobilize its considerable resources in campaigns in all parts of the country. Joe Standa, an NEA official, declares: "We have people in practically every precinct in the country. The NEA has over 9,000 affiliates and we've found an average of 6,200 teachers in every congressional district in the country."[6]

TAX-EXEMPT STATUS

Still a third advantage must be added to the existing (1) contributions of goods and services, which are (2) financed by compulsory dues money—namely, the fact that labor unions are nonprofit, tax-exempt organizations. Section 501 (c) (5) of the Internal Revenue Code grants unions their tax-exempt status. Unions routinely draw upon their tax-exempt resources to aid partisan campaigns. Among the resources so mobilized is the use of the 1.7-cent postage rate to mail campaign literature. In effect, this partisan activity by unions using their tax-exempt resources is a form of public subsidy since the loss of tax revenue caused by unions not having to pay taxes is borne by the American taxpayer.

A significant and inescapable conclusion thus emerges that negates the popular orthodoxy that labor unions exist today primarily to represent the rank and file in collective bargaining. Instead, the truth now penetrating the public consciousness is that organized labor, which annually pulls in over a billion dollars in dues revenue, is a tax-exempt enterprise principally engaged in partisan politics by providing goods and services to endorsed candidates financed from members' compulsory dues.

ASSIGNMENT OF MANPOWER

Of all the tax-exempt resources mobilized by organized labor for partisan political activity, the most important and effective is the assignment of paid union manpower to candidates' campaigns. The AFL-CIO openly admits this and proclaims it as governing policy. In the 1973 report of the AFL-CIO Standing Committee on Organization to the federation's Executive Council are found these policy declarations:

127

In a crucial election year, labor's interests may be best served by placing greater emphasis on political action assignments, and the field staff should be fully prepared to perform such assignments as an integral part of their mission. . . .

There are clearly times when the most effective organizing that can be done is the organizing of support for amendments of the National Labor Relations Act, or for a shift in the balance of power in Congress.

This AFL-CIO policy declaration and the hundreds of examples of paid union personnel being assigned to campaigns that I cited in *The Hundred Million Dollar Payoff* clearly reveal a pattern of illegal activity on the part of unions. The law that is being violated is the Federal Election Campaign Act (Title 18, Section 610 of the U.S. Code), formerly known as the Corrupt Practices Act. Senator Howard Cannon (D–Nev.), chairman of the Senate Rules Committee, which oversees federal election legislation, had this to say, in the debate on April 11, 1974, on the new amendments to the Federal Election Campaign Act:

I simply point out that under section 610 of the Corrupt Practices Act at the present time, it is unlawful for any corporation, whatever, or any labor organization, to make a contribution or expenditure in connection with any election, and so forth. Certainly, if a corporation or a labor union pays the salary of an individual and puts that person to work for a candidate, that is unlawful. It is unlawful under existing law.

WHY NO UNION PROSECUTIONS?

Over nineteen corporations have been prosecuted and over 200 investigated by the Watergate special prosecutor for violations of Title 18, Section 610 by making treasury contributions to candidates for federal offices. Yet there has not been a single prosecution of a labor union despite the immense amount of evidence showing violations of the law. Why did the Watergate special prosecutor fail to prosecute these violations or even investigate them?

Similarly, it should be asked why the Senate Watergate Committee also failed to investigate illegal union political activity when the scope of its mandate included investigating all illegal activities in connection with the 1972 Presidential election, no matter what political party was involved. The final report of the Senate Watergate Committee provides a mass of evidence of illegal corporate contributions to the 1972 cam-

128

paign but is strangely silent on illegal union contributions. The final report does candidly admit: "The Select Committee—whether by the questionnaires or the limited investigations—made no attempt to engage in a comprehensive survey of union political activity." It recommends that an appropriate congressional committee review certain questions posed by the Select Committee but all of the questions completely ignore the scope of illegal in-kind contributions by labor unions. Furthermore, even at the time the Select Committee issued this recommendation it knew the proposal would not be seriously considered since organized labor controls Congress and can easily squelch any such attempt. (See Appendix VIII for members of Congress endorsed by COPE.)

Since the Watergate special prosecutor and the Senate Watergate Committee both failed to investigate illegal union political contributions, why hasn't the Justice Department undertaken such an investigation?

It is the author's belief that the Justice Department under the Nixon and Ford administrations has avoided investigating illegal union political activity because the Republican Party at the national level has skeletons in its closet that it prefers to keep there. Organized labor's campaign contributions—both legal and illegal—go to the Democrats by a ratio of nineteen to one. But this still means that the Republican Party receives about five percent of these union contributions. More investigative journalism is needed into the relationship of the national Republican Party to certain labor unions, but at this time these questions merely are posed to serve to stimulate further research into the subject:

• Why did the Seafarers' Union—which in 1968 supported Humphrey for President—make a $100,000 contribution to the Committee for the Re-election of the President just days before the 1972 election and shortly after a criminal indictment against eight of its top officials had been dismissed by a federal judge because the Justice Department had failed to move in a timely fashion?

• Why was Paul Hall, president of the Seafarers' Union and one of the eight union officials originally indicted, such an ardent supporter of Nixon (in fact, the only supporter) on the AFL-CIO Executive Council until just prior to Nixon's resignation?

• Why was former Teamster president Jimmy Hoffa pardoned shortly after the 1972 election from his prison sentence and set free?

129

- Why did the Teamsters choose former Nixon aide Charles Colson as Washington legal counsel after he left the White House?
- Why was a key meeting of the White House conspirators in the Watergate coverup held at a plush resort in Southern California, which resort was built with Teamster pension funds and which is allegedly run by the mafia?
- Why did the Teamsters make a $25,000 contribution from union treasury funds to a political group opposing Nixon's impeachment?

The Teamsters have customarily supported Republican Presidential candidates while invariably supporting Democratic candidates for Congress. Perhaps the answer to why the Justice Department, which is part of the administration, has done nothing to investigate illegal union political activity lies in the *sub rosa* political relationship between the Teamster hierarchy and the Republicans in the White House.

The close personal and political friendship between Vice President Nelson Rockefeller and George Meany is another significant clue that cannot be ignored.

TWO REALISTIC REMEDIES

Many thoughtful observers believe, therefore, that at the present time only two remedies can be fashioned to end illegal union political activity.

The first is that public opinion be mobilized to force the appointment of a new special prosecutor (or public attorney), one who will investigate illegal union political activity by subpoenaing union leaders and union political directors before a grand jury and through subpoenas *duces tecum* obtain all the files, correspondence, accounting records, canceled checks, and other materials relating to union political operations. If this were done it would be only a matter of weeks or months before the American people would have the full, shocking story of how unions have used the compulsory dues money of their members to corrupt numerous public officials.

The second remedy lies with the courts. All Americans should be heartened by the recent action of the federal judge in California who refused to grant the defendant union's motion for summary judgment in *Ellis-Fails, et al.* v. *Brotherhood of Railway, Airline and Steamship*

Clerks, * a suit brought by union members protesting the use of their compulsory dues money for political activity. For the first time union members will now learn, by the suit being heard in open court, how their dues money is being used to support candidates and ideological causes with which they may be in disagreement. Hopefully, other federal judges will follow this lead in similar cases in the future.

LABOR AND THE DEMOCRATIC PARTY

In February 1975 Meany announced, at a meeting of the AFL-CIO Executive Council in plush Bal Harbour, Florida, that the labor federation would no longer involve itself in political party affairs and would take no part in the selection of delegates to the Democratic National Convention in 1976. Declared Meany: "We have a political party and it's known as COPE, and we are going to continue to improve it, strengthen it, maintain it, in order to try to elect labor friends to the House and Senate and to the state legislatures, irrespective of political parties."[7]

Meany's announcement came as no surprise to those who had followed COPE's persistent feud with Democratic National Committee chairman Robert Strauss. Two months earlier Al Zack, Meany's mouthpiece, had blasted Strauss for not genuflecting to COPE director Al Barkan at the party's charter convention on reforms in Kansas City, Missouri. Zack, evidencing his usual adroitness as AFL-CIO director of public relations, charged: "The Democratic Party structure is now catering exclusively to blacks, browns, youth and women and excluded by that definition are most workers, senior citizens, Jews, Catholics and other segments of what was once a united coalition of forces called the Democratic Party."[8]

Strauss, at the time of Zack's blast, was visibly upset. He told a *New York Times* reporter, "We need George Meany and Al Barkan very badly and anything I can do to keep them involved I'll do."[9]

Barkan and Meany are angry at Strauss because they believe that they should be calling the shots within the Democratic Party, not other special-interest groups. Months earlier Barkan had declared:

*Civil Case Nos. 73–113–N and 73–118–N in the U.S. District Court for the Southern District of California.

131

We're very suspicious. The same groups that brought about Miami are pushing for these reforms. The hell, we want to win. Most labor leaders are Democrats, but we can't rely on the Democratic Party to come up with presidential candidates as we did in the past. We are telling labor leaders that if you want to avoid another '72 you ought to get into the party and fight it out.[10]

Chairman Strauss realizes that labor is the key to a Democratic victory in 1976. Union leaders know this to be true, too. One union leader has been quoted as saying concerning the 1974 special elections: "In the special elections, the Democratic National Committee didn't give a thing—it was almost entirely a labor effort. We don't need the DNC, they need us."[11]

Concerning those special elections, a Democratic source once admitted, "The unions gave twice what they usually give in money, in in-kind services, workers, personnel."[12]

Dean Clowes, Steelworkers' political strategist and a member of COPE's committee on marginal Senate races, said, "If we could concentrate on each district, we could win almost any election."[13]

Meany's declaration that the AFL-CIO was staying out of the Democratic Party's affairs should be kept in perspective. In essence, Meany speaks only for himself and for the federation—not for the 117 unions that belong to the AFL-CIO. At his behest in 1972 the AFL-CIO was neutral in the Nixon-McGovern race but this did not prevent forty-two unions—many of them among the largest and most influential members of the AFL-CIO—from endorsing and supporting the McGovern ticket. Even after Meany's announcement of nonparticipation in February 1975, a number of large unions—including Machinists, Communication Workers, and AFSCME—let it be known publicly that their leadership would not follow Meany's dictate and would continue to work within the Democratic Party for victory in 1976.

7

So Good Men Will Not Say:
" What's the Use ?"

Preceding portions of this book have attempted to show that the new federal election law, rather than being true election reform as it was packaged and sold to the American people, is a cunning, insidious scheme to perpetuate liberals and radicals in power by rigging our Presidential and congressional elections. In its scope and effect the new act eclipses Watergate in its viselike grasp to use our electoral processes and democratic institutions in an illegal and unconstitutional manner to suppress opposing views. That the new law was successfully pushed through Congress, over the protests of a small but courageous minority, by a lobbying cabal of labor unions, "public-interest" organizations, the mass media, and power-hungry politicians should serve to forewarn all our citizens how easily our hard-won liberties can be lost.

The battle has now shifted to the courts with the expectation that the new law's constitutionality or lack thereof will ultimately be decided by the Supreme Court. Should the Supreme Court strike down a number of the law's provisions, then our citizens must turn their attention to enacting a new federal election statute—one arrived at through open discussion and debate and not through hypocritical and deceitful actions by would-be dictators as was the present law.

The drafting of a new federal election law should occupy the finest minds of citizens interested in public affairs. Politics is too important a subject to be left to the politicians. Some outstanding individuals have already focused on what a true campaign law should encompass and, as a starting point, their existing views should be considered.* Here are several of these.

• Former Senator John Williams of Delaware was known as the "conscience of the Senate" until his retirement a few years ago. One of the many cases of public corruption that he investigated and exposed was the infamous Bobby Baker case (which can be distinguished from Watergate in that Baker, when caught, refused to squeal on his higher up). Senator Williams made his campaign reform proposals in an article titled "After Watergate a Plan to Control Campaign Bankrolling," which appeared in the March 1974 issue of *Reader's Digest*. Here in summary is what Senator Williams proposes:

(1) "Shorten the campaign" by having a uniform, nationwide date for primaries and nominating conventions with primary campaigns being held in early August and the general election campaign beginning in early October.

(2) "Grant free television time and mailing rights" to bona fide candidates.

(3) "Get Big Business and Big Labor out of political bankrolling" by enacting new, stringent laws that would effectively bar corporate and union contributions in any form.

(4) "Make small contributors the backbone of political financing" but do not employ public financing.

(5) "Enforce the campaign-funding laws," which, before the new election law, were, on the whole, adequate if impartially and effectively applied. Some of the older laws are still on the statute books.

• The Senate Watergate Committee in its Final Report, released in July 1974, made these eleven campaign financing recommendations:

(1) The committee recommends that the Congress enact legislation to establish an independent, nonpartisan Federal Elections Commission which would replace the present tripartite administration of the Clerk of

*See also Appendix IX for the statement of the National Right to Work Committee to the House Administration Committee on proposed election reform.

the House, Secretary of the Senate, and GAO Office of Federal Elections and would have certain enforcement powers.

(2) The committee recommends enactment of a statute prohibiting cash contributions and expenditures in excess of $100 in connection with any campaign for nomination or election for Federal office.

(3) The committee recommends enactment of a statute requiring each candidate for the office of President or Vice President to designate one political committee as his central campaign committee with one or more banks as his campaign depositories.

(4) The committee recommends enactment of a statutory limitation on overall campaign expenditures of Presidential candidates. The committee proposes a limit on expenditures of 12 cents times the voting age population during a general election.

(5) The committee recommends enactment of a statutory limitation of $3,000 on political contributions by any individuals to the campaign of each Presidential candidate during the prenomination period and a separate $3,000 limitation during the postnomination period. A contribution to a Vice-Presidential candidate of a party would be considered, for purposes of the limitation, a contribution to that party's Presidential candidate.

(6) The committee recommends that the Internal Revenue Code be amended to provide a tax credit in a substantial amount on individual and joint Federal income tax returns for any contribution made in a calendar year to a political party or any candidate seeking election to any public office, Federal, State, or local.

(7) The committee recommends against the adoption of any form of public financing in which tax moneys are collected and allocated to political candidates by the Federal Government.

(8) The committee recommends enactment of a statute prohibiting the solicitation or receipt of campaign contributions from foreign nationals.

(9) The committee recommends that no Government official whose appointment required confirmation by the Senate or who was on the payroll of the Executive Office of the President be permitted to participate in the solicitation or receipt of campaign contributions during his or her period of service and for a period of one year thereafter.

(10) The committee recommends that stringent limitations be imposed on the right of organizations to contribute to Presidential campaigns.

(11) The committee recommends that violations of the major provisions of the campaign financing law, such as participating in a corporate or union contribution or a contribution in excess of the statutory limit, and making a foreign contribution, shall constitute a felony.

• Congressman William Frenzel (R.–Minn.), in the front ranks of those who sought to enact an equitable, fair, and real campaign reform

135

bill in 1974, has proposed new legislation (H.R. 3419) to help remedy the defects of the present law. Here are his thoughtful remarks to the House, from the *Congressional Record* of February 20, 1975:

MR. FRENZEL. Mr. Speaker, today, I am introducing a bill to further reform our system of campaign financing, the Federal Election Campaign Act Amendments of 1975.

The 93rd Congress passed landmark legislation in this area, the Federal Election Campaign Act Amendments of 1974. This law, signed by President Ford on October 15, should have historic, far-reaching effects on our political process. In particular, the establishment of an independent Federal Election Commission should help assure vigorous and judicious enforcement of the new law.

SPECIAL INTEREST MONEY

The 93rd Congress, however, did not finish the job. Most importantly, it did not effectively regulate special interest committees. While special interest committees were limited as to how much they could give a particular candidate—$5,000—the 1974 act did not go nearly far enough.

During the 1974 elections, special interest committees gave more than ever to candidates and their political committees. There are, as of yet, no final totals, but it is likely that special interest giving totaled around $20 million. If campaign contributions are ever used for leverage in the political system, then surely special interest groups head the list of those who may give with the purpose of influencing candidates. These contributions are questionable for several reasons:

First, "Special interests" are exactly what the name implies. Each of these groups has its own special and particular interests which it attempts to promote in the legislative and political process. Ofttimes, these interests may be at odds with the public interest. By giving contributions, these special interests hope to increase their political muscle and gain passage of legislation favorable to their interests, or kill legislation that is unfavorable.

Second. Most of this money goes to incumbents, who are already too well entrenched in office. On the average, over 90 percent of incumbents win in congressional races. Challengers are frequently unable to wage effective campaigns, because they cannot raise sufficient funds to wage an effective campaign. At other times, they raise sufficient funds, but still find themselves far outspent by incumbents with gigantic war chests. The latest figures I have seen indicate that special interest groups gave four times as much money to incumbents as to challengers. Some of the contributions were made after the election was over. This situation is clearly unhealthy, because much of the money is given to incumbents with the knowledge that they will probably win and be in a position to help the special interest groups further their legislative objectives.

Third. Special interest money gives a handful of people disproportionate influence over the political process. In the case of some special interest committees, a handful of people decide where the contributions of thousands of people are to be spent. Many thousands of dollars from thousands of contributors may be collected in these pools, but only an elite few decide where the money is going. Ofttimes, these are the same people who will, in the next Congress, be lobbying on behalf of the special interest group's legislative program.

A key provision of the 1974 act prohibits an individual from giving more than $25,000 to all Federal candidates and political committees in a calendar year. We should not limit what each individual can give from his personal funds to $25,000, but then allow some individuals to allocate hundreds of thousands of dollars of special interest campaign contributions.

Mr. Speaker, the legislation I am introducing today has three provisions which would strictly regulate special interest giving:

First: Since it can be argued that a ban on special interest giving would be unconstitutional, I strongly favor, instead, another approach which would drastically curtail the capabilities of special interests to gain influence through contributions. This proposal would prohibit the pooling of funds and require all contributions made through special interest groups to identify the original donor. In addition, each individual contributor must designate the intended recipient. Special interest groups would only be allowed to act as the agents of individual contributors, thereby reducing considerably whatever influence they gain through campaign contributions.

Second. The second proposal would be to reduce the amount a special interest committee can give to any candidate from $5,000 to $2,500. Special interest groups should not be allowed to contribute five times as much as individuals.

Third. In the past, special interest groups have avoided full disclosure or the gift tax by proliferating the number of their political committees. This same activity could be used to circumvent contribution limitations. Some special interest groups set up 10, 15, or 20 political committees to channel funds to candidates in anticipation of the passage of the 1974 contribution limitations. While the legislative history of the law clearly prohibits such activity, I feel that it is necessary to include specific language in the law banning the proliferation of political committees to circumvent the limitations in order to insure that the courts and administrators have absolutely no latitude in interpreting the law.

DIRTY TRICKS

The 1974 act also failed to include provisions which would specifically outlaw many of the dirty tricks carried out in the 1972 campaign. The Ervin committee made several important recommendations on dirty tricks, many of which are incorporated in this bill. My legislation would:

First. Prohibit Federal and State and local employees from using their official authority in connection with any activity which is financed by subsidies, contract, payments, or other payments of the Federal Government to interfere or affect any Federal election. Present law limits this prohibition only to activities involving loans and grants.

Second. Prohibit election campaign espionage.

Third. Prohibit employees of a candidate or political committee from concealing any campaign abuses or violations of election laws.

Fourth. Forbid the unlawful use of campaign materials, including the embezzlement and stealing of materials from any candidate.

Fifth. Prohibit the infiltration of Federal election campaigns for espionage and sabotage purposes.

Sixth. Prohibit the use of funds to finance violations of any Federal election laws.

Seventh. Make it a separate offense to commit a violation of the criminal code with the intent of interfering with or affecting the outcome of a Federal election.

Eighth. Forbid any personnel of the Executive Office of the President from engaging in investigative or intelligence gathering activity not specifically authorized by statute.

Ninth. Increase penalties for violation of dirty trick provisions from $1,000 to $25,000. The bill also strikes two provisions of title 18. The prohibition on the polling of members of the Armed Forces is eliminated, because this provision has been used to curb the First Amendment rights of military personnel and to harass reporters and other persons who attempt to engage in discussion and debate with members of the Armed Forces.

Section 604, which prohibits solicitation from persons on relief, is also eliminated. This provision discriminates against those who are on relief—

including the unemployed—and has never been enforced. Flagrant abuses, such as coercing persons on relief to give contributions, are still covered by sections 598, 600, and 602.

EXPENDITURE LIMITATIONS

The expenditure limitations in the new law are far too low and help to further entrench incumbents. They have the further effect of limiting political debate and preventing candidates from more fully presenting their views and ideas to the public. The present law also distinguishes between House races, House races in States with only one Representative, and Senate races. Such distinctions are arbitrary and unnecessary. My bill increases the expenditure limitation to $150,000 or 25 cents times the voting age population, whichever is greater, per election for both House and Senate races.

TAX RETURNS

The Federal Election Campaign Act Amendments of 1975 would require full disclosure of any White House request for a tax audit. A report disclosing any such requests must be made annually to the Congress and include the name and office of each officer or employee who makes the request, the name of the taxpayer who is the subject of the request, and a description of any action which the Secretary of the Treasury or his delegate took with respect to the request. Any request made by the President or an officer or employee of the Executive Office of the President, must be made in writing and be maintained on file. The President, Vice President, and any other officer and employee of the Executive Office of the President are barred from having any access to tax returns.

REPEAL OF SECTION 315

Section 315 of the Communications Act, which requires broadcasting stations to grant candidates equal time, is repealed for all Federal elections. Repeal of Section 315 will help give challengers greater exposure to the electorate. Presently incumbents are given considerable coverage between elections, but are able to reduce the visibility of challengers by claiming

139

that television coverage or debate would require the participation of many frivolous, nonserious candidates, because of the requirements of section 315. The discretion of the broadcasting stations, under my proposal, to grant free time would still be limited by the fairness doctrine. Candidates would not have to worry about broadcasting stations excluding them from the air arbitrarily.

VETO OF REGULATIONS

The 1974 act allowed both Houses of Congress to veto any regulation proposed by the Federal Election Commission. While the intent of this provision is to insure that the Commission follows the intent of Congress, it makes the Commission much less independent and allows incumbents to indirectly police their own elections. My bill repeals this provision. By the time any modification of campaign law can be passed, Congress will have enjoyed its veto for at least a year and can be presumed to have rendered valuable initial guidance to the Commission, and provided a good foundation for independent work by the Commission.

LOOPHOLES

The 1974 act made several exceptions to the definitions of contribution and expenditure, thus creating loopholes in the disclosure requirements and contribution and expenditure limitations. Most of these exceptions are unnecessary and are covered by the provisions which allow any person to make up to $1,000 in expenditures independently of a candidate. The legislation I am introducing today would eliminate these loopholes.

DISQUALIFICATION FOR FAILURE TO FILE

Under the 1974 law, candidates will be disqualified from running for Federal office in the next election for failing to file disclosure reports. This section is probably unconstitutional and is an unreasonable penalty that may be used arbitrarily. The bill I am introducing today would eliminate this section.

APPROVAL OF EXPENDITURES BY NATIONAL COMMITTEE

The 1974 Senate version of the bill adopted an amendment by former Senator Marlow Cook which would require the national committee of each political party to approve all expenditures made by its Presidential candidate in excess of $1,000. This requirement would give national parties effective control of groups such as CREEP. Unfortunately, it was dropped in conference. However, I have included it in my package of proposals.

DUTIES OF COMMISSION

The 1974 law eliminated certain duties of the supervisory officers, including those which allow them to publish an annual report and require them to encourage public dissemination of disclosure information. My bill will restore these duties and assign them to the Commission.

Mr. Speaker, despite our excellent bill of last year, total reform of our election campaign law is still an unfinished task. The proposals I have presented today will be another important step forward. They are not the only changes I shall propose. Additional improvements will be introduced later. I urge the Congress, particularly the House Administration Committee and Senate Rules Committee, to hold hearings on this bill. Adoption of these proposals will help to further cleanse our political process and prevent future Watergates.

Epilogue

From there I drove to the White House annex—the old Executive Office Building, in bygone years the War Department and later the Department of State.

Carrying three heavy attaché cases, I entered the Pennsylvania Avenue door, showed my blue-and-white White House pass to the uniformed guards and took the elevator to the third floor. I unlocked the door of 338 and went in. I opened my two-drawer safe, took out my operational handbook, found a telephone number and dialed it.

The time was 2:13 in the morning of June 17, 1972, and the five of my companions had been arrested and taken to the maximum-security block of the District of Columbia jail. I had recruited four of them and it was my responsibility to get them out. That was the sole focus of my thoughts as I began talking on the telephone.

But with those five arrests the Watergate Affair had begun. . . .

After several rings the call was answered and I heard the sleepy voice of Douglas Caddy. "Yes?"

"Doug? This is Howard. I hate to wake you up, but I've got a tough situation and I need to talk to you. Can I come over?"

"Sure. I'll tell the desk clerk you're expected."

"I'll be there in about twenty minutes," I told him and hung up.

From the safe I took a small money box and removed the $10,000 Liddy

had given me for emergency use. I put $1,500 in my wallet and the remain-
ing $8,500 in my coat pocket. The black attaché case containing McCord's
electronic equipment I placed in a safe drawer that held my operational
notebooks. Then I closed and locked the safe, turning the dial several
times. The other two cases I left beside the safe, turned out the light and
left my office, locking the door.

E. HOWARD HUNT
Undercover—Memoirs of an American Secret Agent (Berkley, 1974)

When my telephone rang on that fateful Saturday morning, little did I dream that the act of merely picking up the receiver and answering it was the beginning of a chain of events that would not only completely alter the course of my life, and many other lives, but would ultimately change the course of the history of the world.

A commonly heard phrase is that life turns on being in the right place at the right time. The possibility must also exist of being in the wrong place at the wrong time, or variations of that. In any event, my entrance into the drama of Watergate took place when I was awakened in bed from a sound sleep by my ringing telephone. A more inauspicious method of being thrust into such a dynamic affair can hardly be imagined. Whether my being in bed on that morning was being in the right place at the right time or the opposite, only those years that lie ahead of my present thirty-seven will reveal.

Howard Hunt was both a client whom I had advised on legal matters over the years and a person whom I counted among my close friends, as were his wife Dorothy and their four children. I had known Howard since just before his retirement from the CIA, and when later I entered private practice with a Washington law firm, Howard became one of my first clients.

About half an hour after he called on that June 17, Howard arrived at my apartment, which was located just five minutes from both the White House and Watergate. It took me only a short time to grasp the significance (and horror) of what he had to relate. Apparently, as subsequent events were to reveal, I was the first person after the arrests—next to the seven conspirators themselves—to learn what had really occurred at Watergate and to understand its terrible meaning.

A short time after he arrived, Howard placed a telephone call to G. Gordon Liddy, with whom I had become acquainted in my professional capacity on three or four previous occasions. Howard handed the

144

telephone to me and I too had a conversation with Gordon. Both Howard and Gordon retained me as their legal counsel on that Saturday morning. Later, at about 10:30 A.M. the same day, I—along with my co-counsel—visited the cellblock of the Second Police Precinct; after conversing with the five individuals incarcerated there, we were asked to represent them in the case. The five—James McCord, Bernard Barker, Eugenio Martinez, Frank Sturgis, and Virgilio Gonzales—had been arrested some eight hours earlier within the headquarters of the Democratic National Committee in Watergate.

I served as attorney for the Watergate Seven—the only attorney in the original case to represent all of the defendants—until permission was granted to me to withdraw as counsel in order to avoid a potential conflict of interest in my representing all seven. The issue arose after I had been subpoenaed to appear before the grand jury in an attempt by the prosecution, among other things, to link Hunt and Liddy (who had not yet been arrested or charged with a crime) to the arrested five individuals. This effort by the prosecutors took the form of attempting to extract from my lips as Hunt and Liddy's attorney incriminating information, which I maintained, and still do, is protected by the attorney-client privilege (which protects communications a client has with his attorney) and by the Sixth Amendment, the right to counsel. So strongly did I feel the prosecution was mistaken in this improper course of action that I adopted the legal strategy, after consultation with five senior members of the District of Columbia Bar, of being held in civil contempt by Judge John Sirica in order to obtain an immediate review of the issues by the U.S. Court of Appeals.*

At the first Watergate Seven Trial, in January 1973, I was called as a witness by both the prosecution and the defense. After the trial my name did not emerge again publicly until the Senate Watergate Committee held its televised hearings, which disclosed that I had been the first person approached soon after the break-in to transmit coverup money to the seven defendants. Herbert Kalmbach, President Nixon's personal attorney, who coordinated the approach, testified before the

*I lost on appeal, and on July 19, 1972, went before the grand jury and reluctantly answered questions put to me on matters I felt fell within the attorney-client privilege. The incredible pressures that were brought to bear on me by the prosecutors and by Judge Sirica to violate what I believed to be the sanctity of the attorney-client privilege involve a story about Watergate that has never been disclosed publicly.

Ervin Committee that "there were several telephone calls, but the final wrapup on it was that he [Caddy] refused to receive the funds."

Almost two years later, Kalmbach was again to testify about the circumstances of my being approached to transmit "hush" money. The testimony this time was at the Watergate "coverup" trial of Mitchell, Haldeman, Ehrlichman, Mardian, and Parkinson. As the *Washington Post* of November 13, 1974, reported:

> Judge Sirica waited until he had sent the jurors home for the day to voice his incredulity. Taking over the questioning after the lawyers for all sides were done, Sirica made it plain he could not accept Kalmbach's claims to a slow awakening. The Judge pointed out all of the trouble Kalmbach had with the first $25,000 payment, beginning with Caddy's refusal to take it.
>
> "Didn't that arouse your suspicions somewhat?" the Judge demanded. "Didn't it indicate to you that there must be something wrong?"
>
> "Well, your honor," Kalmbach replied, "I simply felt that there was a misunderstanding in some way."

I had no misunderstanding as to why I believed Kalmbach and his associates wanted me to transmit the coverup money to the defendants. That is precisely why a partner of my law firm was sitting in my office at the time the final telephone call came in, so that I would have a witness to my end of the conversation that I had turned down the solicitation to become part of the conspiracy. Still I found irony in the fact that the same Judge Sirica who held me in contempt of court two years earlier when I sought to protect the attorney-client privilege— and was ever so venal and vicious in disparaging my professional reputation to the packed courtroom—subsequently held up as a standard to Kalmbach my refusal to accept the "hush" money and become a part of the conspiracy. Legal scholars and history will ultimately judge Judge Sirica on whether he gave the original Watergate defendants a fair trial, and the verdict, unless I miss my guess, will be quite unfavorable to Maximum John.

One thing is certain: Watergate for me was a rude awakening to the corruption that permeates American politics today. Much of what the average citizen had long suspected was confirmed as the sordid details of Watergate unfolded. The letdown brought on by the scandal was all the more severe to those of us who had supported the Nixon administration in its early years because of our hopes that it would succeed in reversing the trend toward a regimented, collectivist society and begin the march back to individual liberty.

Shocking as Watergate was to me in revealing the corruptness of the Republican Party, even more shocking was the deceit of the liberal politicians and media barons who vigorously condemned the excesses of power as revealed by Watergate while wrapping themselves in innocence and virtue. It was this patent hypocrisy and deceit, especially by the pliant tools in Congress of the labor bosses, that prompted me to write *The Hundred Million Dollar Payoff*.

And that is why I have written this second exposé, again drawing upon documents and memoranda that are in the public record, to show how in the wake of Watergate radical politicians, acting in concert with vested interest groups, have foisted upon the American people campaign reform legislation that is actually a cunning scheme to rig our elections. *How They Rig Our Elections* is, in many ways, a story of corruption in American politics that in its dimensions makes even Watergate pale.

Appendix I

The Case Against Public
Financing of
Federal Elections

SENATOR ALLEN. Mr. President, many words were spoken, pro and con, about public financing of political campaigns during Senate debates in November and December, 1973, and in April of this year. While many points were made independently during these debates, no effort was made to present a compilation of the various arguments.

At my request, however, Mr. Frederick Pauls, analyst in American National General Research Division, Congressional Research Service, Library of Congress, has compiled arguments against the public financing of political campaigns, and in the process discusses 26 different points.

Mr. President, I believe that this document has great value in the continuing debates surrounding public financing of political campaigns and that it should be given the broadest possible coverage. I ask unanimous consent that this compilation be printed in the *Record.*

There being no objection, the material was ordered to be printed in the *Record,* as follows:

CASE AGAINST PUBLIC FINANCING OF FEDERAL ELECTIONS

Introduction

In the report are noted arguments against the public financing of political campaigns. The report does not attempt to examine each of the various bills which has been introduced in the 93rd Congress to provide public money in one way or another for campaigns. Proposals introduced range from total subsidy for general elections only to partial funding of primary elections as well. In addition, some bills propose government financing of selected campaign costs (e.g., mail, radio-TV). Some bills make public financing optional, some make it mandatory. Rather than examine each of the bills for faults, we have concentrated on arguments which can be made against the general concept of public financing of campaigns. We caution, therefore, that some of the criticisms raised may not apply to certain bills.

Our sources have included hearings held on the subject in 1973 by the Senate Subcommittee on Privileges and Elections, hearings in 1967 on campaign financing by the Senate Finance Committee, and excerpts from various articles, statements, and books. In addition to our discussion of each argument we have quoted for arguments from persons making the same general point. Each quotation is documented. These quotations often develop subsidiary points of an argument.

The report does not review arguments favoring public financing of Federal election campaigns although these have been made. This exclusion of favorable arguments does not represent a position of preference of the Service on the merits of the proposal.

1. *So Radical an Idea Should Be Subject to Careful Scrutiny Before Adoption.*

Twice the Congress has enacted Presidential Election Campaign Fund Acts as amendments to tax bills. A third attempt to attach public-financing-of-all-Federal-elections amendments to the second debt ceiling act of 1973 failed only after the House refused to accept it and several Senators engaged in lengthy debate which forced the provisions to be deleted from the bill. In a fourth attempt by supporters this

---

° *Congressional Record,* June 3, 1974.

year, the Senate passed public campaign financing provisions and the matter now lies in the House Administration Committee.

It can hardly be contended that the concept has been thoroughly aired before congressional committees. In 1966, when the first Presidential Election Campaign Act was passed, a mere two days of hearings in August were held on that idea and on bills to permit tax credits and tax deductions. Only ten persons testified before the Finance Committee when it held those hearings and not all of them spoke to the idea of Federal financing of presidential-election-campaign-fund amendment to the foreign Investors Tax Act. The House acquiesced and the first Presidential Election Campaign Fund Act was established only to be suspended in 1967 when the Senate on reflection found it wanting in many aspects.

Subsequently, in June, the Senate Finance Committee held six days of hearings on various campaign financing proposals, including public financing of presidential and senatorial elections. It reported a bill providing for such assistance on November 1, 1967, but no floor action was taken.

Thereafter, the notion lay dormant until resurrected by the Senate in November, 1971. The House acquiesced and the Presidential Election Campaign Fund Act became operative without adequate hearings having been held on the proposal.

By 1973 some Members of Congress were advocating that all Federal elections be financed in whole or in part from the Treasury. In late June an attempt to repeal the Presidential Election Campaign Fund Act of 1971 failed in the Senate by a vote of 30–62. In late July Senators Kennedy and Scott attempted to amend S. 372, the Federal Elections Campaign Act Amendments of 1973 (passed by the Senate July 30), to provide for public financing of congressional general elections. This effort failed when the amendment was tabled by a 53–40 vote. Senators argued, including some who supported the idea, that hearings should be held on such a radical proposal.

It was not until September of 1973 that four days of hearings by the Privileges and Elections Subcommittee were held on the specific idea of public financing of congressional campaigns. Pursuant to those hearings Senator Pell, the Subcommittee's chairman, introduced Federal Election Campaign Fund bill (S. 2718) on November 16, 1973.

However, proponents of public financing were not content to let the full committee work its will and report the Pell bill, or a clean bill, to the Senate for orderly debate. On November 15, just a day before Senator Pell introduced his bill, the Senate Finance Committee, in a hearing on the Public Debt Limit Act (H.R. 11104), considered an amendment to that bill to provide for full public financing of congressional general elections and partial public financing of presidential primary elections. In late November the Senate accepted the amendment. The House, however, balked and in the end the Senate deleted the offensive provisions from the bill.

In late February 1974 the Senate Rules and Administration Committee reported a public financing bill (S. 3044) to provide public money for presidential and congressional primary and general elections. The Federal Election Campaign Act Amendments of 1974 passed the Senate on April 11, 1974.

No proposal will more dramatically affect the conduct of elections in the United States than this one. Yet the history of congressional consideration of the idea is replete with haste. With the single exception of the 1973 hearings by the Senate Subcommittee on Privileges and Elections, the Senate has failed to hold comprehensive hearings on the subject. Time and again it has attempted, sometimes successfully, to legislate this matter on the floor. Such legislation is almost always ill conceived. In testimony before the Subcommittee, Robert G. Dixon, Jr., an Administration spokesman, urged that Congress await hearings and recommendations on this proposal by a Commission on Federal Election Reform, which President Nixon called for in 1973 and which the Senate voted in July (S.J. Res. 110).

It is unfortunate that the Presidential Election Campaign Fund was adopted through floor amendment. It would be equally unfortunate if congressional public financing became law in a rush for reform. It makes far better sense to establish the Election Reform Commission and let the idea be reflected upon before plunging onward.

Beyond that, the Senate owes the House the opportunity to hold hearings on the subject and to work its will upon a public financing bill in circumstances other than that of having a gun at its head—as was the situation with the public financing proposal attached to the Debt Ceiling Act in November 1973 and the two actions on the Presidential Election Campaign Fund Act.

Only if Congress moves in an orderly fashion can the public be assured that public financing is a sound idea and the evidence on that proposition is far from positive. This area of doubt reinforces the argument that such a proposal should be debated only after the fullest consideration of its wisdom and impact.

* * * * * *

Additional commentary

"The arguments in favor of public financing are not without merit. However, the idea has not received adequate study and the arguments in its favor are not as strong as is commonly thought. Certainly, a proposal that could entail such dramatic change in the political process might have many unforeseeable consequences, and has such powerful arguments both for and against should warrant a most careful examination and evaluation [sic]. Furthermore, proponents of public financing should not forget that the same goals can be achieved by writing responsible rules into a system of private financing. Intensive study of both public financing and alternative means of private financing is needed before we decide which means is best suitable for achieving the goal of open, honest and clear [sic] elections." —William Frenzel (R), Rep. from Minnesota, *Hearings* before Senate Subcommittee on Privileges and Elections, 93rd Cong., 1st Sess., 1973, p. 158.

2. *The Belief That Public Financing Will Purify the Electoral Process in a Way That No Other Reforms Will Is Naive and Untrue.*

Fervent proponents of public financing assume that it will cure all that ails our system of political campaigning. The axiom is that money was the root of all Watergate evils. Take away all that privately given and garnered money, according to this theory, and all those obnoxious, unethical, and illegal political activities engaged in during the 1972 election will disappear.

Certainly we are sophisticated enough not to believe that there is any simple solution to such problems. There is no legislative solution to ill will; no means of curbing those intent upon questionable campaign practices. Those breaking the rules in 1972 knew what the rules were and that they were breaking them, no matter what sophistry they may later have contrived to justify their behavior. Would public financing of campaigns have precluded such activity as occurred in 1972? The honest man must admit that it is uncertain that this would have been the case.

Before adopting public financing of campaigns, it would be better to gauge the effects of the full-disclosure law enacted in 1971 (the Federal Elections Campaign Act); to measure the effectiveness of that Act over a span of elections; and to make such changes in that law as are necessary to regulate properly, fairly, and effectively political campaigns and election finance. In 1973 the Senate passed numerous amendments to the 1972 campaign finance law some of which attempt to make it more difficult for Watergate-type excesses to take place. One such amendment would limit the amount of money which can be contributed in cash. Another would limit the total amount any one individual can annually contribute both to a candidate and to all candidates (see under argument about the constitutionality of limiting campaign contributions). This may be a more sensible route to controlling campaign spending and election practices than public financing and it deserves a fair trial before the private financing system is disposed of.

❧   ❧   ❧   ❧   ❧   ❧

Additional commentary

"It is simplistic to expect that public financing is a panacea for the electoral system, or to believe that fundamental changes in the political structure of electoral processes will not result. Change is desirable, perhaps, urgent, but further thought and dialogue are necessary to a better understanding of what impending changes mean."—Herbert Alexander, Director, Citizens' Research Foundation, in "Watergate and the Electoral Process," a paper delivered at the Center for the Study of Democratic Institutions, Santa Barbara, Calif., Dec. 1973.

❧   ❧   ❧   ❧   ❧   ❧

"There is no magic in public financing. It is not going to do anything mysterious to purify a system that good rules in a private financing system cannot do.

"To state it another way, a lawbreaker will be a lawbreaker, under any system. It is far more important to pass the kind of bill that you passed in July (S. 372, Federal Elections Campaign Act Amendments of 1973) if we are going to assert any law and order in our election system.

"Every evil that is detailed in the testimony of the previous witnesses can be curbed by bills such as you already passed."—William Frenzel (R), Rep. from Minnesota, *Hearings* before the Senate Subcommittee on Privileges and Elections, 93rd Cong., 1st Sess., 1973, p. 142.

      ◇   ◇   ◇   ◇   ◇   ◇

"The abandonment of private financing will not necessarily end campaign abuses. Under public financing, those who are dishonest might still find means of circumventing the law. Events such as Watergate might still occur, because they may be not just a reflection of the way in which we finance our campaigns, but of a mentality and set of attitudes that will persist even with the advent of public financing."— William Frenzel, Rep. from Minn., *Hearings* before Senate Subcommittee on Privileges and Elections, 93rd Cong., 1st Sess., 1973, p. 151.

      ◇   ◇   ◇   ◇   ◇   ◇

"One allegation about providing financial subsidies to political candidates is that the temptation to engage in illegal activities would diminish. Both experience and logic suggest this would not be the case. Experience with subsidies in Puerto Rico demonstrates that the subsidies are used up before the election and that the illegal solicitation of funds, for example, from government employees, ensues. Such a result seems logical, for there is no fixed amount needed for a truly contested campaign. It is a myth to think that the provision of subsidies would change this. In fact, activities such as the Watergate break-in are more likely to occur in campaigns where the level of normal propaganda is lower than in campaigns where extensive activities of the ordinary kind take place. The argument that we can reduce the number of break-ins by limiting the amount of advertising on television and by financing campaigns with public money seems a dramatic non sequitur." —Ralph K. Winter, Jr., "Campaign Financing and Political Freedom" (American Enterprise Institute for Public Policy Research), 1973, pp. 21–22.

3. *Public Financing Is Contrary to Our Tradition of Private Financing, a Tradition Which Both Weeds Out Unviable Candidates and Underpins the Voluntaristic Nature of Our Political System.*

One measure of a candidate's viability is his ability to generate contributions on his behalf for public office. Proponents of public finance portray this process as seedy and sinister at worst, demeaning at best.

155

Some of this reaction may flow from the regrettable excesses of the 1972 elections. It is a fact, however, that private financing has served the Republic well from its beginning. The solicitation of political contributions is a learning process for the office seeker and communications channel for the contributor. It is a means of "putting your money where your mouth is."

Moving to a system of public finance may well encourage those to seek office who would not stand a chance of surviving the "fires" of seeking financial support for their campaigns.

It is questionable whether private financing precludes any viable candidacy from surviving. Senator McGovern's success in 1972 indicates that those with limited initial appeal in opinion poll soundings on potential presidential nominees are not automatically closed off from the money necessary to conduct a campaign, while front runners may fall by the wayside and see their sources of funds dry up. This selecting out process is an essential part of our electoral system. Public financing could alter this process by allowing all to remain in to the very end and, in the case of presidential nominations, might create a situation in which the power brokers at a convention would make the final determination.

Moreover, our party system has always been one which relied on voluntarism, an important ingredient of which has been the solicitation of money to finance the party and its candidates. Adoption of public financing is bound to alter this state of affairs, largely removing this input from the people, thus making politics an affair of the state, possibly more remote from the people than is presently true.

❊ ❊ ❊ ❊ ❊ ❊

Additional commentary

"Private financing is a traditional and useful way to determine candidate attractiveness. It is the old market test, not always effective or fair, but it is not a bad one."

"The enthusiasm of contributors enlivens campaigns and increases voter participation. Also, private financing functions in a manner similar to the free market. It has been one of the traditional ways of determining the popularity and attractiveness of a candidate. Popular candidates rarely have a shortage of funds, while unpopular candidates are usually unable to raise large amounts of funds. Many public financing proposals would give equal amounts of funds to both types of candidates, thereby discriminating against those who are more popular."—William Frenzel (R), Rep. from Minnesota, *Hearings* before the Senate Subcommittee on Privileges and Elections, 93rd Cong., 1st Sess., 1973, pp. 143, 151.

* * * * * *

"Is the use of tax revenues for financing of campaign expenses of political parties and candidates the answer? We think not.

"Indeed, we believe this approach to the problem would be wrong, unfair, and dangerous. Wrong—because it is not compatible with our democratic system which is based on voluntarism. Unfair—because incumbents would have the advantage of public financing of their campaigns on top of free mailing privileges, offices, staffs, phone and travel allowances, to the detriment of challengers. Dangerous—because it may pave the way to profound and unwelcome changes in our democratic system and an undue influence of government in our political process.

"Federal funds applied to Presidential and congressional campaigns, and perhaps later to State and local campaigns, would substantively change the extent of personal participation in politics and significantly alter our political system which has operated with reasonable success for 200 years. It stands to reason that once the campaign finance door is opened to public funding, no matter how slight the crack, ways will be found within the Congress to open it ever wider.

"This Nation's political system is predicated on the proposition that our people are free to group together to pursue legitimate political objectives through a voluntary contribution of time, effort, and money. To sharply diminish that proposition would imply that Congress has lost faith in the American way. Furthermore, now to offer Federal subsidies as the cure-all for our political illnesses might well be compared to the hastily conceived remedy, combined with an improper diagnosis, that killed the patient it was intended to help."—Charles F. Hood, representing the Chamber of Commerce of the U.S., *Hearings* before the Senate Subcommittee on Privileges and Elections, 93rd Cong., 1st Sess., 1973, p. 363.

* * * * * *

"The existence of subsidies might well decrease citizen participation

157

and the morale of those active in politics. Such was the result in Puerto Rico where, over time, party morale declined and voter interest in party activities was correspondingly reduced. The existence of subsidies, in short, might increase the distance between voters and candidates."— Ralph K. Winter, Jr., "Campaign Financing and Political Freedom" (AEI), 1973, p. 24.

4. *Public Financing Will Repose Power over Campaigns in the Bureaucrats Not the People.*

At present financing political elections lies ultimately with the people. They are the source of money and they help to determine who shall run for office and who shall not. Public financing will remove this power from them. It will place that power in the hands of government bureaucrats which, though not an evil *per se,* is less desirable than leaving the matter in the hands of the people.

Voter interest is poor enough (only 55 percent of eligible voters in the last presidential election chose to exercise their voting privilege) without doing more to discourage involvement, which is likely to be a consequence of public financing of campaigns. We should be finding ways to involve the people, not ways to further remove them from the electoral process.

✿　✿　✿　✿　✿　✿

Additional commentary

"The enthusiasm of contributors enlivens campaigns and increases voter participation."

"Depending on the type of public financing, I believe elections would be drab. . . . In my judgment, enthusiasm would decline."

"Bureaucrats would write the rules, control the money, and supervise the law. Our Government would then be leaving the people almost nothing. If we take the elections from the people, we have stolen their heritage.

"That is an overdramatization of the problem, but somebody is going to decide when a fellow made a right report. If he did not, he is not going to get his Federal money."—William Frenzel (R), Rep. from Minnesota, *Hearings* before the Senate Subcommittee on Privileges and Elections, 93rd Cong., 1st Sess., 1973, p. 143.

✿　✿　✿　✿　✿　✿

158

"In our fervor for cleaning up the dirtier aspects of political campaigning, we mustn't make it a sterile operation—too pure and fragile to be touched by the hands of the people. We think that 100 percent public financing would remove an important element of citizen involvement."—Lucy W. Benson, President of the League of Women Voters, as quoted in a *Washington Star-News* article, January 16, 1974 (p. A 15).

✿   ✿   ✿   ✿   ✿   ✿

"And there is one other aspect to the personal involvement and participation in campaigns in America, and that is this: As men who have been elected to public office statewide, each of you is aware of the increasing professionalism in campaigns. Professional managers, consultants and specialists in media, advertising, demographics, research, computers and scheduling are part of nearly every major campaign in this country. Regrettably, however, I fear that much of the citizen involvement and therefore influence is being eroded.

"The use of volunteers is on the decline, which is very sad, but one of the few growing areas of political participation is in the contributing arena. More and more people are participating in campaigns by giving in relatively small amounts of their financial resources, and I do not believe we should in any way discourage this growing trend. Rather, we should congratulate those who have made viable the solicitation of financial support from the many instead of the few, and we should encourage this growth instead of discouraging it.

"As long as campaign financing is on a voluntary basis, the public can exercise some control over the choice of candidates and politics. If politicians do not have to rely on private donations, public influence is weakened over the process of government."—Bernard M. Shanley, Vice Chairman, Republican National Committee, *Hearings* before the Senate Subcommittee on Privileges and Elections, 93rd Cong., 1st Sess., 1973, p. 318.

✿   ✿   ✿   ✿   ✿   ✿

"Here are some of the ways public financing might open the electoral process to manipulation by the federal government: 1) The federal government could set conditions on the candidate's qualifications over and above those already in existence. For various reasons, it could refuse to give federal funds to candidates who were allegedly in 'violation' of the law, classified as 'subversive,' or who were actively opposed to the major parties or the party in power. 2) The federal government could force parties to conform to federal rules and regulations and might eventually gain control of them. 3) Incumbents could purposefully appropriate small amounts of money for political campaigns, thereby making it impossible for the challenger to wage an effective campaign and assuring themselves of victory. 4) Congress and the President might be unable to agree upon how much money to appropriate, in which case there might be little or no funds for political campaign. 5) The federal agency in charge of administering public financing might manipulate the electoral process. It could amend the law by rule without Congress knowing exactly what changes were being made."—William Frenzel, Rep. from Minnesota, *Hearings* before Senate Subcommittee on Privileges and Elections, 93rd Cong., 1st Sess., 1973, p. 150.

✿   ✿   ✿   ✿   ✿   ✿

"Relationships between political parties and voters may be weakened, and citizen interest in working actively in a campaign lost."—Robert G. Dixon, Jr., Asst. Atty. Gen., Dept. of Justice, *Hearings* before Senate Subcommittee on Privileges and Elections, 93rd Cong., 1st Sess., 1973, p. 306.

✿   ✿   ✿   ✿   ✿   ✿

"While the actual cost of administering a program of Federal financing of elections is still unknown, a massive bureaucratic organization would have to be established to supervise the program. Its cost eventually would become exorbitant, and I question seriously that such a program could be realistically and fairly administered. We are all too well aware of the history of bureaucratic involvement in something as open as the political process."—Bernard M. Shanley, Vice Chairman, Repub. National Comm., *Hearings* before Senate Subcomm. on Privileges and Elections, 93rd Cong., 1st Sess., 1973, p. 317.

✿   ✿   ✿   ✿   ✿   ✿

"It is unfortunate that progressive and successful steps to broaden and expand the base of financial support in the campaign last year have been clouded by attention to big money, 'fat cats,' and illegal contributions. The good that took place in 1972 should be a part of our thinking on Federal financing of campaigns. For example, approximately 1 million contributions were received in behalf of President Nixon's reelection. The majority of the contributions were in amounts of $100 or less, with the average of these contributions less than $25. The contributions received in these small amounts totaled more than $15 million.

"Senator McGovern, likewise, raised a similar amount through the financial support of tens of thousands of individuals who contributed in relatively small amounts.

"In contrast, it has been estimated that only 30,000 American citizens contributed to the 1960 campaign of both Presidential candidates. Thus, in only 12 years there has been a sixfold increase in the number of small donors who voluntarily participated in the all-important elective process.

"Campaign reform is necessary. Considering the legislation required for this reform, I urge that you amplify the good while cutting away the bad. Legislation that would force out the small contributor would do irreparable damage to our elective process."—Bernard M. Shanley, Vice Chairman, Republican Nat'l Comm., *Hearings* before Senate Subcom. on Privileges and Elections, 93rd Cong., 1st Sess., 1973, pp. 315–316.

✻ ✻ ✻ ✻ ✻ ✻

"In 1973, almost 85 percent of our total contributions came from the small giver. I think you know, Mr. Chairman, as well as I do, and a lot better, perhaps, that where an individual gives a small amount—I do not care whether it is $1 or $5—to a candidate, he then becomes an advocate, he becomes interested. And this is good, it seems to me, for the electoral process. This is what we want; we do not want to lose them.

"And with the present erosion of both parties—both the Democrat and the Republican Party—we are losing people every day, as opposed to the independents. And we cannot afford it. And the tragedy in this country will be when we lose the two-party system. As you know better than I do, it will be a disaster for this country; it is the basis of our whole system."—Bernard M. Shanley, Vice Chairman, Repub. Nat'l

Comm., *Hearings* before Senate Subcom. on Priv. and Elections, 93rd Cong., 1st Sess., 1973, p. 321.

✻   ✻   ✻   ✻   ✻   ✻

"The current fault of our political system is the shortage of 'people participation.' Too few of our eligible citizens vote. In 1972, 48 million potential voters stayed away from the polls. This number exceeded the votes cast for any candidate.

"Too few work in political campaigns, and too few support financially the party or candidate of their choice. It is estimated that 90 percent of all political contributions come from 1 percent of the population. Here in the world's greatest democracy, such lack of political involvement is deplorable. Public financing would only widen the gap between the electorate and the political process.

"Our greatest need is to develop a sense of obligation and responsibility on the part of more Americans to participate fully in the electoral process—in short, to broaden the popular base of political activity and political giving."—Charles F. Hood, representing the Chamber of Commerce of the U.S., *Hearings* before Sen. Subcom. on Priv. and Elec., 93rd Cong., 1st Sess., 1973, p. 364.

5. *Public Financing Is Yet Another Example of the Subsidy Philosophy.*

Public financing is yet another example of the propensity to attempt solution of national problems with Federal handouts. Subsidization should be employed only if absolutely necessary and that hardly appears to be the case in campaign financing. Other approaches may prove more helpful in controlling campaign costs, e.g., contribution and expenditure limitations, increased or better advertised tax credits and tax deductions, or limited government assistance which treats all candidates in an equal way (say in mail privileges).

✻   ✻   ✻   ✻   ✻   ✻

Additional commentary

Government subsidies for campaigns "would create intractable problems principally because there is no sound underlying theory to justify the subsidy."—Ralph K. Winter, Jr., "Campaign Finances" (AEI Special Analysis, 1971).

162

6. *Public Financing Proposals Prohibiting or Unreasonably Limiting Private Contributions May Violate First Amendment Guarantees of Free Speech.*

Some constitutional scholars and others contend that to prohibit or unreasonably limit contributions by individuals is to violate First Amendment guarantees of free speech. In the contributing context, the giving of money constitutes a "free-speech" act. This argument was perhaps partially responsible for the elimination of limitations on the size of contributions done in the Federal Election Campaign Act of 1971. Public financing proposals which would preclude any private financing seem on their face to violate this constitutional guarantee. Any unreasonable limitation would also seem to violate that guarantee. Such proposals, accordingly, are constitutionally dubious.

S. 372, the Federal Election Campaign Act Amendments of 1973, passed by the Senate July 30, 1973, contain limitations on contributions ($25,000 maximum by an individual to all Federal candidates in any election and $3,000 maximum by an individual to each Federal candidate in any election). How constitutionally valid these limitations are is a question yet to be settled by the courts. Limitations are predicated on Congress' right to regulate Federal elections and to "purify" the electoral process. In any court test the principles of regulations and electoral purity will undoubtedly be weighed against the guarantee of free speech in order to reach a conclusion. This same weighing process would probably occur if a public financing system were brought to court by an individual who felt his First Amendment guarantees were being violated because he was denied, or unreasonably constrained, in his right to contribute to a political campaign.

☼　☼　☼　☼　☼　☼

Additional commentary

"Prohibition, or unreasonable limitation of private contributions is an unconstitutional denial of a long-enjoyed right. It is an obvious discrimination that I do not have to point out to you if we allow one person to volunteer services, and deny another person his right to contribute money. If an accountant, executive or lawyer can contribute $5,000 to my campaign in volunteer services, which they regularly do, how can we tell a person in a wheelchair who wants to give me $5,000

163

that he cannot."—William Frenzel (R), Rep. from Minnesota, *Hearings* before the Senate Subcommittee on Privileges and Elections, 93rd Cong., 1st Sess., 1973, p. 142.

✿ ✿ ✿ ✿ ✿ ✿

"Under some bills, candidates who do not elect to receive a subsidy must nevertheless abide by limitations on contributions and spending. Such limitations may conflict with the First Amendment policy of encouraging as much communication in the political realm as possible."—Robert G. Dixon, Jr., Asst. Atty. Gen., *Hearings* before Senate Subcommittee on Privileges and Elections, 93rd Cong., 1st Sess., pp. 306–307.

✿ ✿ ✿ ✿ ✿ ✿

"Direct subsidies would also raise serious problems of freedom of expression. They would be a form of compulsory political activity which limited the freedom of those who would refrain as well as of those who chose to participate. When an individual in forced, in effect, to make a contribution to a political movement to which he is indifferent or which he finds distasteful, it may fairly be said that a basic freedom is being infringed. When this forced payment is combined with limits on contributions to favored candidates, political freedom is drastically limited. Many who today propose subsidies to political parties or candidates condemn subsidies where religious organizations are concerned. The precise constitutional issues differ but they are sufficiently analogous that one may well question whether the underlying principle is not the same. Indeed, what if a religious party were formed?"

"Public financing of campaigns might run afoul of the Constitution in other ways. Whatever the size of the subsidy, and particularly when combined with a limit on expenditures, the precise amount would be subject to constitutional challenge on the grounds that it discriminated in one fashion or another. The charge would not be less forceful for the fact that it would be entirely up to those in power to say how large the subsidy would be."

"Any formula for determining who gets what subsidy is open to constitutional challenge, for subsidies are inherently inconsistent with a 'free trade in ideas.' One commentator has stated it thus:

The traditional meaning of this concept is that government must not interfere on behalf of either a majority or a minority; if the majority's superior resources give it greater power to express its views through the mass media, this is a natural and proper result of the superior appeal the majority's 'product' has to the public. Government intervention on behalf of minorities would deny First and Fourteenth Amendment rights to members of the majority group by undermining the preponderance which the free market has given them. Likewise, state action calculated to reduce the relative power of minorities to express their views would infringe their constitutional rights. A plan allocating funds to all parties equally would give minorities publicity out of proportion to the size of their following thus discriminating against the majority, and a plan apportioning funds according to party size would give the majority more funds with which to influence uncommitted voters, tending to increase the majority's preponderance.

"This dilemma seems inescapable unless we abandon the tradition that government neither help nor hinder the propagation of the views of a political movement."—Ralph K. Winter, Jr., "Campaign Financing and Political Freedom" (AEI), 1973, pp. 25–26.

7. *Whether or Not Americans Support Public Financing Is Open to Question.*

While a Gallup poll released September 30, 1973, found 65 percent of its respondents thought it a "good idea" that "the federal government provide a fixed amount of money for the election campaigns for the presidency and for Congress and that all private contributions from other sources should be prohibited," a Harris poll released September 24, 1973, found that 73 percent opposed "ending all private contributions to political campaigns, and [having] the federal government finance campaigns out of tax money." Such diametrically opposed findings leave in doubt what actual support there is for the concept among the American people. Moreover, most Americans are so uninformed as to the purposes of and means for public financing of campaigns, not to mention its consequences, that they are in no position to formulate an intelligent opinion. Certainly they are owed an opportunity to be educated in this matter and to register their opinions with the Congress prior to the Government instituting wholesale public financing of national level political campaigns.

Moreover, first year experience with the tax checkoff to finance the Presidential Election Campaign Fund, established by the Revenue Act

165

of 1971, indicates little interest and enthusiasm among the people. Only 3.1 percent of taxpayers submitting returns for 1972 chose to direct that $1 (or $2 on a joint return) of their taxes owed be designated for the Fund. The total amount designated in 1972 was $3.9 million.

Over a four-year period this trend, if it holds, would provide no more than $16 million to be divided among the major and minor party candidates who could qualify for and did choose public financing of their campaigns in 1976. In 1972 George McGovern spent about $28 million in a losing and President Nixon about $55 million in a winning effort. Obviously, if the taxpayer continues to demonstrate apathy for the checkoff there will be hardly enough money available for one decent campaign, let alone more than one. (Note: Early tax returns for 1973 indicate a higher level of participation—14.5 percent. If this high participation rate continues, the Fund would have sufficient amounts by 1976 to finance the general election campaigns of presidential candidates. However, this high rate of checkoff may be a temporary taxpayer reaction to Watergate and enthusiasm could wane in future years.)

At all levels in 1972 it has been estimated that $400 million was expended in political campaigns. All of this money was privately raised, which suggests that private financing is a viable system. It remains to be proven that public financing via the checkoff can do as well.

✿　✿　✿　✿　✿　✿

Additional commentary

"The American public largely ignored the tax checkoff last year, and indications are they will do so again, even though the checkoff form is moved on the form 1040 page of the income tax return. Citizens want to identify directly with the candidate or party of their choice, not through the Treasury Department. Through Federal financing, personal involvement and real participation are lost."—Bernard M. Shanley, Vice Chairman, Repub. Nat'l. Comm., *Hearings* before Senate Subcommittee on Priv. and Elec., 93rd Cong., 1st Sess., 1973, p. 318.

✿　✿　✿　✿　✿　✿

"In a recent poll of our members, we found that: 93 percent favor overall election reform; 94 percent support public disclosure of contributions to, and expenditures by, all candidates for Federal office; 74

percent believe the election campaign law should be administered and enforced by an independent agency; 88 percent favor shorter campaigns; 92 percent would require each candidate to have one central committee for reporting and recordkeeping purposes; 83 percent oppose the granting of free or reduced postal rates to any Federal candidate; 83 percent oppose the present practice of permitting labor and business-related political action groups to contribute unlimited amounts to candidates or parties; and *76 percent favor the continued voluntary funding of political campaigns"* [emphasis supplied].— Charles F. Hood, representing the Chamber of Commerce of the U.S., *Hearings* before the Senate Subcom. on Priv. and Elections, 93rd Cong., 1st Sess., 1973, pp. 365–366.

8. *Public Financing Will Unfairly Work to the Advantage of Incumbents.*

Incumbents enter a campaign with advantages over their opponents. Because of their free mailing privilege they can make known their names in their districts or State through letters, newsletters, and questionnaires. Accordingly, voters are more familiar with them than they are with those who run against them.

A Twentieth Century Fund study, *Electing Congress,* shows that between 1954 and 1968, 92 percent of all House incumbents who sought re-election (3,220 races) were successful, while 85 percent of Senate incumbents won re-election (224 races) during that same period of time. Proponents of public financing claim that it will even the odds between incumbent and opponent. There is a real question as to the validity of that claim. Opponents normally must spend more than incumbents if they are to be successful. Public financing will preclude that possibility and thus benefit the incumbent who already has the advantage. This occurrence is as likely, if not more likely, than that of evening the odds between incumbent and challenger. This is especially true in House races where the challenger must outspend the incumbent if he is to have any chance.

       ✿   ✿   ✿   ✿   ✿   ✿

Additional commentary

"Challengers are at the mercy of incumbents. . . . In the Senate it is said that your challengers can win with less dollars. I will stipulate that. However, in the House it is different. You fellows in the Senate are important big shots. When you fellows run, you dominate the media. When you run every person in the media is hanging on your every word.

"Over in the House we have to fight for a little visibility. Now, in the House an incumbent has access to the media, but the challenger is just another guy. Tables out of a study . . . indicate that a challenger has to spend 10 times as much money as an incumbent to prevail in a House election. I am not sure that I agree with that factor, but I must conclude that in the House it is an unequal struggle with the incumbent heavily favored, and that the House and Senate are two completely different kinds of races."—William Frenzel (R.), Rep. from Minnesota, *Hearings* before the Senate Subcommittee on Privileges and Elections, 93rd Cong., 1st Sess., 1973, p. 142.

✼ ✼ ✼ ✼ ✼ ✼

"A $150,000 limitation for a Congressional campaign may sound huge to reformers or to incumbents whose re-election does not require spending of amounts anywhere near this figure. However, for the challenger, lower limitations impose nearly impossible problems. With today's costs there is no way a challenger can make himself known over a well-identified incumbent when there are stringent expenditure limitations.

"An interesting study by W. F. Lott and P. D. Warner III of the Economics Department of the University of Connecticut written in 1971 is reproduced in the *Congressional Record* of September 23, 1971, on pages 33137 to 33140. Lott and Warner say bluntly that the impact of spending restrictions is 'to insulate the incumbent and for all practical purposes insure his election.'

"Warner-Lott's research 'indicates, for example, that an officeholder who has 40 percent of the total eligible votes in his district registered in his party, can, if he and his opponent are limited to $50,000, expect to receive 60 percent of the total votes cast.'

"Table 4 . . . shows that with a 50 percent party registration, the challenger must spend over $54,000 and the incumbent only $5,000 to have an equal chance of election."

168

Table 4—Maximum Likelihood Point Estimate of Campaign Expenditure Necessary to Give Candidate an Equal a Priori Chance of Election

Voter registration in the party of the candidate, as a percentage of total registration	Expenditures	
	Incumbent	Challenger
30	$31,335.59	$343,960.69
40	11,091.46	121,747.36
50	4,955.96	54,399.96
60	2,566.08	28,167.05
70	1,470.89	16,145.54

"One way to balance the scales under a system of public financing does exist. A candidate would require more money if he was a challenger than he would if he were an incumbent. In order for this alternative to be effective, a measure of the value of incumbency would have to be calculated and the difference paid to the challenger. This system, however, stands little or no chance of passage because Congressmen would not want to see their challengers in a position of beating them at election time."—William Frenzel (R), Rep. from Minnesota, statement submitted to Senate Subcommittee on Privileges and Elections, 93rd Cong., 1st Sess., 1973, p. 157.

❄   ❄   ❄   ❄   ❄   ❄

"I don't go in very strong for public financing. On the face of it, it would give the party in power [or incumbent] what would seem to be an advantage."—Sen. George Aiken, in "Political Report/Public Financing Sought, House Committee Battle Likely over Senate Plan," by Jonathan Cottin, *National Journal Reports,* Nov. 10, 1973, p. 1683.

❄   ❄   ❄   ❄   ❄   ❄

"What would prevent an incumbent President from vetoing or an incumbent Congress from refusing to appropriate money for political campaigns, thereby insuring their own re-election?"—William Fren-

169

zel, Rep. from Minn., *Hearings* before Senate Subcom. on Privileges and Elections, 93rd Cong., 1st Sess., 1973, p. 151.

❖   ❖   ❖   ❖   ❖   ❖

"Federal financing would be of tremendous aid to incumbents and a major disadvantage to challengers, which I think Senator Johnson just indicated, although he did not say it. It would be virtually impossible for an unknown challenger in a large State, such as Texas or California, to unseat an incumbent Senator if he could only spend $175,000, the limit proposed in one bill under consideration. It would take more than that to even get his name known to a majority of the State's voters."—Bernard M. Shanley, Vice Chairman, Repub. Nat'l. Comm., *Hearings* before the Sen. Subcom. on Priv. and Elec., 93rd Cong., 1st Sess., 1973, pp. 317–318.

9. *The Problem of Frivolous Candidacies.*

One of the great problems with all public financing proposals is that they may spawn frivolous candidacies because of the lure of public funds. Three ways have been proposed to discourage the emergence of such candidacies: 1) qualifying petitions, 2) bonds, and 3) matching grants. None of them, however, is without problems.

Petitions present the problem of conflicting laws in the several States and raise questions about what is a valid signature, how to deal with challenges, and who may sign a petition (and how many he may sign). Verification and processing may take so long as to hamper, if not prevent, the granting of money to candidates. Also, the petition method favors those with money and party-backed candidates because these candidates can field the manpower necessary to obtain the needed signatures.

Posting bonds would discriminate against candidates in poor areas because they would find it difficult to obtain the bond. It might also discourage independent candidates who would fear going into deep debt if their bids proved unsuccessful. Finally, it could lead to endless recounts in election after election demanded by candidates who fail to receive enough votes to secure their bond and their subsidy.

Matching grants, while the least objectionable, could lead to washing of funds (e.g., a contributor of $1,000 could increase his contribution 100 percent by having it given under 20 different names at $50 per name, thus qualifying it for matching grants) to help candidates quali-

170

fy for public funds. This method also might fail to produce adequate funds for some races, particularly if combined with stringent contribution limitations. Also, high threshold figures to qualify for matching funds could deter economic and social minority candidacies.

Among general problems inherent in all these approaches are: 1) discouragement of candidacies by those who want to educate the public, 2) discouragement of those who do not want to go through the bureaucratic hassles involved in applying for funds, and 3) discrimination against frivolous candidates by denying them access to the political process.

❄ ❄ ❄ ❄ ❄ ❄

Additional commentary

"When the public financers go further and apply their concept to primary or pre-nomination electioneering, the problems multiply. How do you separate serious from frivolous candidates for a House or Senate seat, particularly when the prospect of public money guarantees candidates an opportunity for exposure at a minimum of cost. Do you require signatures on a petition before a candidate is qualified to get federal funds? A firm can be hired to get them—at $50 per 100 in California. Do you require a prospective candidate to raise some amount in small contributions? How much? Since interest groups already are organized and making just such small contributions upon direction, they could have more clout from their traditional donations, while letting the U.S. Treasury pay part of the costs."—Walter Pincus, "Campaign Financing," *New Republic,* October 27, 1973, p. 18.

❄ ❄ ❄ ❄ ❄ ❄

"A second allegation made on behalf of subsidies is that they would increase 'the opportunities for meaningful participation in . . . electoral contests without regard to the financial resources available to individual candidates. . . .' But how many would become candidates if we subsidized campaigns? Unrestricted access to such subsidies would be an incentive to everyone with a yen for publicity to become a candidate; elections would thus become an anarchic jungle with policy issues wholly obscured. For that reason, many subsidy proposals suggest limitations on eligibility. One formula might call for a subsidy adjusted to performance on previous elections, but that seems unfair to newcomers and overly generous to the "old guard." Another route would be to adjust the subsidy according to performance in the election itself. For example, the Hart bill (which applies only to Senate and House races but could easily be extended to presidential campaigns) would require a security deposit equal to one-fifth of the anticipated subsidy. If the candidate got less than 10 percent of the total vote, the deposit would be forfeited. If he got less than 5 percent, he would have to repay whatever subsidy he had received.

"Such a provision, however, is hardly consistent with the bill's ostensible purpose. A candidate such as Fred Harris, for example, might well have no chance under such a law. If he refused the subsidy, it would be a signal that he did not take his chances seriously. He would then be quite unlikely to raise substantial funds, unless he had a rich patron, an alternative closed off by limits on individual contributions. If he took the subsidy, he would risk bankruptcy. The Hart formula could thus be a Trojan horse to the average candidate.

"What the formula would create, however, would be a temptation for those who anticipated financial gain from running for office. Under the Hart plan, the author/candidate might be encouraged to enter the race to gather material for a book. A publisher's advance could cover the cost of posting the security bond or returning the subsidy. Similarly, many young lawyers would be likely to find it profitable to enter congressional races and take their chances on the subsidy in order to get publicity beneficial to their practices. Even if they might have to forfeit their bond to return the subsidy, it might seem a good risk when the amount was capitalized over the period of time that the anticipated income would accrue. The Hart formula might thus increase the number of non-serious candidates while discouraging those the bill is designed to aid."—Ralph K. Winter, Jr., "Campaign Financing and Political Freedom" (AEI), 1973, pp. 22–23.

10. *There Are Ways for the Government to Assist Candidates Other Than by Total Subsidy.*

If it is felt that the Government ought to provide assistance to candidates for public office, there are more equitable and less complicated ways of doing it than through direct financial assistance. For example, the Government could subsidize part of the mailing costs of candidates; or repeal Section 315 of the Federal Communications Act to permit commercial broadcast of political programs without having to

172

give equal time to all candidates; or meet expenses which are equally shared by candidates. This kind of approach avoids the sticky problems of formulas, enforcement, and inequitableness which attend public financing of campaigns.

* * * * * *

Additional commentary

"All necessary election and primary costs that do not benefit one candidate or party or position on election issues against any other are properly a public responsibility and should be conducted at governmental expense."—Committee for Economic Development, "Restoring Confidence in the Political Process," January 21, 1973, p. 10.

* * * * * *

"A public subsidy for all Federal elections could not be enforced effectively; if granted, it should be confined to specific areas readily monitored.

"Pending bills to determine, among other matters, eligibility of candidates for funds, review of cases where funds are denied, policing records and making investigations involve complicated, protracted and costly administrative and judicial procedures; and enforcement would be difficult."—Robert G. Dixon, Jr., Asst. Atty. Gen., Dept. of Justice, *Hearings* before the Senate Subcommittee on Privileges and Elections, 93rd Cong., 1st Sess., 1973, p. 306.

11. *Tax Credits and Deductions Can Be Increased or Those Existing Better Advertised in Preference to Public Financing.*

The Revenue Act of 1971 allows the taxpayer to claim annually either a tax credit of $12.50 ($25.00 on joint returns) or a tax deduction of $50.00 ($100.00) for political contributions. The purpose of this credit or deduction is to encourage small contributions; as an alternative to public financing efforts should be made (1) to increase the credit and deduction if the present ones are considered insufficient to stimulate giving, and (2) to inform voters of the existence of the credit and deduction in order to encourage contributions in small amounts. If large amounts can be raised in small sums, then the pressure for solicitation of large contributions will be eased and the fear of improper influence because of large contributions abated. The private financing system

173

can continue then to finance elections in America and public financing can be avoided with its many problems and negative features.

* * * * * *

Additional commentary

"We urge the federal government, political organizations, and citizen groups to conduct an extensive campaign to inform voters and taxpayers of the tax incentive provisions in the new law. States levying personal income taxes should adopt tax credits similar to those allowed on the federal income tax. Moreover, we recommend that state tax-credit provisions include contributions to all campaigns on issues subject to popular vote, as well as gifts to primary and general election campaigns."—Committee for Economic Development, "Restoring Confidence in the Political Process," January 21, 1973, p. 9.

* * * * * *

Former Senator Robert F. Kennedy preferred tax incentives to public subsidies. In testimony before the Senate Finance Committee in 1967 he said: "By comparison to tax incentives, I believe individual participation will be discouraged if we use direct subsidies from the Treasury to finance campaigns. I would prefer to have the committee consider moving in the direction of encouraging individual contributions through tax incentives."

In opting for tax incentives the Senator noted seven arguments that favor this approach over public subsidies. These are: (1) incentives would aid candidates prior to the general election while subsidies would "almost necessarily" be limited to activities after the conventions; (2) incentives would encourage contributions for candidates below the presidency, who are future presidential candidates; (3) incentives do not represent the threat to our party system that subsidies do; (4) direct subsidies raise difficult problems regarding who shall qualify, proliferation of candidates, arbitrary formulas that will not work in practice, and interference in state and local party disputes; (5) public subsidies raise constitutional dilemmas not present with tax incentives, in particular ones regarding minor party right to funds and traducing of First Amendment rights of free speech in denying the private citizen the right to contribute; (6) a checkoff permits the taxpayer to earmark how his tax dollar shall be spent, which is contrary to

174

tradition, while direct appropriations would leave a public subsidy system open to the vagaries of the appropriations process; and (7) direct subsidy would "further separate the individual citizen from the political process—insulating the party organization from any need to reach citizens except through the one way communication of television and advertising. The political parties would talk to the citizen; but the individual could not effectively talk back."—Robert F. Kennedy, Sen. from N.Y., in Senate Committee on Finance, Political Campaign Financing Proposals (hearings), 90th Cong., 1st Sess., 1967, pp. 244-248.

✿ ✿ ✿ ✿ ✿ ✿

"Sounder solutions than direct public financing may be available by broadening the base of voluntary citizen participation; examples include tax and other inducements."—Robert G. Dixon, Jr., Asst. Atty. Gen., Dept. of Justice, *Hearings* before the Senate Subcommittee on Privileges and Elections, 93rd Cong., 1st Sess., 1973, p. 306.

✿ ✿ ✿ ✿ ✿ ✿

"To broaden the base of political giving, we urge the Congress to provide for reasonable tax deductions as further incentive to smaller contributors."—Charles F. Hood, representing the Chamber of Commerce of the U.S., *Hearings* before Senate Subcom. on Priv. and Elec., 93rd Cong., 1st Sess., 1973, p. 364.

12. *The Taxpayer's Dollar Will Be Used to Support Candidates He Does Not Favor and Campaign Activities He Abhors.*

The 1971 law establishing the Presidential Election Campaign Fund provided for separate accounts for the two major parties and a general fund for other parties. Presumably this permitted the taxpayer the option of designating to which account he wished to allocate his dollar. The option was included to meet objections to a single fund which would deny the taxpayer the right to earmark his contribution. This segregation of funds was vitiated, however, by a provision of the law which authorized the transfer of funds from the general account to the accounts of each major party 60 days prior to a general election. In other words, a taxpayer who had designated money to the general account, perhaps because he did not want his money to support candidates of either major party, could see some of his money transferred to the accounts of the major parties. This transfer authority made a mockery of the ostensible right to designate one's tax dollar to other than a major party.

In 1973 Congress took yet a further step and obliterated altogether the right of the taxpayer to earmark his dollar. A provision of the first Debt Ceiling Act of 1973 (P.L. 93–53) eliminated the special accounts and provided instead for one general account from which all candidates would draw funds. While this move had the saving grace of excising hypocrisy from the initial act, it made the plan vulnerable to the criticism that the tax checkoff denies to the taxpayer the right to designate who shall benefit from his contribution. The present system of private financing, on the other hand, retains sole power to the contributor in making this determination, a fundamental right which ought not to be denied him.

Obviously, the problem which proponents of the tax checkoff proposal confront is that if they permit the taxpayer final say in the allocation of his dollar, with no provision to transfer money from one fund to the other, the embarrassing situation might arise of insufficient funds being earmarked to finance a candidate of a major party. Their solution is to take away what should be guaranteed.

Others have proposed having no checkoff but instead authorizing the Congress to appropriate such amounts as are necessary to fund public financing of elections. This proposal compounds the problem by removing from the taxpayer any say whatsoever in the matter and by making all taxpayers contributors whether they want to be or not. Accordingly, it is even more unfair than the checkoff.

Yet another problem encountered in public financing is the use of taxpayer dollars to finance campaign activities which he does not approve. The clever and engaging spot advertisement is a favorite of political candidates yet appalls many people. Public financing is not going to change the use of such spots. It will simply use the reluctant taxpayer's dollar to finance them. Even less palatable would be the demagogue financed from the public treasury. The taxpayer might take great exception to him and to financing his type campaign, but unless elaborate, and probably unconstitutional, restrictions were placed upon the speech of candidates nothing could be done to curtail the demagogue. At least under the private financing system his money comes only from those who support him.

✿ ✿ ✿ ✿ ✿ ✿

Additional commentary

"A very basic question, not yet answered, is whether the average citizen wants his tax dollars spent on billboards, campaign flyers and such standard political gimmicks as balloons. Reliability of campaign management would not be increased with Federal financing; the reverse, I am confident, would be true."

"Citizens want to identify directly with the candidate or party of their choice, not through the Treasury Department. Through Federal financing, personal involvement and real participation are lost."—Bernard M. Shanley, Vice Chairman, Republican National Committee, *Hearings* before the Senate Subcommittee on Privileges and Elections, 93rd Cong., 1st Sess., 1973, pp. 317–318.

☆   ☆   ☆   ☆   ☆   ☆

"The use of private money is said to have weakened public confidence in the democratic process. We ought to ask, however, whether confidence is likely to be restored when taxpayers pay for campaigns they regard as frivolous, wasteful, and, in some cases, abhorrent. Would the taxpayer viewing television spots have more confidence because he had to help pay for activities with which he disagreed? What would happen if a racist ran for office and delivered radical and quasi-violent speeches? One result might be cries for even more regulation—in particular, for regulation of the content of political speech. Those calling for public financing often point to polls showing public discontent with the high cost of campaigns. The same polls, however, show as much discontent with 'too much mudslinging.' Indeed, the question, 'Why should the public pay for—?' seems a natural response to repugnant, but subsidized, campaign rhetoric."—Ralph K. Winter, Jr., "Campaign Financing and Political Freedom" (AEI), 1973, p. 24.

13. *Cost of Elections Is Entirely in Keeping with What Is at Stake.*

The favorite adjectives used to describe campaign costs by those seeking public financing of elections are "soaring," "exorbitant," "skyrocketing," "mushrooming." With great lament it is noted that costs have doubled or tripled in recent years. Yet, as a noted authority on the subject, Herbert Alexander, Director of the Citizens' Research Foundation, has pointed out, campaign costs when looked at in perspective are not that extraordinary in our rich, post-industrial society.

In March 1973 he wrote, "political costs need to be considered in perspective. Considered in the aggregate, politics is not overpriced. It is under financed. $400 million [his estimate of the costs of all elections in 1972] is just a fraction of one percent of the amounts spent by governments at all levels, and that is what politics is all about, gaining control of governments to decide policies on, among other things, how tax money will be spent. $400 million is less than the amount spent in 1972 by the two largest commercial advertisers in the United States."

In a post-1972-election interview with *U.S. News & World Report*, Alexander stated that the spending total for 1972 was not excessive for an affluent nation, observing that "it's not much in terms of what is spent on chewing gum and cosmetics." The amount spent in 1972 amounted to less than $3 a head on the basis of nearly 140 million Americans of voting age, or about $5 per actual voter.

Accordingly, how valid is the claim of public financing proponents that our election costs are too high or that the only fair and feasible means of meeting them in the future is through public subsidy? Our rich country is undoubtedly capable of supporting campaigns without recourse to that solution.

✿　✿　✿　✿　✿　✿

Additional commentary

"I do not think we spend too much on elections. Federal elections in this country cost less per voter than elections in many other democratic countries. Total expenditures for Federal elections are only somewhat more than the annual Procter & Gamble advertising budget.

"We ranked in the lower third of the democratic countries in the way we spend money for elections. I think it is darn important, so I do not mind spending as much on our legislative process as we do for soap suds or polished chrome."—William Frenzel (R), Rep. from Minnesota, *Hearings* before the Senate Subcommittee on Privileges and Elections, 93rd Cong. 1st Sess., 1973, p. 143.

✿　✿　✿　✿　✿　✿

"Fourth, it is alleged that public financing will help determine 'the extent to which expenditure levels may be substantially higher than necessary for the conduct of a competitive, informative, and effective campaign. . . .' This statement, too, seems a non-sequitur, since a subsidy tells us nothing about whether present non-subsidized expenditures are excessive. In addition, provision of a subsidy would almost surely increase the amounts spent, as it did in Puerto Rico."—Ralph K. Winter, Jr., "Campaign Financing and Political Freedom" (AEI), 1973, p. 23.

14. *Pernicious Impact of Public Financing on Our Party System.*

No matter what system of public financing is devised it would appear to have an adverse effect on our present party system. Under the present system the parties play a limited role in election campaigns but do not so totally dominate them as to exclude independent-minded candidates from winning elections. If public financing were done exclusively through political parties, power to control dissidents and party independents would accrue to party leaders, potentially smothering a vital force for new ideas and change within a party. Also, because parties would no longer be dependent on private souces for funds, they might be less responsive to popular will.

If, on the other hand, financing were done entirely through candidates, parties could be greatly weakened, splinter candidacies fostered, and the strong two-party system potentially threatened by proliferating third party candidacies. The possibility of financing both candidates and parties would be costly and it might be difficult to maintain an equitable balance between them.

      ❀ ❀ ❀ ❀ ❀ ❀

"If a subsidy is given to individual candidates, party discipline may be impaired. If the subsidy is given to parties, independence of candidates may be lost."—Robert G. Dixon, Jr., Asst. Atty. Gen., Dept. of Justice, *Hearings* before Senate Subcommittee on Privileges and Elections, 93rd Cong., 1st Sess., 1973, p. 306.

      ❀ ❀ ❀ ❀ ❀ ❀

"Public financing would also endanger the delicate balance of our party system. If the subsidy were to go largely to party organizations, they would be immensely stronger than they are now. On the other hand, if it were to go directly to candidates, party organizations would be considerably weakened. The subsidy question thus can be rationally decided only after a number of normative as well as empirical inquiries into the nature of our party system have been satisfactorily resolved. Do we need stronger national parties or stronger state parties? Do we need more candidates independent of existing party organizations, or do we need more organizations such as the Committee to Re-Elect the President? Do we need more party solidarity or will this simply lead to greater executive power?

"There are no settled views on any of these questions. Yet the proposals now before Congress threaten to impose a solution to each and perhaps to change our present system radically and rapidly. The danger is not the less because the effect is random or unintentional—or perhaps even mindless."—Ralph K. Winter, Jr., "Campaign Financing and Political Freedom" (AEI), 1973, pp. 24–25.

15. *Party Responsibility May Decline Because of Public Financing.*
One of the functions of party leaders at the State and local level, and at the national level, is to know the possible sources of financial support for campaigns and to help solicit this money. Remove this function from them and our party system may well die. Proposed systems of public financing which circumvent the party—and most do—may encourage dissolution of parties as we have known them. Historically parties have served as conduits for the various interests of our pluralistic society, binding these together in broad-based coalitions. They have also served to focus voter attention on competing philosophies of government. Thus, they have been a source both of cohesion and of diversity. With their role in promoting and financing candidacies replaced by public funding one wonders whether they could long survive or continue to function in the traditional manner at the national level.

      ✿   ✿   ✿   ✿   ✿   ✿

Additional commentary

"If government funding is provided, the candidate may need to rely less than at present on the party or on party identification. Would relationships between parties and candidates diminish further if candidates receive government financing without reference to parties? Would this, in turn, affect the cohering and unifying roles parties play?"

"When subsidies are extended to Senatorial and Congressional campaigns . . . reduced party loyalty would tend to fragment both majorities and minorities, perhaps leading to new factionalism and splinter parties."—Herbert Alexander, Director, Citizens' Research Foundation, "Watergate and the Electoral Process," a paper delivered at the Center for the Study of Democratic Institutions, Santa Barbara, Calif., Dec. 1973.

16. *Many State Party Leaders Are Opposed to Public Financing.*

A survey by the *U.S. News & World Report* in August 1973 found that "Republican State leaders are virtually unanimous in opposing the use of taxpayers' dollars for political expenses. Democrats are overwhelmingly in favor of the idea." Based on a telegraph and telephone survey of 110 chairmen of State parties (54 of whom responded), they discovered that 28 chairmen (22 Republicans and 6 Democrats) were opposed to public financing of political campaigns, while 20 (all Democrats) favored it, and 6 had no opinion or declined to offer one.

Here is what some of those opposed to public financing had to say about it:

Alabama, J. Richard Bennett, Jr., Repub.: "I am unalterably opposed to the financing of campaigns with public funds. Such a system is unworkable, inconsistent with our system of government, would be impossible to administer fairly, and is fraught with the danger of abuses."

Arizona, Harry Rosenzweig, Repub.: "The use of public funds for national political campaigns would open a Pandora's box of problems."

Florida, L. E. Thomas, Repub.: "The concept of federal funding of campaigns is certainly a form of socialism and is much worse than the present system. The very newspapers and radio and television stations that bemoan the high cost of campaigns could cut campaign costs by as much as two thirds by providing equal advertising space and time to all candidates as a public service."

Hawaii, Carla Coray, Repub.: "The income-tax checkoff is a failure. Citizens want to donate directly to candidates of their choice."

Kansas, Jack Ranson, Repub.: "Federal financing would bring much more federal control, and we need less federal control of all aspects of our lives, not more."

Kentucky, Charles Coy, Repub.: "Generally government supervision should be limited to seeing that elections are fairly conducted."

Kentucky, J. R. Miller, Demo.: "I do not favor federal financing. I favor a strong appeal to the public. Restore confidence in the average person. Instill pride in the U.S., and the money will come."

New Jersey, James Dugan, Demo.: "I have difficulty accepting totally public-financed campaigns. I believe them contradictory to the Constitution."

New Jersey, John Spoltore, Repub.: "The taxpayers have too much to pay for now without the further burden of public financing of campaigns."

New Mexico, Murray Ryan, Repub.: "The use of public money for national campaigns would result in an undesirable bureaucratic maze."

New York, Richard Rosenbaum, Repub.: "The existing federal laws should be more thoroughly assessed before tampering with them by placing stringent limitation on contributions, or providing for either full or partial government financing of political campaigns. The kind of laws frequently discussed today could wind up giving government an inordinately large role in determining who may run for office and how effective any given candidacy may be."

North Carolina, James Sugg, Demo.: "I am not at all certain a system of public funding can be devised that will solve the problem of campaign financing satisfactorily, because of the complexities in choosing candidates eligible for funds."

Oklahoma, Clarence Warner, Repub.: "I am strongly against tax dollars being used in campaigns and against limiting the total amount which can be spent. Both of these proposals work to the advantage of the incumbents."

17. *We Do Not Know What Effect Public Financing Will Have on Pre-nomination Presidential Campaigns.*

It has been suggested and proposed that public financing is desirable for pre-nomination presidential campaigns. This will considerably affect the manner in which such campaigns are conducted and may close out options which exist in the present system. Among questions raised: will public financing include funding the cost of wooing or electing State convention delegates in those states which use the convention system for selecting delegates to national conventions? If so, how are legitimate expenses for that purpose to be defined? If not, will states be forced into primary selection of such delegates against their wishes?

Herbert Alexander has pointed out some options in the present system which may be adversely affected by a system of public financing:

"A movement to draft a potential nominee who had not announced his candidacy or participated in any primaries;

"Dark horse candidates;

"Favorite son and daughter candidates;

"A candidate who loses a primary or two but insists his candidacy is viable and wants continued government assistance;

"A candidate who does not expect to be nominated, but enters the contest in order to dramatize an issue, such as Representative McCloskey in the Republican Party in 1972."

He concludes: "Solutions to many of these contingencies may well be found, but these are (the) kinds of activities that offer safety valves, which would not be closed without considerable scrutiny."

❖ ❖ ❖ ❖ ❖ ❖

Additional commentary

"What about the presidential race, which may begin for any one of a number of hopefuls at least a year before any primary? Do you require a man to raise $100,000 or $250,000 in small contributions before he gets any federal funds? Must he do that before the first primaries have started or can he start after? Can he do it just before the national convention, even if he has no delegates? Can he keep getting federal funds after losing several primaries? Can a favorite son get his small contributors from his own state, then use his federal money to run in other states?"—Walter Pincus, "Campaign Financing," *New Republic,* October 27, 1973, p. 18.

18. *Public Financing in Parliamentary Systems Is Not Analogous to the U.S.*

To draw comparisons between subsidies in parliamentary systems and in the United States overlooks the basic fact that we have an electoral system different from theirs. Subsidies in European countries with parliamentary systems are made to political parties, not to candidates. In these countries, parties control the campaigns of their candidates, supplying most of the money to finance those campaigns. While parties in our country do supply some financial assistance to candidates, they do not exercise the iron control over campaigns that is true in parliamentary systems.

Campaign financing with government subsidy is far less of a threat to the party system of a parliamentary form of government than it is to the political party system in our country. Accordingly, what may work in Norway will not necessarily work in the United States. What particularly distinguishes our electoral system from those of Western European countries is our primary system by which we choose nominees for the general election. This factor complicates the public financing of our campaigns and makes it difficult to finance them fairly. In parliamentary systems parties choose candidates and do not face the difficult problem of primaries in financing elections with public money.

* * * * * *

Additional commentary

"In most of the nations with subsidies, governments fund the parties annually, not only at election time. This is supplemented by free broadcast time, again made to the parties and not to the candidates. Historically, at first, most of the subsidies were given in small amounts to supplement resources already in the political process, and later increased when the system adjusted to the infusion of new funds. Excepting in Puerto Rico, in no country providing subsidies have ceilings been imposed on private contributions. In contrast, efforts are being made in this country to both limit and subsidize. Would that we knew the possibilities of doing both effectively, or the consequences of doing either ineffectively."—Herbert Alexander, Director, Citizens' Research Foundation, in "Watergate and the Electoral Process," a paper delivered at the Center for the Study of Democratic Institutions, Dec. 1973.

19. *Will Public Financing Really Curb the Power of Special Interests?*

Some proponents of public financing believe that it will rid the political process of the corrupting influence of corporate and private wealth. However, it is questionable whether contributions from them are a primary souce of their influence. In this regard two assumptions of those who advocate public financing are more myth than fact. These are: (1) that special interests dominate the political process to the exclusion of the public interest, and (2) that their influence is a direct function of their campaign contributions. Suspicion and accusation, far more than hard evidence, are the foundation for these beliefs.

The Founding Fathers recognized the inevitability of interest groups in society and so created a form of government designed to balance their competing demands. It is both reasonable and acceptable in our political system to have groups petition political leaders on behalf of their interests. Many groups go a step further and solicit from their membership contributions for candidates who look upon their interests with favor. When these contributions cumulate to several thousands of dollars, they become sinister in some people's minds. Actually, they can be thought of as investments which sometimes pay off and sometimes don't. Corporate leaders themselves have spoken of campaign contributions as attempts not to curry favor but to prevent harmful government actions. Regardless of the motivation behind such contributions, no self-respecting Member of Congress nor any President considers himself a lackey for any interest group whose members contribute to his campaign.

Moreover, the power of interest groups will continue to be exercised in the political arena regardless of whether there is public financing of election campaigns. It is doutful that such a system of financing elections will diminish the proper role that groups play or their attempts to persuade legislators to vote in ways favorable to their interests. Nirvana will not come to pass with public financing; nor is it likely that the Congress will somehow become populated with whoever it is the proponents of public financing believe will be elected if their proposal is adopted.

✿ ✿ ✿ ✿ ✿ ✿

Additional commentary

"The assertion that the political process is dominated by the wealthy, vested interests to the exclusion of the public interest is misleading and an oversimplified view of the realities of our democratic processes. While there are numerous examples in which heavily financed interest groups have obtained tax loopholes, subsidies and other government favors, there are also many instances where these interest groups have been frustrated in their attempts to obtain legislation favorable to their interests or to block legislation that was unfavorable. For example, in recent years, there have been:

"The defeat of the aerospace lobby in the battle over the SST;

"Reduction of the oil depletion allowance in the 1969 Tax Reform Act in the face of strong industry opposition;

"Active government efforts to clean up our waters, launched over the intense opposition of industries such as paper and chemicals;

"Passage of Medicare in 1965 in the face of an all-out AMA mobilization against the bill;

"Enactment of stringent air pollution control standards regarding auto emissions despite the opposition of the auto industry;

"Justice Department consent decree requiring ITT to divest a half-dozen major subsidiaries acquired in mergers, despite its vast financial resources and an intense campaign to get the case dropped;

"Opening of the highway trust fund in spite of extensive lobbying efforts by the highway lobbies.

"Nor have these been isolated incidents. Defense and space funding have experienced steady relative declines, despite heavy lobbying and spending by the so-called 'military industrial' complex, while spending for health, education and welfare programs has soared, doubling to around $100 billion.

"These examples are not meant to be an attempt to obfuscate the sometimes excessive and occasionally overwhelming power of the vested interests, but rather they are an effort to place the influence of the special interests vs. the public interest into a more realistic perspective."—William Frenzel (R), Rep. from Minnesota, *Hearings* before the Senate Subcommittee on Privileges and Elections, 93rd Cong., 1st Sess., 1973, pp. 148–149.

✻ ✻ ✻ ✻ ✻ ✻

"Special interest influence is a problem, but campaign contributions are only one of many contributing factors. In fact, political contributions may not be a major or primary source of power for the special and vested interests. There are at least three other factors that are important and significant sources of their power and influence.

"1. The producer groups (usually the special and vested interests) have an inherent advantage over consumer groups (usually the general public). Specifically, producer groups have more time and greater resources which allow them to develop the following attributes that give them an important edge in the struggle for political power:

"Specialized knowledge and expertise in the complex and technical matters in which governmental decisions are required;

"Professional staff and representatives possessing knowledge of the

186

governmental process, and access to the key people who make the decisions;

"A large stake in the limited range of issues that affect their interest, thus allowing for maximum mobilization of resources at the appropriate time and place;

"A certain 'legitimacy,' because the parties most affected by a governmental action should have a large role in determining the outcome;

"Organization networks and structures that facilitate articulation and forceful presentation of their views to both the public and the relevant government decision makers.

"For example, if a public utility wants an increase in rates, it has the time and resources to invest a considerable amount of effort in a campaign to obtain governmental approval. It can develop information that will demonstrate the great need for such an increase. The utility knows the process by which to obtain approval and can easily contact the proper people and decision makers. Having a huge stake in the issue, the entire corporation's resources can be mobilized for this particular effort. Since the company is greatly affected by the possible increase, the government must listen and weigh its case.

"2. Political parties in the United States are relatively weak, broad-based and decentralized. In many other democratic nations, the parties provide a stronger focus and rallying point for the consumer or public interest. The influential special and vested interests in the United States are not often challenged by the political parties. The main check on their powers are the other, conflicting, influential special and vested interests.

"3. Even more importantly, the United States is a highly fragmented, governmental structure. Decisions on particular issues are focused in legislative committees and subcommittees and in executive agencies and bureaus. With the possible exception of the Office of Management and Budget, there is no overall budget control mechanism, no overall view of the allocation of national priorities, and no central agency that can shape and define national public policy. Each special and vested interest merely must concentrate its resources on a handful of committees, agencies or bureaucracies to obtain governmental favors and assistance. Meanwhile, more broadly based groups, such as the consumer and the public interest groups, face the more difficult job of monitoring and overseeing dozens of committees, hundreds of departments, agencies and bureaucracies, and hundreds of thousands of state and local political entities.

"Given these other factors, public financing may fail completely to curb the 'excessive and corrosive' influence of the special and vested interests. Certainly, it will not eliminate or drastically reduce their power and influence."—William Frenzel (R), Rep. from Minnesota, *Hearings* before the Senate Subcommittee on Privileges and Elections, 93rd Cong., 1st Sess., 1973, pp. 149–150.

         ✿   ✿   ✿   ✿   ✿   ✿

"Besides being related to free expression private political contributions provide a means for social or economic minorities, notably business, to gain extra political leverage. This function places campaign giving within the tradition of social pluralism established by the drafters of the U.S. Constitution."—A. James Reichley, "Let's Reform Campaign Financing but Let's Do It Right," *Fortune,* December 1973, p. 158.

         ✿   ✿   ✿   ✿   ✿   ✿

"Finally, we are told that subsidies will reduce the pressure on Congressional candidates for dependence on large campaign contributions from private sources. . . . If, however, one reduces the pressure on candidates to look to the views of contributors, to whom will the candidates look instead? The need to raise money compels candidates to address those matters about which large groups feel strongly. Candidates might well, upon receiving campaign money from the government, mute their views and become even more pre-packaged. Eliminate the need for money and you eliminate much of the motive to face up to the issues. Candidates might then look more to attention-getting gimmicks than to attention-getting policy statements. A subsidy combined with spending limits might insulate incumbents both from challengers and the strongly held desires of constituents."— Ralph K. Winter, Jr., "Campaign Financing and Political Freedom" (AEI), October 27, 1973, pp. 23–24.

20. *It Would Be More Difficult and Probably More Costly to Finance Campaigns Publicly at the Congressional Level Than Under the Present System.*

Leaving aside for the moment the many difficulties involved in financing publicly presidential elections, the problems encountered in financing elections for Congress are even more overwhelming.

The degree and intensity of competition in presidential elections is fairly uniform from election to election. This is not true in congressional elections. In some congressional elections there is little general election competition. Accordingly, elections are really determined at the primary level. Two problems arise from this fact. First, public financing would seem to be required at the primary as well as the general election level in order to realize its stated goal of "purifying" the election finance to the taxpayer. Second, public financing could increase the cost of elections by encouraging excessive intra- and inter-party competition.

Presently, there are several states that are one-party States. Perhaps public financing will change this and create a two-party system in those States, but that is not a certainty. What is more likely is that persons with little chance of victory will nevertheless contest for office because of the availability of funds to them, thus driving up costs, and that candidates who in the past needed to spend small sums to get elected now will spend the total available to them either because of competition or because the money is there for the asking. The one-party-state syndrome also raises the difficult problem of determining whether the candidate of the other "major" party merits major-party funding support since the track record of his party on its face does not indicate that he so qualifies.

Most formulas for public financing depend on the eligible voting age population as the base for determining what money shall be allocated to finance a campaign. Under this formula "x" cents time the EVP produces "y" funds. Unfortunately, election realities may indicate that either more or less money is required in any given race than is produced under the formula. Accordingly, some will be generously treated while others are starved. Candidates A and B in one State may require only several thousand dollars to run a campaign against each other but be allocated far more than that while candidates C and D in another State require more than is prescribed by law for them, hence they are penalized. In other words, there are more variables which figure into the amount of money which is necessary to compete for election than are reducible to a formula for determining that figure. Under current practice these variables (degree of party competitiveness, incumbency of one of the opponents, non-incumbency of either opponent, nature of the State or district involved, cost differential of campaign services across the United States, travel cost differential in States and districts) can be more easily accommodated to, budgeted for, and financed than is true under a system of public finance.

At the primary level, assuming that public financing must also exist there, the devilishly difficult problem arises concerning how to limit the number of candidates who shall be publicly financed. Obviously, it is not financially feasible to fund everyone who runs. Accordingly, lines must be drawn below which the right to funds is denied. Who is the decide at which point some candidate is to be denied public money —below 5 percent of the vote? 10 percent? 15 percent? No one really has a good answer.

Moreover, the process of financing at the primary level is far more difficult than at the general level. Some plans call for candidates to post a bond which they would forfeit if they fail to secure the required percentage of voters to qualify for public financing. Most also have a payback provision, requiring candidates to pay back public funds which they have received if they fail to garner a sufficient number of votes to qualify for assistance. Thus the allocating of funds is complex and the bookkeeping involved is horrendous. Without knowing whether they will receive a vote sufficient to qualify them for assistance, the Government would be giving funds to candidates so they may compete for nomination. It would then have to get back that money from those who fail to qualify. Clearly this is a potential Frankenstein monster.

Bonding and payback provisions are necessary, it is said, to discourage frivolous candidacies while public financing is needed to encourage and aid those to run who might not otherwise be able to. One wonders who are the former and who the latter in this situation? By comparison the present private financing system seems far simpler and more preferable.

Suppose that there is primary competition between third-party candidates. Are they to receive no public funds? If they are to receive funds, what lines of non-eligibility are to be drawn for them? Is the amount to be made available to them to be determined by the total votes they receive? If so, is this fair since it is seldom that primary turnout matches general election turnout with the possible exception of those one-party States where primaries determine general election victors?

190

(For additional comment on the problem of third parties see argument 22 *infra.*)

(NOTE—The problems of incumbency are addressed in argument 8, *supra.*)

✿　✿　✿　✿　✿　✿

Additional commentary

"Public financing plans do not really fit our Federal, pluralistic election system. States vary; districts vary; people vary.

"Are you going to spend money for all the guys that run against Wilbur Mills, George Mahon, Carl Albert, and Wright Patman. They seldom have primary opponents, and yet certainly they will want to use that money.

"And also, the House Members who think they are safe in the House elections will take the money and spend it on the public media, so they will be in a good position to challenge you guys in the Senate the next time around."—William Frenzel (R), Rep. from Minnesota, *Hearings* before the Senate Subcommittee on Privileges and Elections, 93rd Cong., 1st Sess. 1973, p. 144.

✿　✿　✿　✿　✿　✿

"In addition to the problems that I previously have noted with respect to certain of the pending public financing proposals, I would like to point out one other problem, Mr. Chairman, that is present in my State of Louisiana with respect to other proposals that have been made to the committee. My State is favored, or disfavored, depending upon your point of view, with the fact that we have only 3 percent of our registered voters who are Republicans.

"Now, as a believer in the two-party system, I don't believe we ought to forever seal off the chance of Republicans getting elected in our State by saying that they are entitled, under some kind of Federal financing arrangement, to only 3 percent of Federal campaign money.

"On the other hand, I do not think the Federal Government ought to finance a party representing such a small percentage of the registered electorate on an equal basis with Democrats."—J. Bennett Johnston, Sen. from La., *Hearings* before Senate Subcommittee on Privileges and Elections, 93rd Cong., 1st Sess., 1973, p. 312.

✿　✿　✿　✿　✿　✿

191

"Certain of the proposed bills make no provision for financial [sic] primary elections. Thus, would anything really be accomplished by financing general elections from the Federal till while having primaries funded through private donations?"

"There are some sections of the country, may I say, in parenthesis, Senator Pell, that the primary election is the election. And consequently, a primary election by all odds is the most important part of the election process.

"It has been my experience in politics that money spent in primary campaigns probably has greater impact on results than that spent on general elections."—Bernard M. Shanley, Vice Chairman, Repub. Nat'l Comm., *Hearings* before Sen. Subcom. on Priv. and Elec., 93rd Cong., 1st Sess., 1973, p. 317.

✻   ✻   ✻   ✻   ✻   ✻

"There is absolutely no way that the people in my district would accept the spending of $90,000 in a congressional race. It is more than has ever been spent in a general election in the history of the State of Wisconsin.

"Nationally, only a handful of the 831 candidates for the House in the last general election spent that much. That vast majority spent half that amount in the general and primary elections combined. We need to clean up the way we are financing campaigns but not by lavishing candidates with huge amounts of Federal dollars."—David Obey, Rep. from Wisconsin, remarks in the *Congressional Record,* February 13, 1974, p. E607, regarding S. 3044, reported by the Senate Committee on Rules and Administration.

✻   ✻   ✻   ✻   ✻   ✻

"Few of the proposals for public financing are contoured to meet the many peculiarities and idiosyncrasies of the states and localities. Among problems which are encountered: 1) discriminatory petition requirements for third party candidates; 2) deposit requirements favor the wealthy over the poor; 3) spending limitations are unreasonably low for some states, unreasonably high for others; 4) equal amounts for major party candidates may help challenges in Senate races (because incumbents normally outspend challengers) but will hurt challengers in House races (because challengers must outspend incumbents if they are to have a chance); 5) misallocation of funds by giving equal

192

amounts to those in hot races and those in weakly contested races, thus under-financing important races, and over-financing relatively unimportant races." —William Frenzel (R), Rep. from Minn., *Hearings* before the Senate Subcommittee on Privileges and Elections, 93rd Cong., 1st Sess., 1973, p. 152.

21. *Public Financing of Congressional Elections May Adversely Affect the Executive-Legislative Balance of Power.*

Herbert Alexander has raised the interesting point that subsidies for senatorial and congressional campaigns will lead to more independent-minded candidates on the ballot, some of whom will be elected. "At a time when there is concern over Executive-Legislative relationships, when there is concern about Executive encroachment, any further splintering of Congress . . . would ensure the diminishing of the Legislative branch. Checks and balances would be more diffused."

22. *Problems Encountered Because of Minor and New Parties.*

One of the difficulties inherent in any public financing proposal is that it discriminates against minor and new parties. This is so because all plans treat the major parties as equals (even though from election to election and State to State this is untrue) in the allocation of public funds to their candidates while employing a different formula for minor and new parties—usually in their case predicating support either on past performance at the polls or performance in the year for which funds are granted.

Such a differentiation may operate to freeze into place minor and new parties. Correlatively, the present two party system may get locked into place because candidates of these parties will always be guaranteed uniform sums so long as they poll a certain percentage of the vote (usually 25 percent). It is true that the present two party system has existed for more than 100 years and that it may remain that way another 100 years with or without public financing, but at least under a private financing system there is a better chance that one of the major parties might expire for lack of financial support. This need to survive financially is one reason our party system has remained dynamic. It cannot be denied, of course, that even under a public financing system one of the present major parties might pass from existence. However, the security public financing would offer the present major parties would militate against that occurring.

Yet a different consequence is the possibility of third party movements proliferating in the hopes of capturing sufficient votes to obtain public money. Once such support is earned, public finance may then prolong the life of a third party. This possibility does not exist with a private financing system in which minor parties survive only so long as people are willing to contribute to them.

✿　✿　✿　✿　✿　✿

Additional commentary

"Proponents of public financing have failed to arrive at a workable, fair and equitable formula for third and minor parties. They have failed to derive a formula that would make it fairly difficult, but still quite feasible for a third party to receive federal funding. A system (e.g., use of petitions) that might work well for qualifying third and minor parties in California and Oregon might fail miserably in New York and Vermont. A system (e.g., security deposit) that might cause a proliferation of third party and splinter party candidates in one area (e.g., Westchester County) might make it extremely difficult for a third or splinter party to get federal financing in another area (e.g., South Bronx). Proponents have also failed to come up with a formula that will distribute funds fairly and equitably among major and minor parties.

"The treatment of major, minor and third parties raises substantial constitutional questions. Under a system of public financing, must minority parties be guaranteed equal protection? If they are, they would have to receive as much or more than major parties. This would cause a proliferation of minor parties. If they are not given equal protection, the system may be declared unconstitutional. Even if a minor or third party is given as much as a major party, it may still be discriminatory, because the minor party must spend more if it is to do well in an election. To limit the amount a new, minor or third party can receive from the federal treasury to as much as or less than the amount for major parties might severely cripple the ability of these parties to wage successful campaigns. Furthermore, there are ample legal precedents against arbitrary classification of this nature."—William Frenzel, Rep. from Minn., *Hearings* before the Senate Subcommittee on Privileges and Elections, 93rd Cong., 1st Sess., 1973, p. 53.

✿　✿　✿　✿　✿　✿

"A subsidy for a minor party may enable it to survive, although its aims and methods merit an early demise.

"Constitutional objections are also likely to be raised to proposals for a public subsidy to the extent that:

"Major parties receive larger subsidies than minor parties;

"Minor parties are required to make refunds of subsidies if they fail to obtain a certain number of percentage of votes, or to forfeit security deposits whereas similar conditions are not imposed on major candidates."—Robert G. Dixon, Jr., Asst. Atty. Gen., Dep. of Justice, *Hearings* before the Senate Subcommittee on Privileges and Elections, 93rd Cong., 1st Sess., 1973, p. 306.

❋   ❋   ❋   ❋   ❋   ❋

"Splinter and third parties would benefit greatly by Federal financing at the direct expense of the national parties. For instance, if there had been Federal financing in 1968, it is reasonable to assume that Senator McCarthy, denied the Presidential nomination by the Democratic Party, might have formed his own third party, virtually assured of getting at least 5 percent of the vote and being guaranteed retroactive reimbursement of his campaign expenses.

"With the independent vote increasing as it is, the two major parties cannot afford a further splintering of their efforts or of our two-party system, which, in my opinion, makes our Constitution effective. I believe some of the bills being proposed foster erosion of the two great parties in this country by providing for the subsidizing of minority parties in elections."—Bernard M. Shanley, Vice Chairman, Repub. Nat'l Comm., *Hearings* before Sen. Subcom. on Priv. and Elec., 93rd Cong., 1st Sess., 1973, p. 317.

❋   ❋   ❋   ❋   ❋   ❋

"Under a system of public financing, a one-shot third or minor party might poll sufficient votes in an election to assure a sizable subsidy in the next campaign. By the time of the next election, it is feasible that such a party would have spent its fury and be virtually extinct. Yet, it would receive several million dollars which it could decide to spend in a squanderous fashion."—William Frenzel, Rep. from Minn., *Hearings* before Senate Subcom. on Privileges and Elections, 93rd Cong., 1st Sess., 1973, p. 152.

❋   ❋   ❋   ❋   ❋   ❋

"Similarly, direct subsidization of campaigns must have an enormous but uncertain impact on third parties. If a formula like that contained in the Hart bill is employed, third parties would usually have to gamble whether to take the subsidy. The 'seriousness' of a party would have little to do with its decisions since early showings in the polls might augur well—but all third parties suffer late in campaigns from the urge of voters to make their votes 'count.' Declining the subsidy would be taken to mean that the party was not serious and, in any event, the possibility of subsidy would deter further giving. If the formula is based on showings in previous elections, subsidies would sustain third parties long after their appeal had diminished, simply because they once received a significant portion of the vote."—Ralph K. Winter, Jr., "Campaign Financing and Political Freedom" (AEI), 1973, p. 5.

23. *Public Financing Will Either Dry Up Money Available to Local Candidates or Focus the Special Interest Money at the Local Level.*

There is a definite possibility that public financing of national elections will not spur an outpouring of private money to finance state and local elections but will dry up traditional sources of money because it is more difficult to generate contributing enthusiasm at that level. To the degree that this occurs, the so-called special interest may step in, or be called upon, to finance state and local election campaigns. The howl will then go up to finance these elections from public funds and another bite will be put upon the taxpayer if that is enacted. Elections will then become the sole responsibility of the State (Nation) and the voluntary basis of our political system will be wiped away. Is this what we want to see happen?

*   *   *   *   *   *

Additional commentary

"If a system of public financing is adopted, it is very likely that many states would continue with their systems of complete private financing. There are two possible serious consequences of a system of public financing. Such a system could dry up funds for state and local candidates, who already have a difficult time raising adequate funds. Private givers might feel that their responsibility has been satisfied by the National Program. Special interests would not. As a result, state and local candidates and the quality of state and local governments might decrease.

"On the other hand, private contributors—especially special interest groups—might channel the funds formerly used in federal elections into state and local government elections. . . . So if private funds were channeled toward the state and local sector, it might be easy to 'buy' candidates with 'dirty money.' Furthermore, a dramatic increase in spending at the state and local level would probably mean a dramatic increase in overall spending in political campaigns, which is contrary to the goals of many of the proponents of public financing. Chasing 'dirty money' from the nation's capitol to the state capitols and court house would be an ironic by-product of federal financing."—William Frenzel, Rep. from Minnesota, *Hearings* before Senate Subcommittee on Privileges and Elections, 93rd Cong., 1st Sess., 1973, pp. 154–155.

24. *It Is False to Assume That Money Raised Privately Is Necessarily Suspect.*

Proponents of public financing seem to begin with the assumption that money privately contributed to finance campaigns is necessarily suspect. Yet, there is good reason to doubt the validity of that assumption. It is true that interest groups donate with the expectation that those they support who win office will vote in ways beneficial to their interests. But often the candidates they support share a community of interest with them anyway and would vote in their favor on the basis of philosophical predilections irrespective of financial support. Why must the conclusion be drawn that such candidates are "bought" or "unduly influenced" by the funds which come to them from people with whom they share interests? This dark connotation to contributing distorts reality. In some measure it is the "hobgoblin" of liberal minds seeking sinister forces at work to subvert the public interest. These same liberals who see so much wrong in corporate executives contributing to campaigns find nothing sinister in the funds contributed on their behalf by interest groups which favor them. This "good guys"/"bad guys" division among contributors is a false one.

Moreover, whatever faults may exist in the private financing system can be corrected by sensible and effective legislation. The 1971 Federal Election Campaign Act was a step in that direction. Efforts further to perfect it are preferable to junking the private financing system. Public financing as a solution is like throwing the baby out with the bathwater. Much money contributed to finance campaigns in our country is without taint. It is contributed by thousands of Americans who believe in our system of government and want to show their support for the kind of candidates they think should hold office. There is no good reason to deprive them of this opportunity.

✵ ✵ ✵ ✵ ✵ ✵

Additional commentary

"Privately raised money is not necessarily 'dirty' money. Good rules can clean it. I will bet every member of this committee has raised hundreds of thousands of political dollars that they do not think is dirty money."—William Frenzel (R.), Rep. from Minnesota, *Hearings* before the Senate Subcommittee on Privileges and Elections, 93rd Cong., 1st Sess., 1973, p. 142.

25. *Fundraising Is Not Demeaning, but Challenging. The Object Is to Solicit Support Based on Previous Performance and to Constantly Enlarge That Support.*

Underlying the notion of public financing is the idea that fundraising is a shabby, distasteful, and demeaning process. Is this really true? Is not the need to solicit funds one more way in which the officeholder remains in touch with the people? Is it not a means for him to measure public response to his performance in office? Should we insulate the candidate from this process of sufficiently proving himself to the satisfaction of the electorate that they are willing to invest in his candidacy? Perhaps we do need to widen the contribution base in this country —and tax incentives which are on the lawbooks have that goal in mind; but it is questionable that we ought to insulate the candidate from the need to raise money to finance his campaign. This need does not demean him. It does require him to convince people that he merits their financial backing, a requirement that is in keeping with our electoral tradition and one worth preserving.

✵ ✵ ✵ ✵ ✵ ✵

Additional commentary

"Political fundraising is not demeaning to me. It is not easy, and it may never be fun, but I have never been ashamed to ask for money for candidates I support, including myself.

"I wonder if those that are demeaned have as good a product to sell.

"In my State the Republican Party raised $1 million from 68,000 contributors. We get over 10 percent of the members of our parties to contribute, and the biggest fundraising adventure has an average per capital [*sic*] contribution of $7.05.

"I think that is pretty democratic fundraising."

"In support of public financing, proponents assert that private fundraising is a humiliating and degrading experience that political candidates should not be forced to face. While fundraising can be difficult and occasionally embarrassing, proponents fail to recognize its value as a barometer of: 1) a candidate's popular support, 2) public approval of his record while in office, and 3) his seriousness about serving in public office. Furthermore, many public financing proposals might put candidates, especially incumbents, in a position where they would have to do very little to get elected."—William Frenzel, Rep. from Minnesota, *Hearings* before the Senate Subcommittee on Privileges and Elections, 93rd Cong., 1st Sess., 1973, pp. 143, 151.

26. *Definitional Problems Are Encountered in Public Financing Proposals.*

In other arguments presented in this compilation definitional problems have been alluded to. These problems are difficult and raise doubt that fair subsidies can be worked out based on formulas that do not treat candidates as equals. Herbert Alexander, America's foremost analyst of campaign financing, has stated that "presumably, the goal of government subsidy is to help serious candidates, yet retain enough flexibility to permit opportunity to challenge those in power without supporting with significant tax dollars candidates merely seeking free publicity and without attracting so many candidates that the electoral process is degraded. Accordingly, . . . how [do we] define major and minor parties, and distinguish serious and frivolous candidates, without doing violence to equality of opportunity, or to 'equal protection' under the Constitution?" These questions admit of no easy answer. Alexander continues, "Any standards must be arbitrary, and certain screening devices must be used, based upon past vote, numbers of petitions, posting of money bonds, or other means. Some of these means require 'start up' funds or masses of volunteers to get petitions signed, and other plans, such as matching incentives, require popular appeal that can best be achieved through incumbency or years of exposure which also costs money."

❈   ❈   ❈   ❈   ❈   ❈

Additional commentary

"If the amount of the subsidy is based upon previous votes received by the candidate's party, incumbents would receive more money than challengers, who are already at a disadvantage for other reasons. (Under 1966 and 1967 Senate Finance Committee formulas, the parties or candidates qualifying as 'major' would receive equal subsidy assistance.) Subsidies require formulas that raise difficult questions as to what is a 'major' or 'minor' party and why a party is so classified.

"They also bring up the issue of what is a 'qualified candidate,' particularly in the pre-nomination period. Eligibility by petition on a nationwide basis presents problems of validation of signatures and possible harassment by challenging petitions. If subsidies base eligibility on the vote received by a party in the previous election, new parties would not qualify until two or more years after they have organized. To subsidize a minor party after its political activity has peaked could prolong its uselessness; otherwise it might fade away."—Herbert E. Alexander, *Money in Politics* (1972), p. 238.

Appendix II

Common Cause Study Reveals $74 Million Spent by Congressional Candidates Who Ran in 1974 General Elections*

Almost $74 million was reported spent by the 1,161 candidates for Congress who ran in the 1974 general elections, according to a Common Cause study released today. Democrats outspent Republicans, $38.4 million to $32.5 million, in House and Senate races with candidates from both major parties, the study revealed.

An additional $1.7 million in total expenditures was reported by incumbents (62 Democrats, 1 Republican) who did not have major party challengers in the general election. Minor party and independent candidates who ran in the general election reported total spending of some $1.3 million. (See attached Appendix A.)

Democratic incumbents outspent their Republican challengers by an

---

*This study by Common Cause, released on April 11, 1975, is based on cash contributions to congressional candidates. The author of this book, while praising this compilation of election information by Common Cause, must nevertheless point out that in this study, as in past studies by Common Cause, no attempt is made to tabulate and disclose the in-kind contributions of goods and services by organized labor to the candidates it supports, primarily Democrats. In-kind contributions by unions are ten times the amount of their cash contributions; hence, studies such as this one by Common Cause are not definitive.

average of more than two to one. Republican incumbents outspent their Democratic challengers by a margin of three to two.

The study, conducted by the Common Cause Campaign Finance Monitoring Project, covered general election candidates for the period from September 1, 1973, through December 31, 1974. It included 468 Democratic candidates, 407 Republicans and 286 minor party and independent candidates.

HOUSE RACES

Some $45.1 million was reported spent by candidates in the 435 House races. The top House spenders included winners Robert Krueger (D–Tx), $312,000 (included a primary runoff); James Scheuer (D–NY), $301,000; Abner Mikva (D–Ill), $286,000; and defeated Representatives Samuel Young (R–Ill), $251,000 and Joel Broyhill (R–Va), $249,000. (See attached Appendix B for list of top 25 House spenders.)

Of the 810 major party House candidates, only 22 had total expenditures higher than $168,000. This amount represents the combined overall spending limit ($84,000 in a primary and $84,000 in a general election) imposed on future House candidates by the newly enacted campaign finance law. The 22 largest House spenders included 10 incumbents and nine major party candidates in races not involving an incumbent. Only three of the 40 challengers who defeated House incumbents in the 1974 general elections, had total expenditures higher than the $168,000 combined overall limit. The highest total amount spent by the 248 minor party and independent candidates who ran in the general election was $85,680 by Don Elliott (Lib–NY). Elliott, after losing in the Democratic primary, ran as a Liberal in the general election.

Incumbents outspent their major party challengers in almost 80 percent of the 323 House races involving an incumbent and major party challenger. Approximately 70 percent of the 323 major party challengers to incumbents spent less than $50,000.

SENATE RACES

Some $28.9 million was spent in the 34 Senate races. Seven Senate candidates, including five incumbents, spent more than $1 million during their election. Their states ranged in size from South Dakota to

California. The top spenders were incumbents Alan Cranston (D–Ca), $1,336,000; George McGovern (D–SD), $1,173,000; challenger John Glenn (D–Ohio), $1,149,000; incumbents Robert Dole (R–Ks), $1,110,000; Jacob Javits (R–NY), $1,090,000; Birch Bayh (D–In), $1,024,000; and challenger Wendell Ford (D–Ky), $1,007,000. (See attached Appendix C for list of top 10 Senate spenders.)

Of the 65 major party Senate candidates, only 16 had total expenditures higher than the combined overall spending limits to be imposed for future Senate races by the new law. The 16 candidates included eight incumbents, four challengers and four contestants running in a race with no incumbent. Only two of the 38 minor party and independent candidates reported spending more than $100,000. Barbara A. Keating, the Conservative Party candidate in New York, reported spending $192,000 and John Grady, the American Party candidate in Florida, reported spending $148,000.

Incumbents outspent their major party challengers in 24 of the 25 Senate races involving an incumbent and major party challenger. Only two challengers beat Senate incumbents: Wendell Ford (D–Ky), who outspent Senator Marlow Cook $1,007,000 to $525,000; and Gary Hart (D–Col), who spent $353,000 and was outspent by Senator Peter Dominick's $502,000.

The almost $74 million total reported as spent in 1974 by general election Congressional candidates compares with $66.4 million reported as spent in 1972. The 1972 figures covered the period from April 7, 1972, the effective date of the Federal Election Campaign Act of 1971, to December 31, 1972.

In contrast with the $6 million spending margin for Democrats over their Republican opponents in 1974, Republicans outspent Democratic opponents in 1972 by $4.6 million. The party totals in 1972 were $34.2 million for Republicans and $29.6 million for Democrats.

The Common Cause study was based on thousands of disclosure reports filed by 1974 Congressional general election candidates under the 1971 campaign finance law. Common Cause obtained copies of each one of these disclosure reports from the Secretary of the Senate and the Clerk of the House, the federal supervisory officers under the 1971 law for Congressional races.

Campaign finances for each candidate were determined by combining the candidates' reports with the reports of all of the political committees supporting the candidate. House and Senate candidates have

Appendix A

EXPENDITURES REPORTED BY GENERAL ELECTION CANDIDATES IN 1974 CONGRESSIONAL RACES

	HOUSE		SENATE		OVERALL TOTALS	
	No. of Candidates	Expenditures	No. of Candidates	Expenditures	No. of Candidates	Expenditures
Democrats	(434)	23,615,780	(34)	16,585,840	(468)	40,201,620
Republicans	(376)	20,609,762	(31)	11,842,625	(407)	32,452,387
Minor Party/Independents	(248)	826,882	(38)	458,726	(286)	1,285,608
Totals	(1,058)	45,052,424	(103)	28,887,191	(1,161)	73,939,615

	HOUSE		SENATE	
	No. of Candidates	Expenditures	No. of Candidates	Expenditures
Incumbents with Major Party Challengers	(323)	20,463,731	(22)	13,153,649
Major Party Challengers to Incumbents	(323)	12,892,599	(22)	7,316,731
Races with No Incumbents in General Election				
Democrats	(52)	5,644,054	(9)	4,794,221
Republicans	(52)	4,185,069	(9)	2,422,497

been given the opportunity to review the findings and to offer any corrections they felt should be made.

The number of reports, candidates, political committees, and entries covered by these reports make it impossible to guarantee absolute accuracy. The General Accounting Office made this point clear with respect to the studies it released on Presidential finances in the 1972 elections. Common Cause has taken all possible steps to assure the accuracy of its findings.

Appendix B

HOUSE GENERAL ELECTION CANDIDATES

Expenditures Reported by Top 25 Spenders
in 1974 House Races

			(state-cong. dist.)	
†††	1.	Robert Krueger (D)	°° TX-21	**$311,953**
†††	2.	James H. Scheuer (D)	NY-11	301,135
††	3.	Abner J. Mikva (D)	IL-10	286,225
†	4.	Samuel H. Young (R)	IL-10	251,249
†	5.	Joel T. Broyhill (R)	VA-10	248,709
†††	6.	F. W. Richmond (D)	NY-14	245,533
††	7.	Charles J. Horne (D)	VA-09	232,341
††††	8.	Jeff LaCaze (D)	°° LA-06	229,335
†††	9.	Paul Simon (D)	IL-24	223,163
†	10.	Sam Steiger (R)	AZ-03	203,899
†	11.	William H. Hudnut (R)	IN-11	201,673
†	12.	James M. Collins (R)	TX-03	192,058
†	13.	David C. Treen (R)	LA-03	190,135
†	14.	Robin L. Beard (R)	TN-06	189,216
†††††	15.	Lawrence P. McDonald (D)	GA-07	188,093
†††	16.	Norman Y. Mineta (D)	CA-13	185,236
††	17.	Bill Clinton (D)	°° AR-03	180,882
†	18.	J. J. Pickle (D)	TX-10	180,294
†	19.	Robert F. Drinan (D)	MA-04	178,871
††††	20.	Butler C. Derrick, Jr. (D)	SC-03	176,022
††††	21.	Henry J. Hyde (R)	IL-06	175,087
†	22.	Alan Steelman (R)	TX-05	168,457
†	23.	Floyd Spence (R)	SC-02	167,188
†	24.	Paul N. McCloskey (R)	CA-12	166,441
††	25.	Charles Grisbaum, Jr. (D)	LA-03	166,203

Fourteen Democrats and eleven Republicans are listed above.

   † Incumbent
  †† Challenger to incumbent
 ††† Races with no incumbent in general election
†††† Races with no incumbent in general election, where candidate listed defeated an incumbent in the primary
  °° Primary runoff

Appendix C

SENATE GENERAL ELECTION CANDIDATES

Expenditures Reported by Top 10 Spenders
in 1974 Senate Races

† 1. Alan Cranston (D)		CA	$1,336,202
† 2. George McGovern (D)		SD	1,172,831
††† 3. John Glenn (D)		OH	1,149,130
† 4. Robert Dole (R)		KS	1,110,024
† 5. Jacob Javits (R)		NY	1,090,437
† 6. Birch Bayh (D)		IN	1,024,486
†† 7. Wendell Ford (D)		KY	1,006,670
††† 8. Richard Stone (D)	°°	FL	919,787
†† 9. Ramsey Clark (D)		NY	855,576
††10. William Roy (D)		KS	836,927

Eight Democrats and two Republicans are listed above.

Two incumbents who lost in the primary also spent substantial sums: Senator Howard Metzenbaum (D–OH), defeated by John Glenn (listed third above), spent $921,462, and Senator William Fulbright (D–AR) spent $837,481.

    † Incumbent
    †† Challenger to incumbent
    ††† Races with no incumbent in general election
    °° Primary runoff

CAMPAIGN EXPENDITURES IN 1974 HOUSE RACES COMPILED BY THE COMMON CAUSE CAMPAIGN MONITORING PROJECT

This list includes the total campaign expenditure figures for all major party candidates and significantly financed minor party or independent candidates in the 1974 general election.

The source of the information on campaign expenditures is the reports filed under the Federal Election Campaign Act of 1971. The totals cover the period between September 1, 1973, and December 31, 1974. Expenditures for each candidate were determined by combining the reports filed by each candidate with those filed by political committees exclusively supporting that candidate. Expenditures include all money spent by the campaign including debts outstanding (except loans outstanding) as of December 31, 1974. Expenditures do not include funds which have been invested in government bonds or certificates of deposit, or funds which have been used to repay loans made to the campaign. Adjustments have also been made to eliminate all transfers of funds within a campaign.

On the list, winning candidates are listed first. Incumbents are indicated by an asterisk (*). The races printed in *italic* are those in which there was no incumbent in the general election. Candidates indicated by a double asterisk (**) won their primary after a runoff election. The primary vote percentage listed for those candidates is for the runoff. *Congressional Quarterly* is the source of all data on vote percentages.

EXPENDITURES FOR ALL NOVEMBER 1974 HOUSE RACES

Cong. Dist.	SOURCE: *Common Cause* Campaign Monitoring Project	*Primary Vote* %	*General Election Vote* %	*Expenditures*
ALABAMA				
1	Jack Edwards* (R)	No Opp.	59.5	$ 69,347
	Augusta E. Wilson (D)	No Opp.	37.0	57,288
2	William L. Dickinson* (R)	No Opp.	66.1	33,071
	Clair Chisler (D)	No Opp.	33.9	6,134
3	Bill Nichols* (D)	No Opp.	95.9	2,538
4	Tom Bevill* (D)	No Opp.	99.8	5,174
5	Robert E. Jones* (D)	No Opp.	No Opp.	1,262
6	John Buchanan* (R)	No Opp.	56.6	65,235
	Nina Miglionico (D)	64.6	41.0	71,291
7	Walter Flowers* (D)	66.3	91.0	26,604
ALASKA				
1	Donald E. Young* (R)	No Opp.	53.8	140,729
	William L. Hensley (D)	50.2	46.2	136,112
ARIZONA				
1	John J. Rhodes* (R)	No Opp.	51.1	136,038
	Patricia M. Fullinwider (D)	69.1	42.3	20,136
2	Morris K. Udall* (D)	No Opp.	62.0	66,130
	Keith Dolgaard (R)	65.7	38.0	100,581
3	Sam Steiger* (R)	No Opp.	51.1	203,899
	Pat Bosch (D)	50.5	48.9	68,203
4	John B. Conlan* (R)	No Opp.	55.3	97,922
	Byron T. Brown (D)	No Opp.	44.7	55,126

ARKANSAS

1	Bill Alexander* (D)	No Opp.	90.6	$ 19,691
	James L. Dauer (R)	No Opp.	9.3	1,060
2	Wilbur D. Mills* (D)	No Opp.	58.9	71,338
	Judy Petty (R)	No Opp.	41.1	55,573
3	J. P. Hammerschmidt* (R)	No Opp.	51.8	101,709
	Bill Clinton** (D)	69.0	48.2	180,882
4	Ray Thornton* (D)	No Opp.	No Opp.	1,567

  * Incumbent
 ** Primary runoff winner

CALIFORNIA

1	Harold Johnson* (D)	80.1	85.8	30,467
2	Don H. Clausen* (R)	82.9	53.0	75,641
	Oscar Klee (D)	28.8	42.7	53,942
3	John Moss* (D)	No Opp.	72.3	23,145
	Ivaldo Lenci (R)	No Opp.	27.7	2,267
4	Robert Leggett* (D)	No Opp.	No Opp.	11,977
5	John L. Burton* (D)	70.5	59.6	25,457
	Thomas Caylor (R)	61.3	37.7	37,712
6	Phillip Burton* (D)	No Opp.	71.3	32,038
	Tom Spinosa (R)	No Opp.	21.8	10,749
7	*George Miller (D)*	*36.1*	*55.6*	*95,000*
	Gary Fernandez (R)	*No Opp.*	*44.4*	*76,829*
8	Ronald V. Dellums* (D)	69.6	56.6	78,339
	Jack Redden (R)	47.6	39.6	19,878
9	Fortney Stark* (D)	81.1	70.6	60,642
	Edson Adams (R)	No Opp.	29.4	23,778
10	Don Edwards* (D)	77.8	77.0	17,948
	John Enright (R)	51.9	23.0	425
11	Leo Ryan* (D)	83.5	75.8	22,778
	Brainard Merdinger (R)	No Opp.	21.3	2,074
12	Paul N. McCloskey* (R)	49.8	69.1	166,441
	Gary Gillmor (D)	31.9	30.9	37,128
13	*Norman Y. Mineta (D)*	*77.8*	*52.6*	*185,236*
	George W. Milias (R)	*46.3*	*42.4*	*122,239*
14	John McFall* (D)	80.6	70.9	52,268
	Charles Gibson (R)	55.6	24.1	4,154

15	B. F. Sisk° (D)	No Opp.	72.0	$ 55,723
	Carol Harner (R)	No Opp.	28.0	5,303
16	Burt L. Talcott° (R)	No Opp.	49.2	152,455
	Julian Camacho (D)	61.7	47.8	156,084
17	John Krebs (D)	61.5	51.9	130,193
	Robert B. Mathias° (R)	82.2	48.1	136,407
18	William Ketchum° (R)	71.7	52.7	69,806
	George Seielstad (D)	51.4	47.3	48,604
19	Robert J. Lagomersino° (R)	91.0	56.3	74,832
	James Loebl (D)	60.0	43.7	90,337
20	Barry M. Goldwater, Jr.° (R)	91.3	61.2	80,385
	Arline Mathews (D)	42.8	38.8	21,212
21	James C. Corman° (D)	No Opp.	73.5	77,204[1]
	Mel Nadell (R)	No Opp.	26.5	3,603
22	Carlos Moorhead° (R)	86.2	55.8	51,841
	Richard Hallin (D)	66.6	44.2	68,449
23	Thomas M. Rees° (D)	93.1	71.4	80,318
	Jack Roberts (R)	No Opp.	28.6	5,520
24	*Henry A. Waxman (D)*	*74.2*	*64.0*	*95,151*
	Elliott Graham (R)	*30.5*	*33.0*	*22,411*
25	Edward R. Roybal° (D)	No Opp.	No Opp.	24,630
26	John Rousselot° (R)	No Opp.	58.9	66,043
	Paul Conforti (D)	48.9	41.1	8,235
27	Alphonzo Bell° (R)	81.6	63.9	32,270
	John Dalessio (D)	36.1	32.5	29,025
28	Yvonne Burke° (D)	89.8	80.1	29,739
	Tom Neddy (R)	No Opp.	19.9	0
29	Augustus Hawkins° (D)	87.0	No Opp.	6,268
30	George Danielson° (D)	53.6	74.2	64,413
	John Perez (R)	37.7	25.8	5,953
31	Charles H. Wilson° (D)	56.2	70.4	70,813
	Norman Hodges (R)	No Opp.	26.8	38,954
32	Glenn Anderson° (D)	No Opp.	87.7	44,232
33	Del Clawson° (R)	No Opp.	53.4	80,347
	Robert White (D)	21.2	43.1	56,364
34	*Mark W. Hannaford (D)*	*24.1*	*49.8*	*86,981*
	Bill Bond (R)	*44.9*	*46.3*	*82,917*

35	Jim Lloyd (D)	23.4	50.3	$153,087
	Victor V. Veysey° (R)	75.5	49.7	147,861
36	George Brown° (D)	75.7	62.6	43,635
	Jim Osgood (R)	81.8	32.3	21,412
37	Jerry Pettis° (R)	No Opp.	63.2	33,818
	Bobby Ray Vincent (D)	39.9	32.9	9,732
38	*Jerry M. Patterson (D)*	*46.6*	*54.0*	*165,696*
	David Rehmann (R)	*46.1*	*41.3*	*120,744*
39	Charles Wiggins° (R)	74.4	55.3	53,292
	William Farris (D)	38.6	40.4	26,533
40	Andrew J. Hinshaw° (R)	69.5	63.4	72,022
	Roderick Wilson (d)	49.0	30.9	11,781
41	Bob Wilson° (R)	No Opp.	54.5	149,467
	Colleen O'Connor (D)	29.9	43.0	51,980
42	Lionel Van Deerlin° (D)	No Opp.	69.9	38,462
	Wes Marden (R)	No Opp.	30.1	10,555
43	Clair Burgener° (R)	No Opp.	60.4	64,022
	Bill Bandes (D)	49.1	39.6	22,055

[1] According to the office of Rep. James Corman (D–Cal), the total expenditure listed includes congressional office expenses and therefore is not exclusively campaign expenditures.

COLORADO

1	Patricia Schroeder° (D)	No Opp.	58.5	104,126
	Frank K. Southworth (R)	No Opp.	40.8	105,532
2	Timothy E. Wirth (D)	No Opp.	51.9	134,103
	Donald G. Brotzman° (R)	No Opp.	48.0	165,911
3	Frank Evans° (D)	62.1	67.9	30,855
	E. Keith Records (R)	No Opp.	32.1	5,120
4	James P. Johnson° (R)	No Opp.	52.0	53,940
	John S. Carroll (D)	No Opp.	48.0	62,704
5	William L. Armstrong° (R)	No Opp.	57.7	108,701
	Ben Galloway (D)	No Opp.	38.5	32,446

CONNECTICUT

1	William Cotter° (D)	No Opp.	62.7	52,604
	F. Mac Buckley (R)	No Opp.	35.9	28,045
2	*Christopher J. Dodd (D)*	*No Opp.*	*59.0*	*102,209*
	Samuel B. Hellier (R)	*No Opp.*	*39.2*	*87,844*
3	Robert Giaimo° (D)	No Opp.	65.1	40,079
	James Altham, Jr. (R)	No Opp.	31.4	6,556

4	Stewart B. McKinney° (R)	No Opp.	53.2	$ 94,365
	James Kellis (D)	No Opp.	45.2	51,034
5	Ronald A. Sarasin° (R)	No Opp.	50.4	134,440
	William R. Ratchford (D)	61.2	48.0	86,808
6	*Anthony J. Moffett (D)*	*58.0*	*63.4*	*144,806*
	Patsy J. Piscopo (R)	*No Opp.*	*36.1*	*89,328*

DELAWARE

| 1 | Pierre DuPont° (R) | No Opp. | 58.5 | 92,246 |
| | James Soles (D) | No Opp. | 39.6 | 68,839 |

FLORIDA

1	Robert Sikes° (D)	No Opp.	No Opp.	5,740
2	Don Fuqua° (D)	85.7	No Opp.	32,316
3	Charles Bennett° (D)	86.4	No Opp.	2,728
4	Bill Chappell, Jr.° (D)	No Opp.	68.2	63,817
	Warren Hauser (R)	No Opp.	31.8	17,116
5	*Richard Kelley (R)*	*52.9*	*52.8*	*111,194*
	JoAnn Saunders°° (D)	*55.9*	*44.8*	*62,119*
6	C. W. Bill Young° (R)	No Opp.	75.8	32,105
	Herbert Monrose (D)	No Opp.	24.2	4,771
7	Sam Gibbons° (D)	No Opp.	No Opp.	6,228
8	James Haley° (D)	74.8	56.7	15,879
	Joe Lovingood°° (R)	64.7	43.3	45,650
9	Louis Frey, Jr.° (R)	No Opp.	76.7	53,787
	William Rowland (D)	52.9	23.3	5,044
10	Skip Bafalis° (R)	No Opp.	73.7	32,735
	Evelyn Tucker (D)	No Opp.	26.3	4,360
11	Paul Rogers° (D)	85.6	No Opp.	15,517
12	J. Herbert Burke° (R)	74.5	51.0	30,554
	Charles Friedman°° (D)	51.1	49.0	32,038
13	William Lehman°° (D)	67.7	No Opp.	81,915
14	Claude Pepper° (D)	No Opp.	69.1	26,393
	Michael Carricarte (R)	56.8	30.9	18,631
15	Dante Fascell° (D)	No Opp.	70.5	41,957
	S. Peter Capua (R)	No Opp.	29.5	47,775

GEORGIA

1	Ronald B. Ginn° (D)	No Opp.	86.1	27,277
	Bill Gowan (R)	No Opp.	13.9	1,627
2	Dawson Mathis° (D)	No Opp.	No Opp.	16,201

3	Jack Brinkley° (D)	No Opp.	87.7	$ 26,824
	Carl Savage (R)	No Opp.	12.3	12,520
4	Elliott H. Levitas (D)	62.7	55.1	121,724
	Ben B. Blackburn° (R)	No Opp.	44.9	160,151
5	Andrew Young° (D)	No Opp.	71.6	83,481
	Wyman Lowe (R)	No Opp.	28.3	7,713
6	John Flynt, Jr.° (D)	No Opp.	51.5	33,035
	Newt Gingrich (R)	No Opp.	48.5	85,505
7	*Lawrence P. McDonald (D)*	*51.7*	*50.3*	*188,093*
	Quincy Collins (R)	*73.1*	*49.7*	*66,827*
8	Bill Stuckey, Jr.° (D)	59.5	No Opp.	34,674
9	Phil Landrum° (D)	66.6	74.8	17,710
	Ronald Reeves (R)	No Opp.	25.2	2,140
10	Robert Stephens, Jr.° (D)	No Opp.	68.4	17,410
	Gary Pleger (R)	62.5	31.6	18,788

HAWAII

1	Spark Matsunaga° (D)	No Opp.	59.3	165,469
	William Paul (R)	No Opp.	40.7	29,799
2	Patsy T. Mink° (D)	70.0	62.6	97,104
	Carla Coray (R)	No Opp.	37.4	34,089

IDAHO

1	Steven D. Symms° (R)	No Opp.	58.3	125,268
	J. Ray Cox (D)	50.1	41.7	43,784
2	*George V. Hansen (R)*	*53.3*	*55.7*	*120,923*
	Max Hanson (D)	*76.2*	*44.3*	*20,982*

ILLINOIS

1	Ralph Metcalfe° (D)	No Opp.	93.7	37,900
	Oscar Haynes (R)	No Opp.	5.5	833
2	Morgan Murphy° (D)	79.2	87.5	12,299
	James Ginderske (R)	No Opp.	12.5	350
3	Martin A. Russo (D)	No Opp.	52.6	79,420
	Robert Hanrahan° (R)	81.2	47.4	40,912
4	Edward Derwinski° (R)	No Opp.	59.2	41,646
	Ronald Rodger (D)	53.3	40.8	18,301
5	John Kluczynski° (D)	No Opp.	86.0	22,269
	William Toms (R)	No Opp.	14.0	503
6	*Henry J. Hyde (R)*	*48.1*	*53.4*	*175,087*
	Edward V. Hanrahan (D)	*56.1*	*46.6*	*66,284*

7	Cardiss Collins° (D)	No Opp.	87.9	$ 7,292
	Donald Metzger (R)	No Opp.	12.1	16,207
8	Dan Rostenkowski° (D)	No Opp.	86.5	25,720
	Salvatore Oddo (R)	No Opp.	13.5	0
9	Sidney Yates° (D)	No Opp.	No Opp.	11,226
10	Abner J. Mikva (D)	No Opp.	50.9	286,225
	Samuel H. Young° (R)	No Opp.	49.1	251,249
11	Frank Annunzio° (D)	89.0	72.4	58,239
	Mitchell Zadrozny (R)	No Opp.	27.6	33,362
12	Philip Crane° (R)	No Opp.	61.1	60,122
	Betty Spence (D)	No Opp.	38.9	51,594
13	Robert McClory° (R)	71.0	54.5	38,921
	Stanley Beetham (D)	66.3	45.5	39,642
14	John Erlenborn° (R)	No Opp.	66.6	34,214
	Robert Renshaw (D)	47.0	33.4	3,474
15	*Tim L. Hall (D)*	*44.8*	*52.0*	*29,398*
	Clifford D. Carlson (R)	*24.1*	*45.6*	*110,540*
16	John B. Anderson° (R)	No Opp.	55.5	74,346
	Marshall Hungness (D)	No Opp.	28.7	4,587
17	George M. O'Brien° (R)	No Opp.	51.5	80,053
	John Houlihan (D)	73.3	48.5	24,863
18	Robert Michel° (R)	No Opp.	54.8	33,851
	Stephen Nordvall (D)	72.6	45.2	10,776
19	Tom Railsback° (R)	No Opp.	65.3	61,789
	Jim Gende (D)	50.3	34.7	43,533
20	Paul Findley° (R)	No Opp.	54.8	118,162
	Peter Mack (D)	52.7	45.2	53,369
21	Edward Madigan° (R)	No Opp.	65.8	68,372
	Richard Small (D)	52.2	34.2	21,431
22	George Shipley° (D)	No Opp.	59.8	50,328
	William A. Young (R)	71.3	40.2	91,781
23	Melvin Price° (D)	90.3	80.5	27,847
	Scott Randolph (R)	No Opp.	19.5	670
24	*Paul Simon (D)*	*68.4*	*59.6*	*223,163*
	Val Oshel (R)	*57.7*	*40.4*	*50,566*

INDIANA

1	Ray Madden° (D)	74.5	68.6	20,416
	Joseph Harkin (R)	57.4	31.4	10,369

2	Floyd J. Fithian (D)	No Opp.	61.1	$155,580
	Earl O. Landgrebe° (R)	No Opp.	38.9	73,909
3	John Brademas° (D)	79.6	64.1	145,733
	Virginia Black (R)	No Opp.	35.9	16,184
4	J. Edward Roush° (D)	89.8	51.9	57,615
	Walter P. Helmke (R)	68.0	46.5	77,576
5	Elwood Hillis° (R)	No Opp.	56.6	55,490
	William Sebree (D)	27.6	43.4	18,758
6	David Evans (D)	55.4	52.4	15,846
	William Bray° (R)	88.5	47.6	45,434
7	John Myers° (R)	No Opp.	57.1	44,556
	Eldon Tipton (D)	32.9	42.1	13,916
8	Philip Hayes (D)	48.4	53.4	67,429
	Roger H. Zion° (R)	87.0	46.6	122,329
9	Lee Hamilton° (D)	No Opp.	71.1	69,375
	Delson Cox, Jr. (R)	39.5	28.9	7,553
10	Philip R. Sharp (D)	68.5	54.4	74,199
	David W. Dennis° (R)	88.4	45.6	79,840
11	Andrew Jacobs, Jr. (D)	86.4	52.5	47,336
	William H. Hudnut° (R)	94.0	47.5	201,673

IOWA

1	Edward Mezvinsky° (D)	No Opp.	54.4	81,166
	James A. Leach (R)	No Opp.	45.6	89,786
2	*Michael T. Blouin (D)*	*45.4*	*51.1*	*137,750*
	Tom Riley (R)	*69.0*	*48.1*	*107,884*
3	*Charles E. Grassley (R)*	*41.9*	*50.8*	*107,102*
	Stephen J. Rapp (D)	*35.8*	*49.2*	*100,007*
4	Neal Smith° (D)	No Opp.	63.9	0
	Chuck Dick (R)	No Opp.	35.5	55,231
5	Tom Harkin (D)	No Opp.	51.1	120,544
	William J. Scherle° (R)	No Opp.	48.9	103,582
6	Berkley Bedell (D)	No Opp.	54.6	130,742
	Wiley Mayne° (R)	No Opp.	45.4	96,085

KANSAS

1	Keith Sibelius° (R)	No Opp.	58.4	60,893
	Donald Smith (D)	46.0	33.0	64,428
2	*Martha Keys (D)*	*38.4*	*55.0*	*88,959*
	John C. Peterson (R)	*57.6*	*43.9*	*114,214*

214

3	Larry Winn, Jr.° (R)	No Opp.	62.9	$ 77,681
	Samuel Wells (D)	50.6	35.0	26,318
4	Garner Shriver° (R)	No Opp.	48.8	67,446
	Bert Chaney (D)	43.1	42.5	24,467
	John S. Stevens (A)		8.7	2,922
5	Joe Skubitz° (R)	86.9	55.2	63,968
	Franklin D. Gaines (D)	57.6	44.8	99,553

KENTUCKY

1	*Carroll Hubbard, Jr. (D)*	*50.5*	*78.2*	*64,599*
	Charles Banken, Jr. (R)	*41.0*	*18.7*	*1,350*
2	William Natcher° (D)	74.9	73.0	14,505
	Art Eddleman (R)	No Opp.	23.7	21
3	Romano Mazzoli° (D)	90.8	69.7	28,353
	Vincent Barclay (R)	No Opp.	26.6	2,446
4	Gene Snyder° (R)	No Opp.	51.7	86,973
	Kyle Hubbard (D)	52.0	48.3	82,150
5	Tim Lee Carter° (R)	No Opp.	68.2	18,763
	Lyle Willis (D)	45.9	29.3	228
6	John Breckinridge° (D)	83.0	72.1	20,932
	Thomas Rogers III (R)	60.6	24.1	2,217
7	Carl Perkins° (D)	No Opp.	75.6	2,100
	Granville Thomas (R)	No Opp.	24.4	104

LOUISIANA

1	F. Edward Hebert° (D)	80.1	No Opp.	4,712
2	Corinne Boggs° (D)	87.2	81.8	49,846
	Diane Morphos (R)	No Opp.	14.6	7,192
3	David C. Treen° (R)	No Opp.	58.5	190,135
	Charles Grisbaum, Jr. (D)	No Opp.	41.5	166,203
4	Joe D. Waggonner, Jr.° (D)	No Opp.	No Opp.	3,459
5	Otto E. Passman° (D)	73.6	No Opp.	23,902
6	*Henson Moore III (R)*	*No Opp.*	*54.1*	*158,971*
	Jeff LaCaze°° (D)	*51.6*	*45.9*	*229,335*
7	John Breaux° (D)	87.7	89.3	29,991
8	Gillis W. Long° (D)	No Opp.	No Opp.	36,325

MAINE

| 1 | David Emery (R) | No Opp. | 50.2 | 68,040 |
| | Peter Kyros° (D) | 69.1 | 49.8 | 68,094 |

| 2 | William S. Cohen° (R) | No Opp. | 71.4 | $ 91,548 |
| | Markham Gartley (D) | 65.8 | 28.6 | 30,412 |

MARYLAND
1	Robert E. Bauman° (R)	No Opp.	53.0	137,046
	Thomas Hatem (D)	56.2	47.0	48,043
2	Clarence D. Long° (D)	No Opp.	77.1	33,181
	John Seney (R)	No Opp.	22.9	6,234
3	Paul Sarbanes° (D)	No Opp.	83.8	8,765
	William Matthews (R)	No Opp.	16.2	193
4	Marjorie S. Holt° (r)	No Opp.	58.1	99,717
	Fred L. Wineland (D)	54.9	41.9	134,323
5	*Gladys N. Spellman (D)*	*67.1*	*52.6*	*90,144*
	John B. Burcham, Jr. (R)	*74.0*	*47.4*	*39,038*
6	Goodloe Byron° (D)	75.1	73.7	31,308
	Elton Wampler (R)	No Opp.	26.3	11,556
7	Parren J. Mitchell° (D)	No Opp.	No Opp.	22,376
8	Gilbert Gude° (R)	85.0	65.9	48,063
	Sidney Kramer (D)	44.8	34.1	43,889

MASSACHUSETTS
1	Silvio O. Conte° (R)	No Opp.	71.1	47,736
	Thomas R. Manning (D)	55.1	28.9	8,067
2	Edward P. Boland° (D)	No Opp.	No Opp.	56
3	*Joseph D. Early (D)*	*31.8*	*49.5*	*120,584*
	David J. Lionett (R)	*83.2*	*38.4*	*127,978*
	Douglas J. Rowe (Ind)		*12.0*	*69,267*
4	Robert F. Drinan° (D)	No Opp.	50.8	178,871
	Jon Rotenberg (Ind)	No Opp.	34.7	76,576
	Alvin Mandell (R)	No Opp.	14.4	14,322
5	Paul E. Tsongas (D)	72.5	60.6	105,267
	Paul W. Cronin° (R)	No Opp.	39.4	124,049
6	Michael J. Harrington° (D)	74.4	No Opp.	29,810
7	Torbert H. MacDonald° (D)	No Opp.	79.8	15,596
8	Thomas P. O'Neill, Jr.° (D)	No Opp.	87.9	1,414
9	John Joseph Moakley° (D)	No Opp.	89.3	74,237
10	Margaret Heckler° (R)	No Opp.	64.2	71,100
	Barry Monahan (D)	No Opp.	35.8	34,012
11	James A. Burke° (D)	73.1	No Opp.	39,707

12	Gerry Studds° (D)	No Opp.	74.8	$103,350
	J. Alan MacKay (R)	No Opp.	25.2	37,505

MICHIGAN

1	John Conyers, Jr.° (D)	No Opp.	90.7	20,292
	Walter Girardot (R)	No Opp.	8.7	85
2	Marvin L. Esch° (R)	No Opp.	52.3	106,747
	John S. Reuther (D)	31.5	45.4	112,860
3	Garry Brown° (R)	No Opp.	51.2	52,305
	Paul Todd, Jr. (D)	No Opp.	47.6	42,961
4	Edward Hutchinson° (R)	No Opp.	53.1	8,254
	Richard Daugherty (D)	No Opp.	45.5	7,606
5	Richard Vander Veen° (D)	No Opp.	52.6	143,603
	Paul G. Goebel (R)	54.5	43.4	158,891
	Dwight W. Johnson (AIP)		3.7	11,255
6	*Bob Carr (D)*	*72.4*	*49.3*	*157,478*
	Clifford W. Taylor (R)	*42.2*	*48.9*	*119,329*
7	Donald Riegle, Jr.° (D)	81.0	64.7	46,731
	Robert Eastman (R)	No Opp.	33.2	8,902
8	Bob Traxler° (D)	No Opp.	54.8	76,856
	James M. Sparling (R)	89.9	43.4	82,879
9	Guy Vander Jagt° (R)	No Opp.	56.6	51,196
	Norman Halbower (D)	No Opp.	42.1	21,382
10	Elford Cederberg° (R)	77.1	53.7	38,876
	Samuel Marble (D)	No Opp.	45.9	19,974
11	Philip Ruppe° (R)	No Opp.	50.9	45,240
	Francis Brouillette (D)	53.2	48.8	62,656
12	James G. O'Hara° (D)	No Opp.	72.2	22,289
	Eugene Tyza (R)	No Opp.	27.6	997
13	Charles Diggs, Jr.° (D)	No Opp.	87.4	400
	George McCall (R)	No Opp.	11.1	194
14	Lucien Nedzi° (D)	73.8	71.2	14,717
	Herbert Steiger (R)	No Opp.	27.1	0
15	William D. Ford° (D)	No Opp.	78.1	43,458
	Jack Underwood (R)	73.2	20.8	79
16	John Dingell° (D)	No Opp.	77.7	25,410
	Wallace English (R)	56.4	20.5	1,345
17	*William Brodhead (D)*	*27.4*	*69.5*	*55,180*
	Kenneth Gallagher (R)	*62.9*	*29.4*	*97*

18	James J. Blanchard (D)	33.8	58.7	$133,021
	Robert J. Huber° (R)	No Opp.	40.2	120,426
19	William Broomfield° (R)	No Opp.	62.9	34,439
	George Montgomery (D)	No Opp.	36.9	6,357

MINNESOTA

1	Albert Quie° (R)	No Opp.	62.6	67,101
	Uric Scott (D)	63.3	37.4	54,539
2	*Tom Hagedorn (R)*	*72.8*	*53.1*	*148,833*
	Steve Babcock (D)	*51.8*	*46.9*	*142,812*
3	Bill Frenzel° (R)	No Opp.	60.4	104,815
	Bob Riggs (D)	71.9	39.6	33,486
4	Joseph Karth° (D)	No Opp.	76.0	58,551
	Joseph Rheinberger (R)	68.0	24.0	5,740
5	Donald Fraser° (R)	No Opp.	73.8	63,397
	Phil Ratte (D)	No Opp.	24.7	13,340
6	*Richard Nolan (D)*	*69.9*	*55.4*	*139,342*
	Jon Grunseth (R)	*78.4*	*44.6*	*121,048*
7	Bob Bergland° (D)	No Opp.	75.0	92,608
	Dan Reber (R)	No Opp.	25.0	15,082
8	*James Oberstar (D)*	*50.3*	*62.0*	*106,186*
	Jerome Arnold (R)	*68.1*	*26.1*	*38,435*

MISSISSIPPI

1	Jamie L. Whitten° (D)	No Opp.	88.2	3,209
2	David R. Bowen° (D)	81.9	66.1	60,735
	Ben F. Hilburn (R)	No Opp.	27.7	27,000
3	G. V. Montgomery° (D)	No Opp.	No Opp.	0
4	Thad Cochran° (R)	98.5	70.2	83,884
	Kenneth L. Dean°° (D)	50.9	28.8	11,360
5	Trent Lott° (R)	No Opp.	73.0	31,464
	Walter W. Murphy (D)	50.1	14.4	2,163

MISSOURI

1	William Clay° (D)	67.8	68.3	43,810
	Arthur Martin (R)	53.9	31.7	1,881
2	James W. Symington° (D)	71.6	61.0	74,762
	Howard C. Ohlendorf (R)	No Opp.	39.0	43,330
3	Leonor K. Sullivan° (D)	89.5	74.3	27,800
	Jo Ann P. Raisch (R)	67.4	24.3	2,254
4	William J. Randall° (D)	86.7	67.9	19,596
	Claude Patterson (R)	No Opp.	32.1	12,771

5	Richard Bolling° (D)	86.6	69.1	$ 20,590
	John J. McDonough (R)	55.3	29.9	9,247
6	Jerry Litton° (D)	No Opp.	78.9	52,896
	Grover Speers (R)	No Opp.	21.1	745
7	Gene Taylor° (R)	76.0	52.3	96,782
	Richard L. Franks (D)	70.4	47.7	94,173
8	Richard H. Ichord° (D)	84.6	69.9	50,156
	James A. Noland, Jr. (R)	No Opp.	30.1	195
9	William L. Hungate° (D)	No Opp.	66.4	30,091
	Milton Bischof, Jr. (R)	No Opp.	33.6	13,369
10	Bill D. Burlison° (D)	80.1	72.8	28,021
	Truman Farrow (R)	59.6	27.2	2,063

MONTANA

1	Max S. Baucus (D)	43.6	54.8	111,096
	Richard G. Shoup° (R)	No Opp.	45.2	101,118
2	John Melcher° (D)	No Opp.	63.0	57,016
	John K. McDonald (R)	63.6	37.0	32,341

NEBRASKA

1	Charles Thone° (R)	No Opp.	53.3	98,307
	Hess Dyas (D)	No Opp.	46.7	133,261
2	John Y. McCollister° (R)	No Opp.	55.2	92,834
	Daniel C. Lynch (D)	64.2	44.8	87,691
3	*Virginia Smith (R)*	*21.7*	*50.2*	*102,820*
	Wayne W. Ziebarth (D)	*68.9*	*49.8*	*90,123*

NEVADA

1	James Santini (D)	53.8	55.8	122,199
	David Towell° (R)	87.1	36.4	111,697

NEW HAMPSHIRE

1	*Norman E. D'Amours (D)*	*49.8*	*52.1*	*75,128*
	David A. Banks (R)	*39.5*	*47.9*	*108,163*
2	James C. Cleveland° (R)	86.1	64.2	27,102
	Helen L. Bliss (D)	56.5	35.8	15,835

NEW JERSEY

1	James J. Florio (D)	82.8	57.5	97,679
	John E. Hunt° (R)	No Opp.	38.5	57,787
2	William J. Hughes (D)	54.7	57.3	119,864
	Charles W. Sandman, Jr.° (R)	No Opp.	41.3	98,734
3	James J. Howard° (D)	No Opp.	68.9	52,474
	Kenneth W. Clark (R)	No Opp.	29.8	15,231

219

4	Frank W. Thompson° (D)	64.9	66.8	$ 44,542
	Henry J. Keller (R)	No Opp.	33.2	11,891
5	*Millicent Fenwick (R)*	*47.9*	*53.4*	*131,861*
	Frederick Bohen (D)	*57.4*	*43.5*	*117,033*
6	Edwin B. Forsythe° (R)	93.3	52.5	46,521
	Charles B. Yates (D)	34.0	45.5	66,501
7	Andrew Maguire (D)	50.9	49.7	137,280
	William B. Widnall° (R)	63.4	44.4	49,575
	Milton Gralla (Ind)		5.9	26,404
8	Robert A. Roe° (D)	92.7	73.9	36,496
	Herman Schmidt (R)	No Opp.	24.6	415
9	Henry Helstoski° (D)	91.4	64.5	35,192
	Harold A. Pareti (R)	No Opp.	32.9	23,813
10	Peter W. Rodino, Jr.° (D)	89.0	81.0	26,286
	John R. Taliaferro (R)	No Opp.	15.2	0
11	Joseph G. Minish° (D)	No Opp.	69.2	47,606
	William B. Grant (R)	No Opp.	29.4	29,292
12	Matthew J. Rinaldo° (R)	92.6	65.0	128,915
	Adam K. Levin (D)	82.4	32.4	143,895
13	Helen S. Meyner (D)	47.2	57.3	129,289
	Joseph J. Maraziti° (R)	No Opp.	42.7	68,838
14	Dominick V. Daniels° (D)	94.3	79.9	80,556
	Claire J. Sheridan (R)	73.8	16.1	0
15	Edward J. Patten° (D)	No Opp.	71.0	38,113
	E. J. Hammesfahr (R)	No Opp.	27.5	11,165

NEW MEXICO

1	Manuel Lujan, Jr.° (R)	No Opp.	58.6	150,825
	R. A. Mondragon (D)	No Opp.	39.7	113,847
2	Harold Runnels° (D)	No Opp.	66.7	59,733
	Donald W. Trubey (R)	No Opp.	31.9	22,131

NEW YORK

1	Otis G. Pike° (D)	No Opp.	65.0	26,907
	Donald R. Sallah (R)	No Opp.	28.6	4,999
2	Thomas J. Downey (D)	No Opp.	48.8	44,423
	James R. Grover, Jr.° (R)	No Opp.	44.7	11,258
3	Jerome A. Ambro, Jr. (D)	No Opp.	51.8	77,140
	Angelo D. Roncallo° (R)	No Opp.	46.1	68,716
4	Norman F. Lent° (R)	No Opp.	53.6	53,568
	Franklin Ornstein (D)	No Opp.	46.4	70,256

5	John Wydler° (R)	No Opp.	54.2	$ 68,115
	Allard K. Lowenstein (D)	No Opp.	45.8	112,369
6	Lester L. Wolff° (D)	No Opp.	66.7	54,012
	Edythe Layne (R)	No Opp.	33.3	17,919
7	Joseph P. Addabbo° (D)	No Opp.	No Opp.	19,841
8	B. S. Rosenthal° (D)	No Opp.	79.0	14,100
	Albert Lemishow (R)	No Opp.	21.0	880
9	James J. Delaney° (D)	No Opp.	93.0	29,698
10	Mario Biaggi° (D)	No Opp.	82.4	16,524
11	*James H. Scheuer (D)*	*53.4*	*72.2*	*301,135*
	E. G. Desborough (R)	*No Opp.*	*14.2*	*809*
12	Shirley Chisholm° (D)	69.4	80.2	8,947
	Francis J. Voyticky (R)	No Opp.	13.9	0
13	*Stephen J. Solarz (D)*	*43.8*	*81.8*	*67,334*
	Jack N. Dobosh (R)	*No Opp.*	*18.2*	*623*
14	*F. W. Richmond (D)*	*42.1*	*71.3*	*245,533*
	Michael Carbajal, Jr. (R)	*No Opp.*	*11.5*	*1,000*
	Donald Elliott (Lib)	*27.1[1]*	*13.5*	*85,680*
15	*Leo C. Zeferetti (D)*	*50.1*	*58.4*	*53,775*
	Austen Canade (R)	*No Opp.*	*37.9*	*39,133*
16	Elizabeth Holtzman° (D)	No Opp.	78.9	31,746
	Joseph Gentilli (R)	No Opp.	21.1	1,249
17	John M. Murphy° (D)	51.1	57.7	75,272
	Frank J. Biondolillo (R)	No Opp.	25.6	6,760
18	Edward I. Koch° (D)	No Opp.	76.7	57,530
	John Boogaerts, Jr. (R)	No Opp.	18.8	14,156
19	Charles B. Rangel° (D)	No Opp.	96.9	15,536
20	Bella S. Abzug° (D)	No Opp.	78.7	12,655
	Stephen Posner (R)	No Opp.	15.6	224
21	Herman Badillo° (D)	No Opp.	96.7	7,476
22	Jonathan B. Bingham° (D)	No Opp.	85.1	6,545
	Robert Black (R)	No Opp.	9.0	0
23	Peter A. Peyser° (R)	78.4	57.6	73,506
	W. S. Greenawalt (D)	No Opp.	42.4	53,111
24	*Richard L. Ottinger (D)*	*No Opp.*	*57.8*	*120,896*
	C. J. Stephens (R)	*No Opp.*	*42.2*	*60,458*
25	Hamilton Fish, Jr.° (R)	No Opp.	65.3	56,398
	Nicholas B. Angell (D)	No Opp.	33.6	105,404

26	Benjamin A. Gilman° (R)	No Opp.	54.0	$ 91,812
	John G. Dow (D)	No Opp.	38.5	44,465
27	*Matthew F. McHugh (D)*	*50.0*	*52.8*	*56,361*
	Alfred J. Libous (R)	*43.9*	*43.1*	*62,196*
	Franklin B. Resseguie (Con)		*4.1*	*31,904*
28	Samuel S. Stratton° (D)	89.7	80.6	26,618
	Wayne E. Wagner (R)	61.5	17.3	12,232
29	Edward W. Pattison (D)	43.0	54.5	36,227
	Carleton J. King° (R)	59.8	45.5	35,962
30	Robert C. McEwen° (R)	No Opp.	55.0	15,710
	Roger W. Tubby (D)	No Opp.	45.0	25,944
31	Donald J. Mitchell° (R)	No Opp.	59.6	71,642
	Donald J. Reile (D)	51.8	37.7	30,820
32	James M. Hanley° (D)	No Opp.	59.1	70,820
	William E. Bush (R)	No Opp.	40.9	24,942
33	William F. Walsh° (R)	No Opp.	65.3	39,085
	Robert H. Bockman (D)	No Opp.	30.2	4,857
34	Frank Horton° (R)	No Opp.	67.5	68,207
	Irene Gossin (D)	No Opp.	29.0	26,379
35	Barber B. Conable, Jr.° (R)	No Opp.	56.8	75,157
	Margaret Costanza (D)	46.8	39.6	79,560
36	*John J. La Falce (D)*	*69.2*	*59.6*	*65,761*
	Russell A. Rourke (R)	*No Opp.*	*40.4*	*95,249*
37	*Henry J. Nowak (D)*	*No Opp.*	*75.0*	*14,841*
	Joseph R. Bala (R)	*No Opp.*	*24.6*	*22,118*
38	Jack F. Kemp° (R)	No Opp.	72.1	111,609
	Barbara C. Wicks (D)	No Opp.	27.9	11,038
39	James F. Hastings° (R)	No Opp.	60.2	39,974
	W. L. Parment (D)	No Opp.	37.1	7,857

[1] Primary results are for Democratic primary in which Elliott lost to Richmond.

NORTH CAROLINA

1	Walter B. Jones° (D)	90.0	77.5	14,958
	Harry McMullan (R)	No Opp.	22.5	23,729
2	L. H. Fountain° (D)	No Opp.	No Opp.	923
3	David N. Henderson° (D)	No Opp.	No Opp.	560
4	Ike F. Andrews° (D)	63.7	64.7	111,307
	Ward Purrington (R)	No Opp.	34.6	95,418

5	Stephen L. Neal (D)	83.4	52.0	$ 61,107
	Wilmer Mizell° (R)	No Opp.	47.6	62,930
6	Richardson Preyer° (D)	No Opp.	63.7	66,534
	R. S. Ritchie (R)	No Opp.	35.9	85,604
7	Charles G. Rose III° (D)	60.4	No Opp.	39,315
8	W. G. Hefner (D)	No Opp.	57.0	71,793
	Earl B. Ruth° (R)	No Opp.	43.0	35,603
9	James G. Martin° (R)	No Opp.	54.4	128,937
	Milton Short (D)	53.4	44.1	54,071
10	James T. Broyhill° (R)	No Opp.	54.4	78,850
	Jack L. Rhyne (D)	72.4	45.6	19,607
11	Roy A. Taylor° (D)	No Opp.	66.0	18,796
	Albert F. Gilman (R)	No Opp.	34.0	5,999

NORTH DAKOTA

1	Mark Andrews° (R)	78.4	55.7	86,855
	Byron Dorgan (D)	No Opp.	44.3	50,990

OHIO

1	Willis D. Gradison, Jr. (R)	52.1	50.9	126,407
	Thomas Luken° (D)	No Opp.	49.1	79,500
2	Donald D. Clancy° (R)	No Opp.	53.4	33,369
	E. W. Wolterman (D)	50.4	46.6	13,089
3	Charles W. Whalen, Jr.° (R)	No Opp.	No Opp.	2,545
4	Tennyson Guyer° (R)	No Opp.	61.5	26,471
	J. L. Gehrlich (D)	54.0	38.5	8,704
5	Delbert L. Latta° (R)	No Opp.	62.5	26,183
	Bruce Edwards (D)	No Opp.	37.5	7,790
6	William H. Harsha° (R)	No Opp.	68.2	14,306
	Lloyd A. Wood (D)	No Opp.	31.2	9,085
7	Clarence J. Brown, Jr.° (R)	No Opp.	60.5	94,367
	Patrick L. Nelson (D)	62.7	28.7	27,676
8	*Thomas N. Kindness (R)*	*37.0*	*42.4*	*75,516*
	T. Edward Strinko (D)	*34.8*	*38.0*	*72,951*
	Don Gingerich (Ind)		*19.6*	*36,039*
9	Thomas L. Ashley° (D)	78.9	52.8	24,409
	C. S. Finkbeiner, Jr. (R)	51.5	47.2	33,472
10	Clarence E. Miller° (R)	No Opp.	70.4	20,052
	H. Kent Bumpass (D)	No Opp.	29.6	2,423
11	J. William Stanton° (R)	No Opp.	60.5	25,834
	Michael D. Coffey (D)	60.0	39.5	35,009

12	Samuel L. Devine° (R)	No Opp.	50.9	$ 73,858
	Fran Ryan (D)	No Opp.	49.1	94,243
13	Charles A. Mosher° (R)	No Opp.	57.5	17,254
	Fred M. Ritenauer (D)	60.7	42.5	14,889
14	John F. Sieberling, Jr.° (D)	No Opp.	75.4	16,666
	Mark Figetakis (R)	No Opp.	24.6	13,840
15	Chalmers P. Wylie° (R)	No Opp.	61.5	61,241
	Mike McGee (D)	68.9	38.5	21,960
16	Ralph S. Regula° (R)	No Opp.	65.6	61,552
	John G. Freedom (D)	42.9	34.4	15,985
17	John M. Ashbrook° (R)	65.3	52.7	90,357
	David D. Noble (D)	No Opp.	47.3	57,646
18	Wayne L. Hays° (D)	79.5	65.6	32,285
	Ralph Romig (R)	No Opp.	34.4	2,347
19	Charles J. Carney° (D)	76.8	72.7	15,133
	James L. Ripple (R)	No Opp.	27.3	794
20	James V. Stanton° (D)	86.8	86.9	26,109
	Robert A. Frantz (R)	No Opp.	13.1	1,757
21	Louis Stokes° (D)	70.7	82.0	42,214
	Bill Mack (R)	No Opp.	18.0	0
22	Charles A. Vanik° (D)	89.1	78.7	649
	William J. Franz (R)	No Opp.	21.3	4,190
23	*Ronald M. Mottl (D)*	*42.7*	*34.8*	*63,671*
	George E. Mastics (R)	*66.8*	*30.5*	*78,348*
	Dennis J. Kucinich (Ind)		*29.4*	*18,195*

OKLAHOMA

1	James Jones° (D)	81.4	67.9	60,686
	George A. Mizer, Jr. (R)	68.4	32.1	17,878
2	*T. M. Risenhoover °° (D)*	*52.0*	*59.1*	*79,791*
	Ralph F. Keen (R)	*53.8*	*40.9*	*19,395*
3	Carl Albert° (D)	81.7	No Opp.	18,034
4	Tom Steed° (D)	No Opp.	No Opp.	7,451
5	John Jarman° (D)	61.0	51.7	46,295
	M. H. Edwards (R)	No Opp.	48.3	31,255
6	Glenn L. English, Jr.°° (D)	56.4	53.2	78,411
	John N. Camp° (R)	58.1	44.4	53,532

OREGON

1	*Les AuCoin (D)*	*48.9*	*56.0*	*95,168*
	Diarmuid O'Scannlain (R)	*38.8*	*43.9*	*83,659*

2	Al Ullman° (D)	81.2	78.1	$ 49,496
	Kenneth Brown (R)	No Opp.	21.9	629
3	*Robert Duncan (D)*	*34.4*	*70.4*	*84,124*
	John Piacentini (R)	*66.3*	*29.5*	*54,285*
4	James Weaver (D)	35.5	52.9	42,271
	John Dellenback° (R)	No Opp.	47.1	52,614

PENNSYLVANIA

1	William A. Barrett° (D)	No Opp.	75.8	14,729
	Russell M. Nigro (R)	No Opp.	23.3	7,841
2	Robert N. C. Nix° (D)	55.7	74.0	12,122
	Jesse W. Woods, Jr. (R)	No Opp.	26.0	15,833
3	William J. Green° (D)	No Opp.	75.4	51,066
	Richard P. Colbert (R)	No Opp.	24.6	3,082
4	Joshua Eilberg° (D)	76.3	71.0	45,286
	Isadore Einhorn (R)	No Opp.	29.0	4,059
5	*Richard T. Schulze (R)*	*43.5*	*59.6*	*29,965*
	Leo D. McDermott (D)	*53.4*	*40.4*	*39,922*
6	Gus Yatron° (D)	No Opp.	74.6	42,670
	Stephen Postupack (R)	No Opp.	24.0	9,326
7	*Robert W. Edgar (D)*	*65.5*	*55.3*	*38,819*
	S. J. McEwen, Jr. (R)	*50.4*	*43.7*	*110,075*
8	Edward G. Biester, Jr.° (R)	67.1	56.3	9,660
	William B. Moyer (D)	76.3	40.9	24,343
9	E. G. Shuster° (R)	No Opp.	56.5	60,691
	Robert D. Ford (D)	51.6	43.5	32,281
10	Joseph M. McDade° (R)	No Opp.	64.9	34,512
	Thomas J. Hanlon (D)	54.4	35.1	11,146
11	Daniel J. Flood° (D)	No Opp.	74.5	40,699
	Richard A. Muzyka (R)	No Opp.	25.5	3,369
12	John P. Murtha° (D)	85.2	58.1	58,192
	Harry M. Fox (R)	69.2	41.9	42,598
13	R. Lawrence Coughlin° (R)	No Opp.	62.5	62,677
	Lawrence H. Curry (D)	60.0	37.5	22,039
14	William S. Moorhead° (D)	No Opp.	77.4	23,929
	Zachary Taylor Davis (R)	No Opp.	22.5	1,129
15	Fred B. Rooney° (D)	No Opp.	No Opp.	12,261
16	Edwin D. Eshleman° (R)	84.0	63.5	6,996
	Michael J. Minney (D)	No Opp.	35.0	4,507

17	Herman T. Schneebeli° (R)	No Opp.	52.1	$ 47,611
	Peter C. Wambach (D)	50.3	47.9	38,899
18	H. John Heinz III° (R)	No Opp.	72.1	89,449
	Francis J. McArdle (D)	57.7	27.9	23,727
19	*William F. Goodling (R)*	*39.8*	*51.4*	*42,944*
	Arthur L. Berger (D)	*25.5*	*47.6*	*67,162*
20	Joseph M. Gaydos° (D)	No Opp.	81.7	24,778
	Joseph J. Anderko (R)	No Opp.	18.3	101
21	John H. Dent° (D)	No Opp.	69.9	26,636
	C. L. Sconing (R)	57.4	30.1	5,324
22	Thomas E. Morgan° (D)	31.8	63.6	64,572
	J. R. Montgomery (R)	93.4	31.7	173
23	Albert W. Johnson° (R)	54.4	52.7	50,758
	Yates Mast (D)	28.2	47.3	10,870
24	Joseph P. Vigorito° (D)	68.7	58.6	16,327
	Clement R. Scalzitti (R)	No Opp.	41.4	3,619
25	Gary A. Myers (R)	30.9	53.8	33,064
	Frank M. Clark° (D)	56.2	46.2	88,588

RHODE ISLAND

1	Fernand J. St. Germain° (D)	No Opp.	72.9	59,244
	Ernest Barone (R)	No Opp.	27.1	3,556
2	*Edward Beard (D)*	*51.8*	*78.2*	*20,583*
	Vincent J. Rotondo (R)	*No Opp.*	*21.8*	*41,113*

SOUTH CAROLINA

1	Mendel J. Davis° (D)	No Opp.	72.7	40,729
	George B. Rast (R)	No Opp.	25.9	0
2	Floyd Spence° (R)	No Opp.	56.1	167,188
	Matthew J. Perry (D)	57.1	43.0	92,813
3	*Butler C. Derrick, Jr. (D)*	*65.2*	*61.8*	*176,022*
	Marshall J. Parker (R)	*No Opp.*	*38.2*	*105,897*
4	James R. Mann° (D)	No Opp.	63.3	26,536
	Robert L. Watkins (R)	No Opp.	36.7	13,994
5	*Kenneth L. Holland°° (D)*	*53.0*	*61.4*	*96,834*
	Len Phillips (R)	*No Opp.*	*37.8*	*44,759*
6	John W. Jenrette, Jr. (D)	No Opp.	52.0	150,887
	Edward L. Young° (R)	No Opp.	48.0	145,823

SOUTH DAKOTA

1	Larry Pressler (R)	51.3	55.3	58,106
	Frank E. Denholm° (D)	No Opp.	44.7	20,583

| 2 | James Abdnor* (R) | No Opp. | 67.8 | $ 66,250 |
| | Jack M. Weiland (D) | No Opp. | 32.2 | 58,907 |

TENNESSEE

1	James H. Quillen* (R)	No Opp.	64.2	10,683
	Lloyd Blevins (D)	No Opp.	35.8	2,013
2	John J. Duncan* (R)	95.6	70.9	28,825
	Jesse James Brown (D)	65.8	29.1	0
3	Marilyn Lloyd (D)	[1]	51.1	44,920
	LaMar Baker* (R)	No Opp.	45.9	96,717
4	Joe L. Evins* (D)	No Opp.	99.9	4,776
5	Richard Fulton* (D)	76.2	99.8	34,502
6	Robin L. Beard* (R)	No Opp.	56.7	189,216
	Tim Schaeffer (D)	48.9	43.3	96,288
7	Ed Jones* (D)	70.7	No Opp.	74,880
8	Harold E. Ford (D)	54.7	49.9	146,940
	Dan Kuykendall* (R)	81.9	49.4	132,411

[1] Mrs. Lloyd replaced her husband, deceased, as the nominee.

TEXAS

1	Wright Patman* (D)	53.4	68.6	141,936
	J. W. Farris (R)	No Opp.	31.4	111,902
2	Charles Wilson* (D)	No Opp.	No Opp.	18,405
3	James M. Collins* (R)	82.4	64.7	192,058
	Harold Collum (D)	58.9	35.3	79,372
4	Ray Roberts* (D)	No Opp.	74.9	16,337
	Dick LeTourneau (R)	No Opp.	25.1	28,765
5	Alan Steelman* (R)	No Opp.	52.1	168,457
	Mike McKool (D)	51.4	47.9	122,086
6	Olin E. Teague* (D)	No Opp.	83.0	7,249
	Carl A. Nigliazzo (R)	No Opp.	17.0	1,203
7	Bill Archer* (R)	No Opp.	79.2	80,941
	Jim Brady (D)	76.8	20.8	10,827
8	Bob Eckhardt* (D)	76.3	72.2	12,841
	Donald D. Whitefield (R)	No Opp.	27.8	10,008
9	Jack Brooks* (D)	No Opp.	61.9	79,023
	Coleman R. Ferguson (R)	No Opp.	38.1	12,805
10	J. J. Pickle* (D)	67.7	80.4	180,294
	Paul A. Weiss (R)	No Opp.	19.6	500

11	W. R. Poage° (D)	80.5	81.6	$ 8,606
	Don Clements (R)	No Opp.	17.2	190
12	Jim Wright° (D)	No Opp.	78.7	118,839
	James S. Garvey (R)	No Opp.	21.3	65,161
13	John Hightower (D)	64.2	57.6	124,132
	Robert Price° (R)	No Opp.	42.4	157,697
14	John D. Young° (D)	No Opp.	No Opp.	2,861
15	Eligio de la Garza° (D)	No Opp.	No Opp.	1,562
16	Richard White° (D)	No Opp.	No Opp.	11,373
17	Omar Burleson° (D)	No Opp.	No Opp.	9,200
18	Barbara Jordan° (D)	No Opp.	84.8	19,825
	Robbins Mitchell (R)	No Opp.	14.0	4
19	George Mahon° (D)	No Opp.	No Opp.	2,044
20	Henry B. Gonzalez° (D)	No Opp.	No Opp.	8,993
21	*Robert Krueger°° (D)*	*51.5*	*52.6*	*311,953*
	Douglas Harlon (R)	*60.8*	*45.2*	*164,675*
	Ed Gallion (A)		*2.2*	*9,260*
22	Bob Casey° (D)	68.4	69.5	133,623
	Ron Paul (R)	No Opp.	28.4	16,206
23	Abraham Kazen, Jr.° (D)	71.4	No Opp.	44,737
24	Dale Milford° (D)	58.0	76.1	63,103
	Joseph Beaman, Jr. (R)	No Opp.	20.4	1,285

UTAH

1	K. Gunn McKay° (D)	No Opp.	62.6	25,611
	Ronald Inkley (R)	52.7	31.5	10,938
2	*Allan T. Howe (D)*	*55.8*	*49.5*	*95,540*
	Stephen M. Harmsen (R)	*59.7*	*46.9*	*103,717*

VERMONT

1	*James Jeffords (R)*	*39.5*	*52.9*	*55,883*
	Francis Cain (D)	*42.8*	*40.0*	*47,037*

VIRGINIA

1	Thomas Downing° (D)	No Opp.	99.8	2,897
2	G. William Whitehurst° (R)	No Opp.	60.0	83,545
	Robert R. Richards (D)	No Opp.	40.0	44,418
3	David Satterfield III° (D)	No Opp.	88.5	4,406
4	Robert W. Daniel, Jr.° (R)	No Opp.	47.2	79,134
	Lester E. Schlitz (D)	No Opp.	35.9	79,837

5	W. C. Daniel° (D)	No Opp.	99.4	$ 1,165
6	M. Caldwell Butler° (R)	No Opp.	45.1	63,622
	Paul J. Puckett (D)	No Opp.	27.0	25,933
	Warren D. Saunders (A)	No Opp.	26.1	57,819
7	J. Kenneth Robinson° (R)	No Opp.	52.6	96,443
	George H. Gilliam (D)	No Opp.	47.1	62,839
8	Herbert Harris (D)	52.5	57.6	101,299
	Stanford E. Parris° (R)	No Opp.	42.4	149,450
9	William C. Wampler° (R)	No Opp.	50.9	116,944
	Charles J. Horne (D)	No Opp.	49.1	232,341
10	Joseph L. Fisher (D)	42.2	53.6	144,751
	Joel T. Broyhill° (R)	No Opp.	45.2	248,709

WASHINGTON

1	Joel Pritchard° (R)	No Opp.	69.5	84,093
	Will Knedlick (D)	37.3	28.6	7,108
2	Floyd Meeds° (D)	No Opp.	59.7	65,954
	Ronald Reed (R)	63.3	38.9	14,317
3	*Don Bonker (D)*	*36.0*	*60.9*	*81,853*
	A. Ludlow Kramer (R)	*No Opp.*	*38.1*	*136,810*
4	Mike McCormack° (D)	78.4	58.9	52,217
	Floyd S. Paxton (R)	77.4	41.1	106,726
5	Thomas S. Foley° (D)	84.9	64.3	48,059
	Gary Gage (R)	64.0	35.7	12,228
6	Floyd Hicks° (D)	72.3	71.8	10,357
	George M. Nalley (R)	No Opp.	28.2	8,185
7	Brock Adams° (D)	No Opp.	71.1	46,122
	Raymond Pritchard (R)	56.9	28.9	2,309

WEST VIRGINIA

1	Robert H. Mollohan° (D)	87.1	59.7	62,952
	Joe A. Laurita, Jr. (R)	57.2	40.3	105,927
2	Harley O. Staggers° (D)	No Opp.	64.4	15,484
	William H. Loy (R)	No Opp.	35.6	30,995
3	John M. Slack, Jr.° (D)	59.6	68.5	54,008
	William L. Larcamp (R)	No Opp.	31.5	8,123
4	Ken Hechler° (D)	No Opp.	No Opp.	449

WISCONSIN

1	Les Aspin° (D)	No Opp.	70.5	30,443
	Leonard W. Smith (R)	No Opp.	29.5	7,629

2	Robert W. Kastenmeier° (D)	No Opp.	64.8	$ 17,663
	Elizabeth T. Miller (R)	No Opp.	35.2	16,658
3	Alvin J. Baldus (D)	39.7	51.1	72,958
	Vernon W. Thomson° (R)	No Opp.	47.4	87,902
4	Clement J. Zablocki° (D)	No Opp.	72.5	9,852
	Lewis H. Collison (R)	No Opp.	23.8	5,986
5	Henry S. Reuss° (D)	No Opp.	80.0	2,073
	Mildred A. Morries (R)	No Opp.	20.0	459
6	William A. Steiger° (R)	No Opp.	59.5	51,495
	Nancy J. Simenz (D)	No Opp.	35.4	6,128
7	David R. Obey° (D)	No Opp.	70.5	25,807
	Josef Burger (R)	No Opp.	29.4	12,683
8	Robert J. Cornell (D)	56.6	54.4	63,736
	Harold V. Froelich° (R)	No Opp.	45.6	93,272
9	*Robert W. Kasten (R)*	*56.9*	*52.9*	*91,770*
	Lynn S. Adelman (D)	*59.4*	*45.0*	*104,934*

WYOMING

1	Teno Roncalio° (D)	No Opp.	54.7	52,860
	Tom Stroock (R)	76.8	45.3	98,581

Campaign Expenditures in 1974 Senate Races Compiled by the Common Cause Campaign Monitoring Project

This list includes the total campaign expenditure figures for all major party candidates and significantly financed minor party or independent candidates in the 1974 general election.

The source of the information on campaign expenditures is the reports filed under the Federal Election Campaign Act of 1971. The totals cover the period between September 1, 1973, and December 31, 1974. Expenditures for each candidate were determined by combining the reports filed by each candidate with those filed by political committees exclusively supporting that candidate. Expenditures include all money spent by the campaign including debts outstanding (except

230

loans outstanding) as of December 31, 1974. Expenditures do not include funds which have been invested in government bonds or certificates of deposit, or funds which have been used to repay loans made to the campaign. Adjustments have also been made to eliminate all transfers of funds within a campaign.

On the list, winning candidates are listed first. Incumbents are indicated by an asterisk (*). The races printed in *italic* are those in which there was no incumbent in the general election. Candidates indicated by a double asterisk (**) won their primary after a runoff election. The primary vote percentage listed for those candidates is for the runoff. *Congressional Quarterly* is the source of all data on vote percentages.

EXPENDITURES FOR ALL NOVEMBER 1974 SENATE RACES

(The winning candidate is listed first. The contests printed in *italic* are those in which there was no incumbent; those printed in roman had an incumbent candidate. —in Primary Vote % column means candidate was nominated by state convention.)

SOURCE: *Common Cause Campaign Monitoring Project*

	Primary Vote %	General Election Vote %	Expenditures
ALABAMA			
James Allen* (D)	82.6	95.8	$ 37,328
ALASKA			
Mike Gravel* (D)	53.2	58.3	469,300
C. R. Lewis (R)	53.0	41.7	353,701
ARIZONA			
Barry Goldwater* (R)	No Opp.	58.3	394,042
Jonathan Marshall (D)	53.7	41.7	129,260
ARKANSAS			
Dale Bumpers (D)	*65.2*	*84.9*	*335,874*
John Jones (R)	*No Opp.*	*15.1*	*18,651*
CALIFORNIA			
Alan Cranston* (D)	83.4	60.5	1,336,202
H. L. (Bill) Richardson (R)	64.5	36.2	702,767
COLORADO			
Gary Hart (D)	39.3	57.2	352,557
Peter Dominick* (R)	No Opp.	39.5	502,343
CONNECTICUT			
Abraham Ribicoff* (D)	—	63.7	435,985
James H. Brannen (R)	—	34.3	66,162

231

FLORIDA
Richard Stone°° (D)	51.0	43.4	$ 919,787
Jack Eckerd (R)	67.3	40.9	421,169
John Grady (A)		15.7	148,495

GEORGIA
Herman Talmadge° (D)	81.2	71.7	65,207
Jerry Johnson (R)	No Opp.	28.2	12,856

HAWAII
Daniel Inouye° (D)	No Opp.	82.9	205,265

IDAHO
Frank Church° (D)	85.6	56.1	300,300
Robert Smith (R)	72.0	42.1	127,926

ILLINOIS
Adlai E. Stevenson III° (D)	82.6	62.2	757,329
George M. Burditt (R)	82.7	37.2	488,556

INDIANA
Birch Bayh° (D)	—	50.7	1,024,486
Richard G. Lugar (R)	—	46.4	619,678[1]
Don L. Lee (A)		2.8	19,194

IOWA
John Culver (D)	No Opp.	52.0	470,970
David Stanley (R)	66.6	47.3	336,067

KANSAS
Robert Dole° (R)	No Opp.	50.9	1,110,024
William R. Roy (D)	84.7	49.1	836,927

KENTUCKY
Wendell H. Ford (D)	84.9	53.5	1,006,670
Marlow Cook° (R)	87.1	44.1	524,569

LOUISIANA
Russell Long° (D)	74.5	No Opp.	498,774

MARYLAND
Charles Mathias (R)	75.7	57.3	329,845
Barbara Mikulski (D)	40.4	42.7	74,311

MISSOURI
Thomas F. Eagleton° (D)	87.3	60.1	647,143
Thomas Curtis (R)	81.8	39.3	362,804

NEVADA
Paul Laxalt (R)	81.3	47.0	385,861
Harry Reid (D)	59.9	46.6	410,553

NEW HAMPSHIRE
John H. Durkin (D)	50.0	49.7	128,389
Louis Wyman (R)	83.2	49.7	138,605

[1] According to Lugar, the Indiana Republican State Central Committee expended an additional $418,000 in behalf of the Lugar for U. S. Senate Committee.

232

NEW YORK

Jacob K. Javits° (R)	No Opp.	45.3	$1,090,437
Ramsey Clark (D)	47.8	38.2	855,576
Barbara A. Keating (C)		15.9	192,462

NORTH CAROLINA

Robert B. Morgan (D)	*50.6*	*62.1*	*781,201*
William E. Stevens (R)	*65.5*	*37.0*	*385,527*

NORTH DAKOTA

Milton Young° (R)	No Opp.	48.4	300,121
William Guy (D)	82.9	48.3	115,561
James R. Jungroth (Ind)		2.9	13,187

OHIO

John H. Glenn (D)	*54.5*	*64.6*	*1,149,130*
Ralph Perk (R)	*63.7*	*30.7*	*292,838*

OKLAHOMA

Henry Bellmon° (R)	86.9	49.4	622,480
Ed Edmondson (D)	58.5	48.9	195,429

OREGON

Robert Packwood° (R)	No Opp.	54.9	333,004
Betty Roberts (D)	—	44.2	80,193

PENNSYLVANIA

Richard S. Schweiker° (R)	No Opp.	53.0	799,499
Peter Flaherty (D)	46.1	45.9	256,483

SOUTH CAROLINA

Ernest F. Hollings° (D)	No Opp.	69.5	227,835
Gwenyfred Bush (R)	No Opp.	28.6	6,754

SOUTH DAKOTA

George McGovern° (D)	No Opp.	53.0	1,172,831
Leo K. Thorsness (R)	52.2	47.0	528,817

UTAH

E. J. Garn (R)	—	*50.0*	*363,162*
Wayne Owens (D)	—	*44.1*	*445,500*

VERMONT

Patrick Leahy (D)	*76.3*	*49.5*	*152,817*
Richard Mallary (R)	*59.7*	*46.4*	*90,617*

WASHINGTON

Warren Magnuson° (D)	92.5	60.7	463,116
Jack Metcalf (R)	59.9	36.1	63,153

WISCONSIN

Gaylord Nelson (D)	No Opp.	61.8	247,551
Thomas Petri (R)	84.8	35.8	80,590

° Indicates incumbent
°° Indicates primary runoff winner

Appendix III

"MNPL Organizing Early for 1976 U.S. Elections"*

(From Committee on '76 Elections.)

In 1976 we will be electing a President, 33 U.S. Senators, and all 435 U.S. Representatives.

The past six years of Republican administration have caused the working men and women of the United States immeasurable damage and loss of buying power. Instead of the standard of living for workers rising, it has gone down. There is no question that the blame can be laid directly at the feet of the past and present Republican administrations. There is also no doubt in our minds that the only way to change these disastrous policies is to change administrations.

The Democratic Party has numerous good candidates that are either announced or unannounced seekers of their party's nomination. It is our recommendation that every IAM member who is a member of the Democratic Party should take an active interest in helping their chosen candidate win the Democratic nomination. We further recommend that the national MNPL attempt to meet with all candidates who are seek-

*Action Program adopted in February 1975 by the National Planning Committee of the Machinists Non-Partisan Political League of the International Association of Machinists and Aerospace Workers (from the *Machinist*, February 13, 1975).

234

ing the Presidential nomination and attempt to determine their qualifications for that office. The national MNPL will then be able to properly
advise the IAM membership of the qualifications and abilities of the
various candidates.

U.S. SENATE RACES

In 1976, there will be 33 U.S. Senate seats up for election. These 33
seats are presently held by 21 Democrats, 10 Republicans, one Conservative and one Independent. The majority of these seats are held by
friendly incumbents who, in some cases, will need early support. A
few of the seats are held by out-and-out enemies of organized labor.
Perhaps they can be defeated for reelection by a friendly candidate.

It is recommended that in each state, where there is a U.S. Senate
race, a committee be set up by the Machinists State Council to determine the situation in that state as regards the race and to communicate
that information as soon as possible to the national MNPL.

U.S. HOUSE RACES

Most of the 92 new members were elected by majorities that will
place them on the marginal Congressional District list. However, the
majority of seats, both Democratic and Republican, will be considered
safe. An initial look at all the House seats shows that there are 118 that
should be considered marginal. These are seats that were won by 55%
or less, or changed parties in 1974. These 118 marginal seats are the
greatest number in MNPL history.

A look at the list shows some revealing facts. First, 63 of them are
Democrats and 58 Republicans. A majority of them (68) are newly
elected Representatives. MNPL supported 57 of the Representatives
on the marginal list. Of that 57, 50 are newly elected Representatives.
Even more startling is the fact that 46 of the newly elected Representatives supported by MNPL on the marginal list were involved in elections that changed the seat from the Republican Party to the
Democratic Party. This points out the need for a special effort.

EARLY PREPARATION

We recommend a program to be started early in 1975 immediately following the adjournment of the National Committee meeting. This program is to be aimed at the marginal Senatorial seats and House of Representatives districts.

HELPING INCUMBENT FRIENDS

In those marginal Senate seats and House districts where an incumbent friend will have major opposition and problems getting reelected, we recommend that the state council, IAM district and/or local lodge, whatever the case may be, take the initiative role in seeing that the Senator or Representative in question gets early organizational help from both MNPL and state and central body COPEs.

A well-organized registration program should be planned using the central body COPEs and other allies such as Frontlash, A. Philip Randolph Institute, Concerned Seniors, the Labor Council for Latin American Advancement and other groups interested in registration drives. We should support efforts this year to enact a Federal postcard registration law.

Early plans should be made to provide full-time and part-time help in the IAM's areas of responsibility in registration, education and get-out-the-vote efforts.

Plans should be made to meet with the Senators and Representatives to advise them of our plans and activities. Plans must be made to carry-out an early fund-raising effort to supply the necessary funds for the organizational efforts and financial assistance for the Senators and Representatives involved.

OPPOSING UNFRIENDLY INCUMBENTS

In those seats presently held by unfriendly Senators and Representatives, we recommended that MNPL, with the help and cooperation of state and county central body COPEs, determine if our endorsed candidate from the previous election should be the candidate to challenge the incumbent enemy. If the determination is made that he or she should be our endorsed candidate, then we should take the necessary

236

steps to try to insure that our candidate gets the nomination of his or her party. If this is not the case, we recommend, again with the help and cooperation of the state and county central body COPEs, that a search be made for a qualified candidate to challenge the unfriendly incumbent.

We further recommend that all of these efforts be coordinated through the national MNPL as well as with state and county central body COPEs involved.

Appendix IV

Admission of AFL-CIO Partisan Political Activities by Thomas Harris, Member of Federal Election Commission

[Note: Thomas Harris, a federal election commissioner, signed the following stipulation in 1973 as associate general counsel, AFL-CIO, admitting the use by the AFL-CIO of tax-exempt dues money for political activity. The document is Exhibit 3889 filed in the case of *George L. Seay, et al.* v. *Grand Lodge International Association of Machinists and Aerospace Workers, et al.,* civil case nos. 67–1394-HP and 71–498-HP (C.D. Calif., Dec. 19, 1973) in the United States District Court for the Central District of California.]

The AFL-CIO is a labor federation. It has many functions which are set out in Article II of its Constitution, a number of which include political and legislative activities, including the advocacy of legislation which it deems to be in the interest of organized labor and the election of candidates favorable to its legislative policies. One of its largest departments, the Committee on Political Education, is devoted exclusively to such matters. In addition to the activities carried on by COPE, the President and the Secretary-Treasurer and some other representatives and employees of the AFL-CIO devote a portion of their time to furthering the political and legislative objectives of the organization and in pursuing activities designed to secure maximum support for these objectives by affiliated unions, and state and local AFL-CIO councils and committees, including their involvement in and planning and preparing for political activities. . . .

National COPE seeks to coordinate the political activities of the national and international unions affiliated with the AFL-CIO and of state and local AFL-CIO central bodies. COPE's national staff is headquartered on the 6th floor of the AFL-CIO building in Washington, D.C. The Administrative Committee of COPE is headed by the President of the AFL-CIO, and consists of members of the AFL-CIO Executive Council. The operations of COPE are under the immediate direction of Alexander E. Barkan, its national director, Joseph M. Rourke, Deputy Director, and John Perkins, Assistant Director. The headquarters staff includes a research director and an assistant research director, a national field coordinator, a data processing director, a publications director, and various other staff assistants. COPE currently has 18 area directors and field representatives stationed in various areas of the country, and having responsibility for COPE activities in specific states. Included among the 18 field staff are field coordinators for minority groups and women. . . .

With minor exceptions, the expenses of COPE, including salaries of the COPE staff personnel, travel expenses, office supplies, telephone and telegraph, printing, and general overhead expenses are paid by the AFL-CIO out of the general fund of the AFL-CIO, a fund which is derived principally from per capita taxes received from affiliated national and international unions. . . .

In addition to the expenditures of COPE referred to in the foregoing paragraph, some of the other departments of the AFL-CIO including the public relations department, the publications department, the research department, the education department, the civil rights department and the legislative department carry out some functions and activities which are integrated with the political and legislative activities of the AFL-CIO and COPE. No records or accounts are maintained by AFL-CIO in a manner which would permit a proportionate allocation of the expenses of these various departments to the political and legislative activities and functions of AFL-CIO and COPE.

The official newspaper of the AFL-CIO, the *AFL-CIO News,* and some of the printed materials prepared and distributed by the Educational Department and other departments of the AFL-CIO seek to in-

239

fluence the reader toward political and ideological positions favored and supported by AFL-CIO and COPE. . . .

AFL-CIO and COPE officials seek to maintain close liaison with political party officials in various states and in various congressional districts, and COPE officials sometimes participate in the process of selecting candidates, campaign planning and policy decisions respecting the mechanics and strategy of the election campaigns of candidates for national state and local offices. Through coordination with affiliated international unions and their state and local representatives, COPE assists in providing financial, organizational and manpower resources for the campaigns of such candidates. In congressional and senatorial election years COPE divides the marginal congressional districts and key Senate races and approximately 10 of the major national and international unions affiliated with AFL-CIO generally accept special responsibility for specific congressional districts of Senate races. These affiliated unions, in turn, assign staff representatives to these strategic areas. In order to provide these staff representatives with necessary training in political strategy and techniques COPE conducts political seminars and conferences at various locations throughout the county at various times during the year. Such conferences and seminars are held in off-years as well as in election years in order to insure the existence of a large corps or politically trained union staff personnel available for assignment to actual campaign operations. . . .

A portion of COPE Educational Fund monies, derived ultimately from membership dues are frequently used for the preparation, printing and dissemination of political brochures and other materials which support particular candidates for federal office. Such funds are also used for the purpose of making direct cash contributions to candidates for non-federal offices, such as state gubernatorial races. . . .

One of COPE's major operational tools is voter registration. By using its computerized voter identification program, COPE seeks to determine whether union members are registered and to which political party the union member belongs. The use of this program greatly facilitates the registration of union members and their families. COPE registration drives are now carried on in various states according to the laws of such states, throughout the year, utilizing staff personnel made available by affiliated unions. . . .

240

Appendix V

Speech by Congressman Robert Michel (R.—Ill.) Exposing Union "In-Kind" Contributions in Four Special Congressional Elections in 1974*

One final point I would like to make in transgressing upon the Member's time in general debate here is what I see is left out of the bill and which I would like to have seen offered in the form of an amendment to appropriately treat the in-kind services and goods, for the special interest groups often make substantial contributions by providing in-kind services and goods, such as telephones, cars, airplanes, computer time, staff "volunteers," and the like.

The committee bill would exempt these contributions from both the limitation and in some cases the disclosure requirements.

To prevent this type of campaign abuse, the amendment I had intended to offer before adoption of the closed rule would have prevented or prohibited such in-kind contributions in excess of $100.

I might say that in the four particular special elections for seats in the House of Representatives that were held earlier in the year it has been estimated with pretty good justification, and I will insert with my remarks, when I have asked for permission to revise and extend, some documents that will lead us to believe in just those four special elec-

* *Congressional Record*, August 7, 1974.

tions the in-kind services provided actually approached or exceeded the amount of hard contributions.

Current law defines the word "contribution" to exclude "services provided without compensation by individuals volunteering a portion or all of their time on behalf of a candidate or political committee," and the committee bill further exempts certain other limited personal services, so my amendment would have had no effect on truly voluntary efforts by individuals on behalf of a candidate.

The amendment would, however, have curbed the type of "in-kind" contributions of special interest groups that have resulted in millions of dollars' worth of what are, in effect, unreported campaign contributions.

Such contributions have been extensively documented in past campaigns, and represent a serious violation of the spirit, if not the actual letter, of our campaign law.

While several legislative methods of dealing with this problem have been suggested, a flat prohibition of "in-kind" contributions in excess of $100 is by far the most effective since it would eliminate, beyond the $100 level, the inevitable questions that arise over the worth or dollar value of such services to a candidate.

It seems to me if we hope to maintain any measure of credibility in our efforts at campaign reform, we must certainly take the steps necessary to curb abuses such as this.

Mr. Chairman, I am inserting in the RECORD the material I referred to earlier.

PENNSYLVANIA'S 12TH DISTRICT

The documented record of the race between Democrat John Murtha and Republican Harry Fox reveals that literally tens of thousands of union dollars were poured into the campaign by Murtha for former Representative John Saylor's (R.–Pa.) seat in the 12th District.

Contributions were of two types:

1. "Hard" contributions, in the form of cash donations, from thirty-two different union political action committees in the amount of $25,450.00 that were made to the Citizens for Murtha Committee.

2. "Soft" contributions, in the form of full time union staff personnel from national COPE, state COPE, the Pennsylvania state AFL-CIO and various other unions, the mailing by unions in behalf of Murtha,

organizational activity at Indiana University that was clearly coordinated with Frontlash and supervised by a union "volunteer," last minute get-out-the-vote activities, polls conducted by the state AFL-CIO, and other such "soft" contributions. The amount identified in this area —by no means a full tally since the records for most of these hidden contributions remain in the hands of private organizations—comes to over $40,000—or nearly double the amount of hard contributions made by union officials.

Staff Time

It is clear that at least 20 union officials contributed time and effort during the campaign. They were:

1. Alexander Barkan, Director, COPE, $32,274.00 annual salary and $6,727.23 expenses.

2. Joseph Ferguson, Business Agent, International Ladies Garment Workers, $11,388.00 in annual salary, and $1,274.46 expenses.

3. Douglas Allen, Pennsylvania State AFL-CIO, salary unknown.

4. Mike Trbovich, Vice President, United Mine Workers, $31,100.57 annual salary and $3,049.04 expenses.

5. John Vento, Pennsylvania State AFL-CIO, salary unknown.

6. Carl Stellmack, Pennsylvania State AFL-CIO, salary unknown.

7. Harry Boyer, Pennsylvania State AFL-CIO, salary unknown.

8. Bernard Lurye, Assistant Manager, Garment Workers, $12,855.00 salary and $938.25 expenses.

9. James Myers, Organizer, AFSCME, $8,793 salary and $8,563.05 expenses.

10. Andrew Koban, District 15, Steelworkers, $17,314.59 salary and $4,179.56 expenses.

11. Edward Monborne, District 2, and International Exec. Board Member NMU, $22,491.73 salary and $4,600.61 expenses.

12. Frank Kulish, District 2 President, UMW, $15,314.17 salary and $87.22 expenses.

13. Mike Johnson, Vice President, Pennsylvania State AFL-CIO, salary unknown.

14. Robert Spence, International Representative, COMPAC, salary unknown.

15. Walter Carmo, Pennsylvania Education Assoc., salary unknown.

16. Chuck Krawetz, UMW, salary unknown.

17. Arnold Miller, President, UMW, $36,283.79 salary and $3,966.71 expenses.

18. Irwin Aronson, staff Pennsylvania State AFL-CIO, salary unknown.

19. Tom Reddinger, President, Indiana Labor Council (IAM), union salary, if any, unknown.

20. Dana Henry, member, IAM, no union salary.

Each of these individuals was identified—either through newspaper accounts, internal memos or union newsletters and papers—as having spent from one day to as much as five weeks promoting the Murtha candidacy.

One unionist, Tom Reddinger, identified by the *Johnstown Tribune-Democrat* as President of the Indiana County Central Labor Council, admitted in a personal interview, that he took five weeks of unpaid leave time from his job at Fisher-Scientific Company, Indiana, Pa., to work in the Murtha campaign. He further stated that all his expenses during this time were paid for by the Pennsylvania State AFL-CIO, including the cost for four telephones at headquarters, that, according to a General Telephone Company spokesman in Johnstown, would cost $126.80 during the five-week period. Based on Reddinger's rate of pay with Fisher, his "in-kind" contribution in salary during the five-week period would come to approximately $1,000.

Where salaries are available, the union official involved was pro-rated at the actual salary (plus identifiable expenses), for the period of time he was involved; where no salary was available, a reasonable figure of $15,000 per annum was assigned (a low figure in light of the bulk of identified salaries of union officials).

On this basis, it was determined that salaries involved amounted to $5,902.78 and expenses to $2,317.73, for a total of $8,220.51.

Printing

There were four mailings to the 66,000 union members in the district and 6,500 active and retired teacher union members by the Pennsylvania AFL-CIO COPE and the Political Action Committee for Education (PACE), political arm of the state teachers union (Penn. State Education Association).

The two mailed under Permit #1, Harrisburg (the permit is held by Speed Mail, Inc.) were costed out by reputable printers at the following rates:

244

1. Mailing of January 18, 1974 to 1,000 retirees only:

Printing, $10 and postage, $80 (mailed first class); totals $90.

Mailing of January 25, 1974 to 6,500 active and retired educators:

Printing at $10/m, $650 and postage, $520 (mailed first class), totals $1,170.

Two additional mailings were sent out at the non-profit organization rate (1.7 cents per piece) under permit #668 at Pittsburgh, Pa., a permit registered to the Pennsylvania State . . . Costs of these two mailings, were as follows:

Mailing to 66,000 union members in District by United Labor Committee:

Printing at $27/m, $1,782; postage at 1.7c, $112; and postage $191, totals $2,025.

The second quoted postage cost is the difference between a non-profit mailing rate of 1.7c and what the candidate would have had to pay if the mailing had gone out regular bulk mail rates.

Mailing to same members in district of flyer with four halftones:

Printing at $40/m, $2,640; postage at 1.7c, $112; and postage, $191; totals $2,943.

Thus, the total value of mailings by unions in behalf of the Murtha candidacy came to $6,288.00.

Other Contributions

Other "soft" contributions by unions to the Murtha race included:

1. At least 15,000 telephone calls by the Indiana County Central Labor Committee to members of the union in the county. (Source—interview with Tom Reddinger.)

2. "At least $12,000 is expected to go into the district from labor for last minute campaign expenses and election day activities." (*Philadelphia Bulletin*, February 3, 1974.)

3. "$14,000 which . . . the state and national AFL-CIO and COPE committees spent to house and feed staff members at a downtown Johnstown motel during the election campaign." (*Johnstown Tribune-Democrat*, January 30, 1974.)

4. The AFL-CIO was "operating out of 15 rooms at the Sheraton Inn, on Market Street." (*Johnstown Tribune-Democrat*, December 18, 1973.)

5. The state AFL-CIO conducted a telephone poll for Murtha in the 12th District (*Johnstown Tribune-Democrat*, December 18, 1973.)

6. Democratic telephone bank workers use facilities of Gautier Hall,

which is owned by the Steelworkers Union (photo in the *Johnstown Tribune-Democrat,* February 5, 1974).

Summary

By category, identifiable soft contributions by unions to the Murtha campaign are as follows:

Staff time, salaries and expenses deferred	$ 8,220.51
Printing and postage for mailings	6,288.00
Student activities	369.53
Other:	
Last minute get-out-the-vote	12,000.00
Costs at the Sheraton	14,000.00
Subtotal	$40,878.04

When one includes the "hard" (reported) contributions of $28,-450.00, it can be seen that the value of the total union effort in the district is at least $66,328.04, or nearly as much as Murtha reported for his entire campaign.

OHIO'S FIRST DISTRICT

There is very little doubt that, both in and off the record, union officials and their political organizations had a tremendous impact on the race between the Democrat, Tom Luken, and the Republican, Bill Gradison, on March 5th.

Direct contributions by union political organizations to the Luken for Congress Committee were made by thirty-three separate union organizations in the amount of $30,875.00.

The scope and significance of the indirect contributions by union officials are captured in the February 8, 1974 edition of the *Chronicler,* a bimonthly publication of the Cincinnati AFL-CIO Labor Council, which is distributed to 2,000 labor officials in the Cincinnati area.

In it, an announcement is made of the "most important business meeting for all union stewards and committeemen geared to their vital part in labor's effort to insure the election of Tom Luken to Congress." It goes on to note that "materials will be furnished and *definite assignments outlined* for the action required to build a Luken victory . . ." (emphasis supplied).

The cost of the space devoted in the *Chronicler* to Luken over the January 8–March 25 period represents an indirect cost of $360 alone.

In addition, William Sheehan, head of the Labor Council, disclosed that at least 4 national and state staffers were in for the election—or as George Meany put it on "Face the Nation" on March 3rd concerning the race, "We're putting in the usual—we're sending in outsiders. Some of our COPE men. . . ."

Among those in Cincinnati were Ray Alverez, Area Director of COPE ($2,085.46 contribution in salary and expenses under previous formula); Ruth Colombo, COPE ($1,977.19 pro-rated salary and expenses for one month); Jane Adams Ely, Ohio State AFL-CIO (salary unknown); W. C. Young, National Field Director, COPE (salary $20,373.50, expenses $8,659.84). Ely and Young were in for an undisclosed period of time, but the bare minimum of salary and expenses for even one day's stay could reasonably be put at $500.00.

Thus, identifiable staff time and expenses for union officials came to $4,562.65.

Moreover, Alverez stated in an interview that at least 84,000 telephone calls were made from the phone banks at the Central Labor Council to union members in the District. If the cost of those calls were projected at the same 4½ cents per call rate used in Michigan, that would place their value at $3,780.00.

As in other districts, there were many mailings to union members:

1. At least two—one dated February 18, 1974 and another February 28, 1974—were sent out to members of District 30, United Steelworkers of America.

2. Another mailer dated February 28, 1974 was sent to all members of Local 863, UAW.

3. Yet another mailer dated February 18, 1974 was sent to members of the Amalgamated Clothing Workers.

4. Space was devoted in local union papers to promoting the candidacy of Luken.

In all at least $8,342.65 in paid staff time and telephone costs on a projected basis were pumped into the Luken campaign.

MICHIGAN'S EIGHTH DISTRICT

As in the case with other special, off-year elections, the race between Democrat Robert Traxler and Republican Jim Sparling was signifi-

247

cantly influenced by the infusion of "hard" and "soft" contributions made by union officials to the Traxler campaign.

Hard contributions amounted to nearly $29,000 with the United Auto Workers—an independent union based in the state—contributing nearly half the "hard" labor money, as reported by the Traxler for Congress Volunteer Committee.

Some 22 labor political action groups contributed $28,880 in "hard" money to the campaign, a figure that every cursory research shows does not realistically measure the contribution on the part of the union hierarchy in behalf of the Traxler campaign.

Staff

A minimum of eight national, state and local union officials contributed their salaried staff time (plus expenses) to the project of getting Traxler elected.

Those officials were:

James George, United Auto Workers (UAW), Detroit, annual salary $17,093.80, expenses $4,285.06.

Sam Fishman, UAW, salary $23,088.10, expenses $6,219.25.

Ray Alverez, Area Director, AFL-CIO COPE, salary $19,772.50, expenses $6,868.17.

Ernest Dillard, UAW, Detroit, salary $18,294.64, expenses $6,-246.37.

W. C. Young, National Field Director, COPE, salary $20,373.60, expenses $8,659.84.

John Dewan, UAW, Madison Heights, Michigan, salary $16,943.80, expenses $3,992.16.

Ruth Colombo, Assistant Area Director, Women's Activities Program (COPE), salary $20,360.50, expenses $3,365.90.

In addition, Wallace J. "Butch" Warner, 2575 N. Orr Rd., Hemlock, Michigan, was off his job (unpaid) from January 14, 1974 through the election (April 16, 1974) to work as coordinator on the campaign for the "Traxler for Congress Labor Coordinator."

An employee of Michigan Bell and a paid staffer as President of Communications Workers of America Local No. 4108, Warner's worth to the campaign (he is a cable splicer and earns $235 per week under terms of the union contract) comes to $3,202.50.

Warner disclosed in an interview that he had indeed worked with COPE and UAW personnel, identifying Sam Fishman as having been on the scene for at least one week, W. C. Young for 10 days, Ruth Colombo as having supervised for "at least 10 days" the phone banks used to contact the 43,000 UAW members, 5,000 retirees and 25,000 AFL-CIO members in the district.

For various reasons—such as an unlisted number, personnel moving, etc.—some 50 percent of the 73,000 union members, according to Warner, were not contacted. Thus, some 43,800 calls were made, many of them twice, once they were identified as in the Traxler camp. Assuming $1/2$ of those contacted were in this category, that means approximately 65,200 phone calls to union members alone at the rate of $4^{1}/2$ cents per call (as billed in Michigan) for a net cost of $2,922.

In terms of paid staff time, we must weigh in the appropriate pro rata share of Ray Alverez' salary and expenses. Alverez candidly admits he was assigned to work in three congressional districts (Ohio 1, Michigan 5 and Michigan 8) from January 3 through April 16—or 28 percent of his annual time.

Thus, in all three races, his "in-kind" contribution was $6,256.40, a third of which ($2,085.46) is allocated to the race in Michigan 8.

Applying the same pro rata formula, the "in-kind" contributions for other COPE and UAW operatives are as follows:

W. C. Young had salary of $738.00 and expenses of $309. which total $1,047.

Ruth Colombo had salary of $738.00 and expenses of $309. which total $1,047.

Sam Fishman had salary of $444.00 and expenses of $120. which total $564.

In summary, a cursory glance will establish at least $7,945.96 in "soft" contributions of paid staff time to the Traxler campaign.

Printing

In addition to the identifiable staff time and expenses involved, a substantial "soft" contribution came in the form of four separate mailings, three of which were sent "To all UAW members in Michigan's 8th Congressional District." Copies of those mailings are attached as "A."

Two different mailing permits were used at the non-profit organization rate, with permit #3333, which belongs to American Mailers and Binders of Detroit, on two mailings, and the UAW's own permit #8000 being used for the third.

In terms of cost, as estimated by a Michigan printer, here is what each of the mailings would cost:

Mailing of March 30, 1974 to 43,000 UAW members:

Printing at $28.80/m, $1,238.40; postage at 1.7c, $73.10; and postage, $124.70, totals $1,436.20.

Mailing of April 2, 1974 to 43,000 UAW members (it is noteworthy that this mailing, made from Detroit under permit #3333, contained as an insert a six-panel brochure allegedly paid for by the Traxler for Congress Volunteer Committee):

Printing a two-page letter at $38.30/m, $1,668.40; postage at 1.7c, $73.10; and postage at 2.9c, $124.70, totals $1,866.20.

Mailing of April 6, 1974 to 43,000 UAW members:

Printing, $1,668.40; postage at 1.7c, $73.10; and postage at 2.9c, $124.70, totals $1,866.20.

Mailing of "8th Congressional District Special Election Edition" of Michigan *AFL-CIO News* (Vol. 35, No. 37, April 16, 1974) to UAW members in the 8th District.

(In this eight-page tabloid, five pages are devoted unabashedly to promoting the candidacy of Traxler. Taking $1/8$th of the costs the "in-kind" contribution is shown below.)

Printing, $2,750.00; and postage $200.00, totals $2,950.00.

Thus, total soft printing costs contributed by the UAW and Michigan State AFL-CIO to the candidacy of Traxler came to a total of $8,118.60.

Summary

It is therefore reasonable to state that many thousands of dollars in soft contributions were funneled into the Michigan 8 race by the unions and union officials.

The contributions break down as follows:

"Hard" contributions from labor sources, $28,880. "Soft" contributions:

Staff time and expenses	$ 7,945.96
Printing	8,118.60
Telephone costs	2,922.00
Total	$18,986.56

This "investment" is over and above the reported money, for a grand total union contribution of $47,866.56.

Additionally, three union officials were identified as being on the scene, whether as paid or unpaid is not clear. The three were: James George, UAW, Detroit (annual salary of $17,093.80); Ernest Dillard, UAW, Detroit (annual salary of $18,294.64); and John Dewan, UAW, Madison Heights (annual salary $16,943.80).

MICHIGAN'S FIFTH DISTRICT

The race for Vice President Gerald Ford's former seat in Congress was somewhat different from the other three special elections, in that a professional firm—headed by John Martilla—took over direction and management of the Vander Veen campaign.

Nevertheless, the union influence directing the campaign was exercised in both a direct and indirect fashion, much as it was in all other special elections.

1. Direct contributions as filed by the treasurer of the Vander Veen for Congress Committee list some 12 separate union political action groups contributed a total of $18,711.00 to the Vander Veen campaign —or approximately 38 percent of the total direct reported contributions of $49,588.70.

2. Indirect contributions. Perhaps because a professional consulting firm was retained to direct the Vander Veen campaign, the "high profile" maintained by union officials while working in other special elections was not as evident. However, Ray Alverez, area Director of the AFL-CIO's Committee on political education (COPE), admitted to having been in Michigan's 5th District. Under the same formula developed for Michigan's Eighth District some $2,085.46 of Alverez' annual salary and expenses of $26,640.67 could be considered an indirect campaign contribution.

The printing area was one that afforded a good deal of "in-kind" support for the Democrat. Curiously, the same format, type face, halftones, paper, three of the pages are exactly the same and appeared in a tabloid-type mailer that went out under *both* the permit number of the candidate (#552) and the permit of the Western American mailers (#1), which mailed the piece in behalf of Region 1-D, United Auto Workers, Box H, Grand Rapids, Mich.

In terms of specific mailings and costs, the following were sent during the course of the campaign:

Two page letter, enclosing a xeroxed "fact sheet" on Vander Veen plus a postage paid return card under Permit #4721 addressed to Region 1-D, UAW, soliciting workers for the Vander Veen campaign.

Printing, $1,151.70; postage at 1.7c, $374.00; and postage at 2.9c, $638.00, totals $2,163.70.

Tabloid mailer (mentioned previously) sent to all UAW members in the district.

Printing $2,373.00; postage at 1.7c, $374.00; and postage at 2.9c, $638.00, totals $3,385.00.

In addition a separate tabloid mailer was also prepared that is, once again, similar and identical in places to the other two tabloids. The difference is that this is printed on offset stock instead of newsprint and in all likelihood mailed at an estimated cost of $3,315.00 to all UAW members in the district.

Thus total "in-kind" printing and contributions to the Vander Veen Campaign came to $8,863.70; combined with the salary for just one member of the COPE staff, Ray Alverez, the total in-kind contributions in their quietest of the districts comes to at least $10,949.30.

Obviously, not all "soft" contributions are covered in the report on this district—telephones, etc.—but the low profile maintained by union officials during the race makes them almost impossible to detect.

Appendix VI

Reported Union Campaign Contributions to Members of the House Education and Labor Committee, 94th Congress

(Compiled by the National Right to Work Committee) SOURCE: Clerk of the House

*Michael Blouin (D–Iowa) $36,900 4
*Paul Simon (D–Ill.) $34,400 4
John Dent (D–Pa.)... $29,275 2,3,4
*Robert Cornell (D–Wis.).. $29,175 4
Frank Thompson (D–N.J.) $26,300 2,3,4
*Ron Mottl (D–Ohio) $23,830 4
Lloyd Meeds (D–Wash.)... $22,550 2,4
Peter Peyser (R–N.Y.) $21,555 4
William Clay (D–Mo.) $18,850 2,3,4
John Brademas (D–Ind.).. $18,700 2,4
*Ted Risenhoover (D–Ok.) $18,600 4
William Lehman (D–Fla.) $18,550 4
*Leo Zeferetti (D–N.Y.)... $15,062 4
James O'Hara (D–Mich.)... $14,300 2,4
Phillip Burton (D–Cal.)... $13,050 2,4
Dominick Daniels (D–N.J.) $12,550 2,3,4
*George Miller (D–Cal.)... $12,000 4
*Tim Hall (D–Ill.) $11,150 1,4
William Ford (D–Mich.).. $10,650 2,3

Mario Biaggi (D–N.Y.)... $ 7,400 2,3,4
Joseph Gaydos (D–Pa.)... $ 6,450 2,4
Ike Andrews (D–N.C.)... $ 6,250
*Edward Beard (D–R.I.) .... $ 5,350 1,4
Patsy Mink (D–Hawaii).. $ 3,560 2
Ronald Sarasin (R–Conn.)... $ 2,350
Shirley Chisholm (D–N.Y.) .... $ 2,125 2,3,4
Al Quie (R–Minn.) .... $ 2,000
Alphonzo Bell (R–Cal.).. $ 1,900
Marvin Esch (R–Minn.).. $ 1,900
Augustus Hawkins (D–Cal.)... $ 1,400 2
John Ashbrook (R–Ohio).. $ 500
*Bill Goodling (R–Pa.)... $ 500
Carl Perkins (D–Ky.)... $ 500 2,3,4
John Buchanan (R–Ala.).. None
John Erlenborn (R–Ill.) .... None
Edwin Eshleman (R–Pa.)... None
*James Jeffords (R–Vt.) .... None
*Larry Pressler (R–S.D.).. None
*Virginia Smith (R–Neb.).. None
          TOTAL.. $429,632

° First term Congressman elected in 1974.
¹ Public statements indicate support of compulsory unionism in public sector.
² Voted in 1970 against the Right to Work provision in the Postal Reorganization Act.
³ Has sponsored legislation which would compel federal, U.S. postal service, or state, county and local government employees to support unions in order to work for their own government.
⁴ Received ten percent or more of total campaign contributions from union sources.

254

Appendix VII

Affidavit of Jerry Wurf,

President, AFSCME, on Political Activity

Superior Court of the District of Columbia

Mamie Adams, et al.,	✲
	✲
Plaintiffs,	✲
	✲
v.	✲ Misc. No. 56–72
	✲
City of Detroit, AFSCME	✲
Council 77, et al.,	✲
	✲
Defendants.	✲
	✲

The undersigned, Jerry Wurf, as President of the American Federation of State, County and Municipal Employees, AFL-CIO, being duly sworn, makes the following statement:

1. The American Federation of State, County and Municipal Employees, AFL-CIO (hereinafter AFSCME) receives revenues in the

form of per capita tax payments of $1.50 per member per month from its local unions, as set forth in Article IX, Section 7 of the International Constitution currently in effect. Per capita tax revenues so received are co-mingled in the general fund of AFSCME and used for its programs and activities, including political action and legislative action programs.

2. The per capita payments required by the AFSCME Constitution to be transmitted to AFSCME by its affiliated local unions also include payment in the same amount, $1.50 per month, for each non-member agency fee payer, and all such payments are co-mingled and used as described in the foregoing paragraph.

3. In carrying on its political action programs and activities AFSCME utilizes its officers and salaried staff personnel. A portion of the salaried time and reimbursed expenses of staff personnel and of the costs of office space, office supplies, telephone and telegraph, printing and general overhead and administration expenses of AFSCME are either directly related to its political action programs and activities or provide administrative support for such programs and activities.

4. In recent years, the political programs and activities of AFSCME have been closely related to one of the two major political parties, particularly at the national level. Some AFSCME officers and staff personnel hold official positions in that party at the national, state or local level, and participate in the election campaigns of candidates of that party. Through coordination with other international unions and their state and local representatives AFSCME and its PEOPLE Committee assist in providing financial, organizational and manpower resources for voter registration drives, preparation and dissemination of campaign literature, and get-out-the-vote activities in support of candidate campaigns. These activities are at times coordinated with those of other organizations with similar objectives.

5. The cost of publication of the *Public Employee,* which is the official newspaper of AFSCME, is paid for out of AFSCME general funds.

6. One of the departments of AFSCME, the Department of Legislation and Political Action, consists of a staff of professional and clerical employees engaged in political training and education programs and in dealing with legislative developments of interest to AFSCME. All salaries and expenses including office overhead and administration of such Department are paid for out of the general funds of AFSCME.

256

7. Contributions are made from the general funds of AFSCME to candidates for state and local offices where such contributions are not prohibited by law and where AFSCME has determined that such support is in the interest of public employees. For the purposes set forth in Article VIII, Section 5 of its Constitution, AFSCME has established a PEOPLE Committee (Public Employees Organized to Promote Legislative Equality) which is administered by its officers. This Committee received voluntary financial contributions from AFSCME members. The constitutional provision directs that these voluntary contributions are to be used for the achievement of the legislative goals of AFSCME. For this purpose the PEOPLE Committee furnished financial assistance to some candidates for federal office. The expenses of voluntary fund-raising activities of the PEOPLE Committee including staff salaries and expenses and use of physical facilities, are to the extent legally permissible, paid for from the general funds of AFSCME.

8. The Department of Education has assisted in training of the Legislation and Political Action staff in use of educational techniques and has assisted in the presentation of its programs. The salaries and expenses of staff personnel and the cost of operation is paid for out of AFSCME general funds.

Jerry Wurf
International President
American Federation of State, County
and Municipal Employees, AFL-CIO

Appendix VIII

Members of Congress
Endorsed and Supported by .COPE

(• = COPE Endorsement)

ALABAMA
Senators
•John J. Sparkman (D)
James B. Allen (D)

Representatives
1. Jack Edwards (R)
2. William L. Dickinson (R)
3. Bill Nichols (D)
•4. Tom Bevill (D)
•5. Robert E. Jones, Jr. (D)
6. John H. Buchanan (R)
7. Walter Flowers (D)

ALASKA
Senators
Ted Stevens (R)
•Mike Gravel (D)

Representative (At Large)
Don Young (R)

ARIZONA
Senators
Paul J. Fannin (R)
Barry Goldwater (R)

Representatives
1. John J. Rhodes (R)
•2. Morris K. Udall (D)
3. Sam Steiger (R)
4. John B. Conlan (R)

ARKANSAS
Senators
John L. McClellan (D)
•Dale Bumpers (D)

Representatives
•1. Bill Alexander (D)
•2. Wilbur D. Mills (D)
3. John P. Hammerschmidt (R)
4. Ray Thornton (D)

CALIFORNIA

•Alan Cranston (D)
•John V. Tunney (D)

Representatives
• 1. Harold T. Johnson (D)
    2. Don H. Clausen (R)
• 3. John E. Moss (D)
• 4. Robert L. Leggett (D)
• 5. John L. Burton (D)
• 6. Phillip Burton (D)
• 7. George Miller (D)
• 8. Ronald V. Dellums (D)
• 9. Fortney H. (Pete) Stark (D)
•10. Don Edwards (D)
•11. Leo J. Ryan (D)
•12. Paul N. McCloskey, Jr. (R)
•13. Norman Y. Mineta (D)
•14. John J. McFall (D)
•15. B. F. Sisk (D)
   16. Burt L. Talcott (R)
•17. John Krebs (D)
   18. William M. Ketchum (R)
   19. Robert J. Lagomarsino (R)
   20. Barry Goldwater, Jr. (R)
•21. James C. Corman (D)
   22. Carlos J. Moorhead (R)
•23. Thomas M. Rees (D)
•24. Henry A. Waxman (D)
•25. Edward R. Roybal (D)
   26. John H. Rousselot (R)
•27. Alphonzo Bell (R)
•28. Yvonne Brathwaite Burke (D)
•29. Augustus F. Hawkins (D)
•30. George E. Danielson (D)
•31. Charles H. Wilson (D)
•32. Glenn M. Anderson (D)
   33. Del Clawson (R)
•34. Mark W. Hannaford (D)
•35. Jim Lloyd (D)
•36. George E. Brown, Jr. (D)
   37. Vacant
•38. Jerry M. Patterson (D)
   39. Charles E. Wiggins (R)
   40. Andrew J. Hinshaw (R)
   41. Bob Wilson (R)
•42. Lionel Van Deerlin (D)
   43. Clair W. Burgener (R)

COLORADO

Senators
•Floyd K. Haskell (D)
•Gary Hart (D)

Representatives
•1. Patricia Schroeder (D)
•2. Timothy E. Wirth (D)
•3. Frank E. Evans (D)
   4. James T. Johnson (R)
   5. William L. Armstrong (R)

CONNECTICUT

Senators
•Abraham A. Ribicoff (D)
   Lowell P. Weicker, Jr. (R)

Representatives
•1. William R. Cotter (D)
•2. Christopher J. Dodd (D)
•3. Robert N. Giaimo (D)
   4. Stewart B. McKinney (R)
   5. Ronald A. Sarasin (R)
•6. Anthony Toby Moffett (D)

DELAWARE

Senators
   William V. Roth, Jr. (R)
•Joseph R. Biden, Jr. (D)

Representative (At Large)
   Pierre S. duPont IV (R)

FLORIDA

Senators
•Lawton Chiles (D)
•Richard Stone (D)

Representatives
• 1. Robert L. F. Sikes (D)
• 2. Don Fuqua (D)
• 3. Charles E. Bennett (D)

- 4. Bill Chappell, Jr. (D)
  5. Richard Kelly (R)
  6. C. W. Bill Young (R)
- 7. Sam Gibbons (D)
- 8. James A. Haley (D)
  9. Louis Frey, Jr. (R)
  10. L. A. (Skip) Batalis (R)
  11. Paul G. Rogers (D)
  12. J. Herbert Burke (R)
- •13. William Lehman (D)
- •14. Claude Pepper (D)
- •15. Dante B. Fascell (D)

GEORGIA

Senators
•Herman E. Talmadge (D)
•Sam Nunn (D)

Representatives
- 1. Bo Ginn (D)
  2. Dawson Mathis (D)
- 3. Jack Brinkley (D)
- 4. Elliott Levitas (D)
- 5. Andrew Young (D)
  6. John J. Flynt, Jr. (D)
  7. Larry McDonald (D)
  8. W. S. (Bill) Stuckey, Jr. (D)
  9. Phil M. Landrum (D)
- •10. Robert G. Stephens, Jr. (D)

HAWAII

Senators
 Hiram L. Fong (R)
•Daniel K. Inouye (D)

Representatives
•1. Spark M. Matsunaga (D)
•2. Patsy T. Mink (D)

IDAHO

Senators
•Frank Church (D)
 James A. McClure (R)

Representatives
1. Steven D. Symms (R)
2. George Hansen (R)

ILLINOIS

Senators
 Charles H. Percy (R)
•Adlai E. Stevenson III (D)

Representatives
- 1. Ralph H. Metcalfe (D)
- 2. Morgan F. Murphy (D)
- 3. Martin A. Russo (D)
  4. Edward J. Derwinski (R)
  5. Vacant
  6. Henry J. Hyde (R)
- 7. Cardiss Collins (D)
- 8. Dan D. Rostenkowski (D)
- 9. Sidney R. Yates (D)
- •10. Abner J. Mikva (D)
- •11. Frank Annunzio (D)
  12. Philip M. Crane (R)
  13. Robert McClory (R)
  14. John N. Erlenborn (R)
- •15. Tim L. Hall (D)
  16. John B. Anderson (R)
  17. George M. O'Brien (R)
  18. Robert H. Michel (R)
  19. Tom Railsback (R)
  20. Paul Findley (R)
  21. Edward R. Madigan (R)
- •22. George E. Shipley (D)
- •23. Melvin Price (D)
- •24. Paul Simon (D)

INDIANA

Senators
•Vance Hartke (D)
•Birch Bayh (D)

Representatives
- 1. Ray J. Madden (D)
- 2. Floyd J. Fithian (D)
- 3. John Brademas (D)
- 4. J. Edward Roush (D)
  5. Elwood Hillis (R)
- 6. David W. Evans (D)
  7. John T. Myers (R)
- 8. Philip H. Hayes (D)
- 9. Lee H. Hamilton (D)

•10. Philip R. Sharp (D)
•11. Andrew Jacobs, Jr. (D)

IOWA
Senators
•Dick Clark (D)
•John C. Culver (D)

Representatives
•1. Edward Mezvinsky (D)
•2. Michael T. Blouin (D)
3. Charles E. Grassley (R)
4. Neal Smith (D)
5. Tom Harkin (D)
6. Berkley Bedell (D)

KANSAS
Senators
•James B. Pearson (R)
Robert Dole (R)

Representatives
1. Keith G. Sebelius (R)
•2. Martha Keys (D)
3. Larry Winn, Jr. (R)
4. Garner E. Shriver (R)
5. Joe Skubitz (R)

KENTUCKY
Senators
•Walter Huddleston (D)
•Wendell H. Ford (D)

Representatives
•1. Carroll Hubbard, Jr. (D)
•2. William H. Natcher (D)
•3. Romano L. Mazzoli (D)
4. Gene Snyder (R)
5. Tim Lee Carter (R)
•6. John B. Breckinridge (D)
•7. Carl D. Perkins (D)

LOUISIANA
Senators
•Russell B. Long (D)
J. Bennett Johnston, Jr. (D)

Representatives
•1. F. Edward Hebert (D)
•2. Lindy (Mrs. Hale) Boggs (D)
3. David C. Treen (R)
4. Joe D. Waggonner, Jr. (D)
5. Otto E. Passman (D)
6. W. Henson Moore (R)
•7. John B. Breaux (D)
•8. Gillis W. Long (D)

MAINE
Senators
•Edmund S. Muskie (D)
•William D. Hathaway (D)

Representatives
1. David F. Emery (R)
2. William S. Cohen (R)

MARYLAND
Senators
•Charles McC. Mathias, Jr. (R)
J. Glenn Beall, Jr. (R)

Representatives
1. Robert E. Bauman (R)
•2. Clarence D. Long (D)
•3. Paul S. Sarbanes (D)
4. Marjorie S. Holt (R)
•5. Gladys Noon Spellman (D)
6. Goodloe E. Byron (D)
•7. Parren J. Mitchell (D)
•8. Gilbert Gude (R)

MASSACHUSETTS
Senators
•Edward M. Kennedy (D)
•Edward W. Brooke (R)

Representatives
1. Silvio O. Conte (R)
• 2. Edward P. Boland (D)
• 3. Joseph D. Early (D)
• 4. Robert F. Drinan (D)
5. Paul E. Tsongas (D)
• 6. Michael J. Harrington (D)

261

- 7. Torbert H. Macdonald (D)
- 8. Thomas P. O'Neill, Jr. (D)
- 9. Joe Moakley (D)
- •10. Margaret M. Heckler (R)
- •11. James A. Burke (D)
- •12. Gerry E. Studds (D)

MICHIGAN
Senators
•Philip A. Hart (D)
 Robert P. Griffin (R)

Representatives
- • 1. John Conyers, Jr. (D)
- 2. Marvin L. Esch (R)
- 3. Garry Brown (R)
- 4. Edward Hutchinson (R)
- • 5. Richard F. Vander Veen (D)
- • 6. Bob Carr (D)
- • 7. Donald W. Riegle, Jr. (D)
- • 8. Bob Traxler (D)
- 9. Guy Vander Jagt (R)
- 10. Elford A. Cederberg (R)
- 11. Philip E. Ruppe (R)
- •12. James G. O'Hara (D)
- •13. Charles C. Diggs, Jr. (D)
- •14. Lucien N. Nedzi (D)
- •15. William D. Ford (D)
- •16. John D. Dingell (D)
- •17. William M. Brodhead (D)
- •18. James J. Blanchard (D)
- 19. William S. Broomfield (R)

MINNESOTA
Senators
•Walter F. Mondale (D)
•Hubert H. Humphrey (D)

Representatives
- 1. Albert H. Quie (R)
- 2. Tom Hagedorn (R)
- 3. Bill Frenzel (R)
- •4. Joseph E. Karth (D)
- •5. Donald M. Fraser (D)
- •6. Richard Nolan (D)

•7. Bob Bergland (D)
•8. James L. Oberstar (D)

MISSISSIPPI
Senators
 James O. Eastland (D)
 John C. Stennis (D)

Representatives
- 1. Jamie L. Whitten (D)
- •2. David R. Bowen (D)
- 3. G. V. (Sonny) Montgomery (D)
- 4. Thad Cochran (R)
- 5. Trent Lott (R)

MISSOURI
Senators
•Stuart Symington (D)
•Thomas F. Eagleton (D)

Representatives
- • 1. William Clay (D)
- • 2. James W. Symington (D)
- • 3. Leonor K. (Mrs. John B.) Sullivan (D)
- • 4. William J. Randall (D)
- • 5. Richard Bolling (D)
- • 6. Jerry Litton (D)
- 7. Gene Taylor (R)
- • 8. Richard H. Ichord (D)
- • 9. William L. Hungate (D)
- •10. Bill D. Burlison (D)

MONTANA
Senators
•Mike Mansfield (D)
•Lee Metcalf (D)

Representatives
•1. Max S. Baucus (D)
•2. John Melcher (D)

NEBRASKA
Senators
 Roman L. Hruska (R)
 Carl T. Curtis (R)

Representatives
1. Charles Thone (R)
2. John Y. McCollister (R)
3. Virginia Smith (R)

NEVADA
Senators
•Howard W. Cannon (D)
Paul Laxalt (R)

Representative (At Large)
•Jim Santini (D)

NEW HAMPSHIRE
Senators
•Thomas J. McIntyre (D)
Vacant

Representatives
•1. Norman E. D'Amours (D)
2. James C. Cleveland (R)

NEW JERSEY
Senators
•Clifford P. Case (R)
•Harrison A. Williams, Jr. (D)

Representatives
• 1. James J. Florio (D)
• 2. William J. Hughes (D)
• 3. James J. Howard (D)
• 4. Frank Thompson, Jr. (D)
5. Millicent Fenwick (R)
6. Edwin B. Forsythe (R)
• 7. Andrew Maguire (D)
• 8. Robert A. Roe (D)
• 9. Henry Helstoski (D)
•10. Peter W. Rodino, Jr. (D)
•11. Joseph G. Minish (D)
•12. Matthew J. Rinaldo (R)
•13. Helen S. Meyner (D)
•14. Dominick V. Daniels (D)
•15. Edward J. Patten (D)

NEW MEXICO
Senators
•Joseph M. Montoya (D)
Pete V. Domenici (R)

Representatives
1. Manuel Lujan, Jr. (R)
•2. Harold Runnels (D)

NEW YORK
Senators
•Jacob K. Javits (R)
James L. Buckley (C)

Representatives
• 1. Otis G. Pike (D)
• 2. Thomas J. Downey (D)
• 3. Jerome Ambro, Jr. (D)
4. Norman F. Lent (R)
5. John W. Wydler (R)
• 6. Lester L. Wolff (D)
• 7. Joseph P. Addabbo (D)
• 8. Benjamin S. Rosenthal (D)
• 9. James J. Delaney (D)
•10. Mario Biaggi (D)
•11. James H. Scheuer (D)
•12. Shirley Chisholm (D)
•13. Stephen J. Solarz (D)
•14. Frederick W. Richmond (D)
•15. Leo C. Zeferetti (D)
•16. Elizabeth Holtzman (D)
•17. John M. Murphy (D)
•18. Edward I. Koch (D)
•19. Charles B. Rangel (D)
•20. Bella S. Abzug (D)
•21. Herman Badillo (D)
•22. Jonathan B. Bingham (D)
•23. Peter A. Peyser (R)
•24. Richard L. Ottinger (D)
25. Hamilton Fish, Jr. (R)
26. Benjamin A. Gilman (R)
•27. Matthew F. McHugh (D)
•28. Samuel S. Stratton (D)
•29. Edward W. Pattison (D)
30. Robert C. McEwen (R)
31. Donald J. Mitchell (R)

•32. James M. Hanley (D)
•33. William F. Walsh (R)
•34. Frank Horton (R)
35. Barber B. Conable, Jr. (R)
•36. John L. LaFalce (D)
•37. Henry J. Nowak (D)
38. Jack F. Kemp (R)
39. James F. Hastings (R)

NORTH CAROLINA
Senators
Jesse A. Helms (R)
•Robert Morgan (D)

Representatives
1. Walter B. Jones (D)
2. L. H. Fountain (D)
3. David N. Henderson (D)
• 4. Ike F. Andrews (D)
• 5. Stephen L. Neal (D)
• 6. Richardson Preyer (D)
• 7. Charles G. Rose (D)
• 8. W. G. Hefner (D)
9. James G. Martin (R)
10. James T. Broyhill (R)
•11. Roy A. Taylor (D)

NORTH DAKOTA
Senators
Milton R. Young (R)
•Quentin N. Burdick (D)

Representative (At Large)
Mark Andrews (R)

OHIO
Senators
Robert Taft, Jr. (R)
•John Glenn (D)

Representatives
1. Willis D. Gradison, Jr. (R)
2. Donald D. Clancy (R)
• 3. Charles W. Whalen, Jr. (R)
4. Tennyson Guyer (R)
5. Delbert L. Latta (R)

6. William H. Harsha (R)
7. Clarence J. Brown (R)
8. Thomas N. Kindness (R)
• 9. Thomas L. Ashley (D)
10. Clarence E. Miller (R)
11. J. William Stanton (R)
12. Samuel L. Devine (R)
13. Charles A. Mosher (R)
•14. John F. Seiberling, Jr. (D)
15. Chalmers P. Wylie (R)
16. Ralph S. Regula (R)
17. John M. Ashbrook (R)
•18. Wayne L. Hays (D)
•19. Charles J. Carney (D)
•20. James V. Stanton (D)
•21. Louis Stokes (D)
•22. Charles A. Vanik (D)
•23. Ronald M. Mottl (D)

OKLAHOMA
Senators
Henry Bellmon (R)
Dewey F. Bartlett (R)

Representatives
•1. James R. Jones (D)
•2. Theodore M. Risenhoover (D)
•3. Carl Albert (D)
•4. Tom Steed (D)
•5. John Jarman (R)
•6. Glenn English (D)

OREGON
Senators
Mark O. Hatfield (R)
Bob Packwood (R)

Representatives
•1. Les AuCoin (D)
•2. Al Ullman (D)
•3. Robert Duncan (D)
•4. James Weaver (D)

PENNSYLVANIA
Senators
Hugh Scott (R)
•Richard S. Schweiker (R)

264

Representatives
- 1. William A. Barrett (D)
- 2. Robert N. C. Nix (D)
- 3. William J. Green (D)
- 4. Joshua Eilberg (D)
  5. Richard T. Schulze (R)
- 6. Gus Yatron (D)
- 7. Robert W. Edgar (D)
- 8. Edward G. Biester, Jr. (R)
  9. Bud Shuster (R)
- •10. Joseph M. McDade (R)
- •11. Daniel J. Flood (D)
- •12. John P. Murtha (D)
  13. Lawrence Coughlin (R)
- •14. William S. Moorhead (D)
- •15. Fred B. Rooney (D)
  16. Edwin D. Eshleman (R)
  17. Herman T. Schneebeli (R)
- •18. H. John Heinz III (R)
  19. William F. Goodling (R)
- •20. Joseph M. Gaydos (D)
- •21. John H. Dent (D)
- •22. Thomas F. Morgan (D)
  23. Albert W. Johnson (R)
- •24. Joseph P. Vigorito (D)
  25. Gary A. Myers (R)

RHODE ISLAND
Senators
•John O. Pastore (D)
•Claiborne Pell (D)

Representatives
•1. Fernand J. St. Germain (D)
•2. Edward P. Beard (D)

SOUTH CAROLINA
Senators
Strom Thurmond (R)
•Ernest F. Hollings (D)

Representatives
•1. Mendel J. Davis (D)
 2. Floyd Spence (R)
•3. Butler Derrick (D)
•4 James R. Mann (D)

•5. Kenneth L. Holland (D)
•6. John W. Jenrette, Jr. (D)

SOUTH DAKOTA
Senators
•George McGovern (D)
•James Abourezk (D)

Representatives
1. Larry Pressler (R)
2. James Abdnor (R)

TENNESSEE
Senators
Howard H. Baker, Jr. (R)
Bill Brock (R)

Representatives
1. James H. Quillen (R)
2. John J. Duncan (R)
•3. Marilyn Lloyd (D)
•4. Joe L. Evins (D)
5. Richard Fulton (D)
6. Robin L. Beard (R)
•7. Ed Jones (D)
•8. Harold E. Ford (D)

TEXAS
Senators
John G. Tower (R)
Lloyd M. Bentsen (D)

Representatives
- 1. Wright Patman (D)
- 2. Charles Wilson (D)
  3. James M. Collins (R)
  4. Ray Roberts (D)
  5. Alan Steelman (R)
  6. Olin E. Teague (D)
  7. Bill Archer (R)
- 8. Bob Eckhardt (D)
- 9. Jack Brooks (D)
  10. J. J. Pickle (D)
  11. W. R. Poage (D)
  12. Jim Wright (D)
•13. Jack Hightower (D)

14. John Young (D)
15. E. de la Garza (D)
16. Richard C. White (D)
•17. Ømar Burleson (D)
18. Barbara Jordan (D)
19. George H. Mahon (D)
20. Henry B. Gonzalez (D)
•21. Robert Krueger (D)
22. Bob Casey (D)
•23. Abraham Kazen, Jr. (D)
24. Dale Milford (D)

UTAH
Senators
•Frank E. Moss (D)
Jake Garn (R)

Representatives
•1. Gunn McKay (D)
•2. Allan T. Howe (D)

VERMONT
Senators
Robert T. Stafford (R)
•Patrick J. Leahy (D)

Representative (At Large)
James M. Jeffords (R)

VIRGINIA
Senators
Harry F. Byrd, Jr. (I)
William L. Scott (R)

Representatives
1. Thomas N. Downing (D)
2. G. William Whitehurst (R)
3. David E. Satterfield, III (D)
4. Robert W. Daniel, Jr. (R)
5. Dan Daniel (D)
6. M. Caldwell Butler (R)
7. J. Kenneth Robinson (R)
• 8. Herbert E. Harris II (D)
9. William C. Wampler (R)
•10. Joseph L. Fisher (D)

WASHINGTON
Senators
•Warren G. Magnuson (D)
•Henry M. Jackson (D)

Representatives
•1. Joel Pritchard (R)
•2. Lloyd Meeds (D)
•3. Don Bonker (D)
•4. Mike McCormack (D)
•5. Thomas S. Foley (D)
•6. Floyd V. Hicks (D)
•7. Brock Adams (D)

WEST VIRGINIA
Senators
•Jennings Randolph (D)
Robert C. Byrd (D)

Representatives
•1. Robert H. Mollohan (D)
•2. Harley O. Staggers (D)
•3. John M. Slack (D)
•4. Ken Hechler (D)

WISCONSIN
Senators
•William Proxmire (D)
•Gaylord Nelson (D)

Representatives
•1. Les Aspin (D)
•2. Robert W. Kastenmeier (D)
•3. Alvin Baldus (D)
•4. Clement J. Zablocki (D)
•5. Henry S. Reuss (D)
6. William A. Steiger (R)
•7. David R. Obey (D)
•8. Robert J. Cornell (D)
9. Robert W. Kasten, Jr. (R)

WYOMING
Senators
•Gale W. McGee (D)
Clifford P. Hansen (R)

Representative (At Large)
•Teno Roncalio (D)

Appendix IX

Statement of
National Right to Work Committee
to House Administration Committee
on Proposed Election Reform

Honorable John H. Dent
Chairman
Subcommittee on Elections
Committee on House Administration
U.S. House of Representatives
Suite H-326, U.S. Capitol
Washington, D.C. 20515

Dear Mr. Chairman:

This statement is in response to your request of November 19, 1973, that we submit our testimony on election reform in written form. We are extremely distressed that on a matter of such vital importance we have been denied the opportunity to testify in person.

The National Right to Work Committee is a single-purpose, citizens' organization, comprised of both employers and employees, devoted to the concept that no individual should be compelled to pay money to any private organization as a condition of employment.

Like most Americans, we recognize the serious need for further careful examination and reform of the practices under which political campaigns are financed. Therefore, we applaud the initiative taken by those members of the U.S. Senate and House of Representatives who have introduced campaign reform legislation in this First Session of the 93rd Congress.

Some of this proposed legislation, such as S. 372, is in the form of amendments to the Federal Election Campaign Act of 1971. Some of it goes further, such as H.R. 7612, and provides for public financing of federal election campaigns.

However, in our opinion, these various proposals all have a common shortcoming. They fail to deal adequately with the most serious of all election campaign abuses, namely the use of compulsory union dues for partisan political purposes. Consequently, we believe these bills would do more harm than good if passed in their present form. Their provisions would restrict certain selected areas of campaign support while leaving others relatively untouched. In our opinion, the present language in these bills would compound an injustice adversely affecting millions of America's working people.

Testifying before the Senate Subcommittee on Privileges and Elections this year in support of legislation that would have federal election campaigns financed out of the public treasury, AFL-CIO Legislative Director Andrew J. Biemiller unwittingly acknowledged the very point we are making here:

> We want the Congress to put the AFL-CIO out of the business of making campaign contributions. We would be delighted if the AFL-CIO never had to raise another dime for a candidate.
>
> Without fund-raising headaches, we would be able to better fill our members' needs for registration assistance, providing them information about candidates and issues, and finally getting our members out to vote their consciences on Election Day. [*Daily Labor Report,* 9/27/73, p. A-14.]

What Mr. Biemiller really meant was that union officials would prefer not to have to spend compulsory dues money to pay the costs of raising "voluntary" funds which can legally be contributed to candidates for federal offices. Freed from the costs of fund-raising, these officials then would have considerably more compulsory dues money to spend on partisan registration and get-out-the-vote drives and on propagandizing members and other voters in support of certain candidates and in opposition to others.

Under a unique grant of special privileges by the federal government to union officials, close to two billion dollars in union dues is collected each year from wage earners who are forced to pay that money or lose their jobs. Union officials then invest a substantial part of that money in political activities, many of which are opposed by those who, under federal law, have been compelled to pay up or be fired.

Only the most naive persons can any longer accept the discredited notion that union politicking is financed exclusively by voluntary contributions. The record is clear that much money for politics comes directly from revenue derived from union dues.

Twelve years ago, Justice Hugo Black in his dissent in *IAM* v. *Street,* 367 U.S. 740 (1961), said: "There can be no doubt that the federally sanctioned union-shop contract here, as it actually works, takes a part of the earnings of some men and turns it over to others, who spend a substantial part of the funds so received in efforts to thwart the political, economic and ideological hopes of those whose money has been forced from them under authority of law." And the situation continues to worsen.

The United Auto Workers has publicly admitted spending union dues for partisan political purposes and will—subject to a highly questionable internal union procedure—rebate $3.68 per member per year on request (*UAW Administrative Letter,* Vol. 24, No. 9, August 2, 1972). That is roughly $5,000,000 in dues money a year for one union, as compared with less than $900,000 in "voluntary" expenditures reported by that same union to the Clerk of the House in 1972 (*Daily Labor Report,* August 22, 1973, p. A-6). The fact that only 100 of the 1.4 million members currently demand such rebates according to the UAW is another story—suffice it to say that the shoe is on the wrong foot: can you imagine the courage it takes to stand up in a union hall and demand part of your dues back!

The AFL-CIO Committee on Political Education reported $1,-270,075 in expenditures of "voluntary" funds in 1972 to the Clerk of the House (*Daily Labor Report,* August 22, 1973). The AFL-CIO's most recent financial report shows that the AFL-CIO's expenditure of dues money for COPE was $1.8 million for the fiscal year ending June 30, 1972 and $1.7 million for the fiscal year ending June 30, 1973 (Report of the AFL-CIO Executive Council to the Tenth Convention, October 18, 1973). These figures do not include the dues money spent on politics by the many AFL-CIO state and local central bodies, nor do they include the expenditures of any of the individual unions affiliated with the AFL-CIO.

Rather than burdening the Subcommittee with page after page of evidence of massive union politicking with compulsory dues money, I will merely cite from the AFL-CIO's own description of COPE's role in the 1972 elections. We are prepared, however, to provide for the record as much additional documentation as this Subcommittee wishes. In its Report to the Tenth Convention, October 18, 1973, the AFL-CIO Executive Council boasts:

> By any standard of measurement, the COPE program in 1972 exceeded any previous year—more volunteer manpower and womanpower and *more full-time staff assigned by international unions; increased funding; more effective and better-organized registration and get-out-the-vote campaigns, improved precinct-level organization.*
>
> COPE-supported non-partisan programs aimed at union members in the minorities community under the aegis of the A. Philip Randolph Institute, in the youth community under Frontlash, and among seniors through the National Council for Senior Citizens, all functioned with great effect and impact in their respective areas.
>
> In addition, *the special program under which members of the Executive Council assumed responsibility for guidance and assistance to COPE's program in states with marginal Senate and House races contributed significantly to successful election results.* The U.S. was divided into 10 geographic regions, with one or more members of the Executive Council assigned to work with state and local councils in each region.
>
> With the help of the council members and a special COPE project that provided early organization of COPE programs in marginal districts, 51 of 83 candidates endorsed in marginal House races, and 10 out of 19 in Senate races, won. *Most of these were extremely close elections, and the margin of victory was clearly provided by labor's efforts.*

✧ ✧ ✧ ✧

Major progress was achieved in the nuts-and-bolts programs that are essential to any successful political effort, registration and getting out the vote, and in these areas COPE's computerized Voter Identification Project was of immense value. *Twenty-three states participated in the data processing program which permitted sorting and printing of nearly 10 million names in a format compatible with local registration records.*

270

In COPE's registration campaign, and the election period get-out-the-vote effort, more than 110,000 volunteers—union members and members of their families—participated, devoting more than a million hours to checking lists, canvassing, telephoning, preparation and distribution of materials, conducting election day carpools and baby-sitting operations. This was the highest number of volunteers ever involved in COPE activities.

Total funding of COPE programs, including contributions to endorsed candidates, reached a record high of more than $2 million, 25 percent over the best previous year of 1970. Many international unions reached or exceeded 100 percent of the voluntary COPE quota.

Besides manpower and money to conduct an effective political education campaign, COPE assisted state and local central labor bodies by providing other tools needed to reach and motivate members.

Hundreds of thousands of leaflets and flyers, special radio announcements in support of labor-backed candidates, a million copies of voting records in various marginal races—these were some of the services COPE made available to AFL-CIO members.

Layouts and Photographs of the candidates were prepared for use by unions as special inserts in their official journals.

The AFL-CIO Department of Public Relations helped in developing and producing informational materials on COPE-endorsed candidates. *The hundreds of thousands of letters and other literature generated under this program were paid for, signed and distributed to their members by local unions.* [Emphasis added.]

In evaluating the above summary of COPE's activities in the 1972 campaign, it is wise to remember that the AFL-CIO would not wittingly admit to the use of dues money for political purposes. Also, it must be noted that the AFL-CIO was neutral in the 1972 presidential election, and thus that the above description does not include the efforts which many unions exerted on behalf of George McGovern. As for the monetary value of the total aid that comes from union treasuries to support candidates, Victor Riesel, an authoritative labor columnist, has estimated that union officials spent some $60 million in the 1968 elections (Riesel column, Nov. 6, 1968) and $50 million in 1972 (Riesel column, Nov. 3, 1972) for their chosen candidates.

Predictably, union officials have challenged the accuracy of Mr. Riesel's estimates. On November 3, 1973, he publicly responded to one such challenge at the request of the Orlando (Fla.) *Sentinel-Star:*

In measuring the value of campaign contributions, the unions do not admit that there is far more than cash gifts to be considered. . . .

If you apply cost accounting to what the unions do in a political way, . . . you will find that the non-cash contributions consist of staff time— meaning union officials who are assigned to campaigns for months on end —printing costs, postage, telephone and various other support services financed entirely with compulsory union dues and fees.

For example, during the recent Democratic telethon, the Communications Workers of America furnished 10,000 telephone operators to take calls. They were supposed to be volunteers, but were they? Who paid their carfare?

How do you "cost out" the value of 72,000 house-to-house canvassers by labor in the 1968 election, or the 95,000 election day car pool drivers and baby sitters?

The Carpenters' Union sent letters to 900,000 people urging them to vote Democratic. Think of the expense of that. There were 600 political organizers from the steelworkers, a similar number from the auto workers. In 638 localities throughout the country there were 8,000 telephone banks manned by a total of 25,000 persons. There were 94,000 distributors of material.

It is time and services, not just cash contributions alone, which I consider in making my estimates. I know my estimates are right. I know they spent the time and money. Let them open their books if they say they didn't.

As members of the Subcommittee know, Mr. Riesel is justifiably regarded as a genuine friend of organized labor. He is famed for his unrelenting crusades against union racketeers, and it will long be remembered that one such crusade cost him his sight.

The use of compulsory union for political purposes corrupts the election process. It destroys the independence of many elected officials, making them virtual prisoners of a few union chieftains who dole out tens of millions of dollars for political campaigns in manpower, materials, and outright cash.

David Broder got to the heart of the matter in his perceptive column on campaign financing in the December 3, 1973 edition of the *Washington Post*. Broder wrote: ". . . money is just one of the sources of influence on a political contest. If access to large sums is eliminated as a potential advantage . . . then the election outcome will likely be determined by the ability to mobilize other forces." Broder's point, of course, is that eliminating the dollar influence on politics is not enough for that automatically enhances the influence of those who can provide manpower or publicity for the campaign.

We think that compelling America's working people to contribute, as a condition of employment, enormous sums for politics each year is the most disgraceful of all election campaign abuses. For this reason, it is our view that a campaign reform bill which fails to deal with this problem is worse than no bill at all.

The federal government is responsible for having created this problem. We think it is time for the federal government to undo the wrong it has done.

The role of the federal government in creating these injustices is two-fold: First, the full authority of federal law stands behind the firing of workers who refuse to pay dues to unions which use that money for political causes the workers oppose; Second, extra tax privileges have been extended to labor unions under which, unlike officers of any other organization, union officials can collect and spend tax-exempt money for partisan political purposes.

Let me emphasize that I am addressing this Subcommittee on behalf of a cross-section of the American people. We represent no special-interest group. Rather, I am speaking for the millions of America's union members who object to having their compulsory dues used for politics. I am also speaking for the millions of voters who object to having their government dominated by unrepresentative union officials whose political control is based on the conscripted dues of their forced followers. That millions of voters believe too much power already is concentrated in the hands of labor union officials has been demonstrated convincingly by a nationwide survey conducted by Opinion Research Corporation in 1972. Results of that survey show that 68 percent of the U.S. public—including a majority of the members of union families—think union bosses hold too high a concentration of power.

We respectfully request that this subcommittee amend the legislation you are now considering with language which would clearly, explicitly and unequivocally foreclose the possibility that the compulsory dues paid by any American wage earner can be used directly or indirectly for any kind of partisan political activity.

Section 610 of Title 18, United States Code, as amended by the Federal Election Campaign Act of 1971, allows three exceptions to its prohibition on the use of dues money by unions for political purposes:

(1) communications to union members and their families;
(2) non-partisan registration and get-out-the-vote drives aimed at members and their families; and
(3) the establishment, administration, and solicitation of contributions to separate segregated funds.

Union political operatives have driven an entire fleet of campaign bandwagons fueled by compulsory union dues through these three loopholes.

With respect to the first exception, in *U.S.* v. *CIO*, 335 U.S. 106 (1948), the Supreme Court said that if the section of the Federal Corrupt Practices Act (since enacted into positive law as 18 U.S.C. §610 and further amended) forbidding expenditure of union funds for political purposes "were construed to prohibit the publication, by corporations and unions in the regular course of conducting their affairs, of periodicals advising their members, stockholders or customers of danger or advantage to their interests from the adoption of measures or the election to office of men, espousing such measures, the gravest doubt would arise in our minds as to its constitutionality."

The Court in *CIO* did not rule on the constitutionality of a ban on the use of *compulsory* dues for partisan political purposes. In fact, the Court indicated that it had in mind only the case of voluntary union membership:

> Members of unions paying dues and stockholders of corporations know of the practice of their respective organizations in regularly publishing periodicals. It would require explicit words in an act to convince us that Congress intended to ban a trade journal, a house organ or a newspaper, published by a corporation, from expressing views on candidates or political proposals in the regular course of its publication. *It is unduly stretching language to say that the members or stockholders are unwilling participants in such normal activities,* including the advocacy thereby of governmental policies affecting their interests, and the support thereby of candidates thought to be favorable to their interests. [Emphasis added.]

Futhermore, the extent of present union political activity in this area is far greater than anything suggested in the 1948 *CIO* case. The Supreme Court there was dealing with a regular issue of a union newspaper, distributed "in regular course to those accustomed to receive copies of the periodical," containing a front page endorsement of a

274

congressional candidate. The Court did not have before it a specially produced campaign brochure mailed just before the election, at heavily tax-subsidized non-profit organizational postal rates, to all members of all unions in a given election district, nor was it considering a COPE sample ballot passed out to all voters at the polls on election day. The Court specifically noted the narrowness of the issue before it:

> It is one thing to say that trade or labor union periodicals published regularly for members, stockholders or purchasers are allowable under [610] and quite another to say that in connection with an election occasional pamphlets or dodgers or free copies widely scattered are forbidden.

There are indeed First Amendment questions which must be dealt with in this connection, but they should more properly be raised in the name of the union members who are compelled to pay dues under compulsory union shop contracts and who do not wish to have their dues money used to support candidates, or a political party, they oppose. What is to be said about the rights of the several million union members who favored the candidacy of Richard Nixon in 1968 at the same time that their union leaders and union salaried staff personnel were working feverishly, with the aid of their dues dollars, to defeat him? Isn't it a fact that their freedom of speech, their freedom of conscience, and their freedom of political thought and action were being sacrificed?

Moreover, there is reason to question the whole idea of protected free speech as applied to the union political efforts. Is this type of activity an expression of free speech by the rank and file members, or simply a case of the union members being manipulated to serve the political preferences of the union officers? In an article on the 1968 campaign COPE Director Alexander Barkan admits that a majority of union members favored Wallace at the outset, and the mail effort of the union professionals was to switch them over from Wallace to Humphrey (Barkan, "Political Activities of Labor," *Issues in Industrial Society,* Vol. 1, No. 2, 1969). Can this kind of manipulation of the rank and file members come within the constitutionally protected range of free speech, or isn't it a case of the union officers actually frustrating the exercise of free speech by the members? Viewed in proper context, the only constitutional rights a union may be said to have are derivative rights, that is, derived from the rights of the individual members to associate together for a common objective, namely, collective bargaining. It cannot be assumed that when a worker joins a union he transfers to the union his right to express himself on political matters. How then can it be said that the union, as an entity, can claim a protected right of free speech when it isn't speaking in the name of the members?

It can thus be concluded that the free speech protection of the First Amendment cannot logically be extended to the kind of partisan political activities which are undertaken by unions, and that if this question were presented to the Supreme Court in this framework the Court would hold that Congress can properly prohibit such expenditures. Further, since millions of workers are involuntarily required to pay union dues under compulsory union shop contracts the Court might well find that the use of their compulsory dues to finance partisan election campaigns abridges *their* First Amendment rights of freedom of speech, freedom of association, and freedom of political thought and action.

The Federal Election Campaign Act of 1971 amendment to 18 U.S.C. §610, by legalizing such expenditures, weakens the protections originally intended for rank and file union members by Congress, encourages broader penetration by unions into the field of politics, and indirectly sanctions such abridgement of the rights of the rank and file workers. We therefore propose that Section 610's first exception should be narrowed to prohibit the use of compulsory dues for communications supporting or opposing candidates for federal office.

The second exception is a problem of enforcement. Section 610 permits only *non-partisan* registration and get-out-the-vote drives and only those aimed at the union membership. In fact union registration drives are neither non-partisan nor solely member-directed. Al Barkan, Director of AFL-CIO COPE, in describing organized labor's role in the 1968 elections stated, "In many states labor did the registration job for Humphrey single handedly; the Democratic Party had abandoned the field" (Barkan, *supra*). Though the Report of the AFL-CIO Executive Council to the Tenth Convention, October 18, 1973, pays lipservice to Section 610 by characterizing union registration and get-out-the-vote drives as "non-partisan," this characterization is belied by the very words of the Report:

> The political programs of the trade union movement in 1972 achieved their primary goal: to retain a progressive Congress.

276

—uncommitted in the presidential campaign, the AFL-CIO was thus enabled to devote all of its time, energy and political resources to the critical battle for Congress.

—COPE's program in states with marginal Senate and House races contributed significantly to successful election results.

—51 of 83 candidates endorsed in marginal House races, and 10 of 19 in Senate races, won. Most of these were extremely close elections, and the margin of victory was clearly provided by labor's efforts.

No new legislation is required in this area. Proper enforcement by the Justice Department of Section 610 as it now stands would end the practice of partisan voter registration and election day activities financed by compulsory union dues. If the Justice Department vigorously prosecuted violations, few union officials would risk flouting the law.

The third exception allows unions to pay the overhead costs of running political committees from dues money, in effect subsidizing the fund-raising which results in direct cash contributions and indirect services to political candidates. This is not an insubstantial sum of money. Administrative costs of the average political committee generally run close to 50 percent of the committee's total expenditures—it costs $1.00 to raise $2.00. In addition, dues money pays the salaries and expenses of political operatives who perform direct and indirect unreported services for candidates. Such subsidization of direct or indirect political contributions cannot be justified on First Amendment grounds; it is a violation of the First Amendment rights of the individual employees whose dues and service fees are used for political purposes against their desires. Accordingly, we recommend that Section 610's third exception should be narrowed to prohibit the use of compulsory union dues to pay the overhead costs of union political committees. For example, the present Section 19 of S. 372 could be renumbered Section 19(b) and our proposal inserted as Section 19(a); or our proposal could be added as Section 302 of Title II of H.R. 7612.

In conclusion, we specifically suggest amending Section 610 of Title 18, United States Code, by adding at the end of the second paragraph thereof the following:

Provided further, That it shall be unlawful for money or anything of value secured by physical force, job discrimination, financial reprisals, or the threat of force, job discrimination, or financial reprisal, or by dues, fees, or other monies required as a condition of employment, to be used to pay the costs of: 1) communications by a corporation to its stockholders and their families or by a labor organization to its members and their families supporting or opposing any candidate for any of the offices referred to in this section, or supporting or opposing any political party or political committee, or 2) establishing, administering, and soliciting contributions to a separate segregated fund to be utilized for political purposes by a corporation or labor organization.

This suggested amendment would not prohibit the use of dues of voluntary members for either purpose, nor would it prohibit the use of compulsory dues for any communications to members other than those communications supporting or opposing candidates, parties, or political committees. The language of this proposed amendment could be easily incorporated in the campaign reform legislation now pending before this Subcommittee.

The use of compulsory union dues for political purposes seriously jeopardizes our system of representative government. It dilutes every citizen's political freedom and outrageously violates the basic rights of workers whose money is being misused. Our Committee believes that there can be no meaningful campaign reform legislation unless it contains provisions which will put a stop to these political spending abuses.

We submit that our proposal will go far to right these serious wrongs that have been allowed to go unchecked for too long a time. We urge that you give favorable consideration to this proposal.

Sincerely yours,
    /s/
Reed Larson
Executive Vice President
National Right to Work Committee   December 13, 1973

Notes

For further research and reference on federal election campaigns, three sources are suggested: (1) *Federal Election Campaign Laws,* a compilation of present federal statutes by the Senate Library for the Senate Rules and Administration Committee (January 1975), and available from the Superintendent of Documents, U.S. Government Printing Office, Washington, D.C. 20402 ($1.30); (2) studies and analyses of federal elections published by the Citizens' Research Foundation of Princeton, New Jersey, whose Washington affiliate, the National Information Center on Political Finance (Room 213, 1414 Twenty-second Street, N.W., Washington, D.C. 20037), provides copies of the reports filed by candidates for federal office listing contributions and expenditures; (3) *Federal Election Law Manual* ($50.00), published by the Republican National Committee (310 First St., SE, Washington, D.C. 20003), and used by Republicans, Democrats, and Independents to find out how to comply with the new law.

Chapter 1
1. *Wall Street Journal,* September 6, 1974.
2. *Human Events,* January 4, 1975.
3. *Washington Post,* January 14, 1975.

4. *Human Events,* October 26, 1974.
5. *Washington Post,* November 25, 1974.
6. From a report by UPI's Richard Rashker, quoted in "A Wrinkle in the Campaign Law" by Ronald Goldfarb, *Washington Post,* January 27, 1975.
7. *Washington Post,* April 2, 1975.
8. April 15, 1971.
9. AP dispatch, February 13, 1975.

Chapter 2
1. This chapter is based upon a summary titled "Highlights of Federal Laws Relating to Financing and Conducting Federal Election Campaigns," prepared by the Republican National Committee, January 24, 1975.

Chapter 6
1. *Memo from COPE,* May 11, 1974.
2. *National Journal,* November 16, 1974.
3. *California AFL-CIO News,* November 23, 1974.
4. See Appendix IV.
5. *Public Employee,* October 1974.
6. Walter N. Lang, "The NEA and Politics," *Human Events,* October 12, 1974.
7. *New York Times,* February 19, 1975.
8. *Miami Herald,* December 14, 1974.
9. *New York Times,* December 13, 1974.
10. *Congressional Quarterly,* February 9, 1974, p. 298.
11. *Congressional Quarterly,* June 8, 1974, p. 1478.
12. Ibid.
13. Ibid.